Social Work Response to Environment and Disasters

Social Work Response to Environment and Disasters

Edited by
Sanjai Bhatt
Neera Agnimitra

SHIPRA

Rs. 850; US$ 42.50

ISBN: 978-81-7541-746-5

First Published in India in 2014

Social Work Response to Environment and Disasters

Published by:
SHIPRA PUBLICATIONS
H.O.: LG 18-19, Pankaj Central Market, Patparganj,
I.P. Ext., Delhi-110092, Tel: 91-11-2223 5152, 2223 6152
Br.Off.: 4617/18, Ansari Road, Darya Ganj,
New Delhi-110002, Tel: 9650028065, 9810522367
E-mail: info@shiprapublications.com
www.shiprapublications.com

Dedicated to

Prof. Surendra Singh

A well known social work educator, researcher, activist and administrator who served the social work education and profession five decades, also as the First President, National Association of Professional Social Workers in India and First President of First Indian Social Work Congress, 2013

Preface

The 75th Jubilee Year of social work education in India has gone by. In seven and a half decades of its existence, social work education has witnessed many significant developments, momentous changes and innumerable achievements. It is not that the road has been smooth, for there have been hurdles and shortcomings. In the beginning, up to the setting up of the UGC Second Review Committee, the number of social work educational institutions was limited, but since the 1990s, there has been a mushrooming of social work institutions. While some of them are indeed contributing to the cause of the profession, many of them have sub-standard facilities, untrained and under-qualified teaching faculty, inadequate curricula and fieldwork prescription, among other incongruities. There is a need to review the situation and take corrective action to strengthen the overall state and profile of social work education and practice in the country.

In the last two decades, a sea change has occurred as far as the economic, political and social realities across the globe are concerned. The national context is also changing, largely on account of the global transformation, and also on account of the fact that the Indian society, economy and polity are experiencing rapid changes. Under the circumstances, the social work profession has also been impacted by these changes. The increasing complexities of life and an ongoing adjustment to the rapid transition in the context of our professional functioning have compelled us to assume a new persona and to secure new ways to help the needy and the strife ridden groups and communities. The changing context is also leading to a reformulation of the functional role of social workers. Professional social work is gradually enhancing its boundaries and spreading its wings to include new and challenging areas of practice. However, even as the educators and practitioners strive hard to acclimatize and to establish their position in the new context, it is not easy going. Even after 75 years of the historical traverse of social work education in India, the professional identity of social workers still remains nebulous and contestable. We are yet to attain our true professional space and credibility. This implies that trained social workers are yet to establish themselves as capable and equipped practitioners to engage with the multifarious contemporary issues that deserve our engagement. The reasons for this scenario are many and they range from a sense of inertia in aligning the syllabi and field practicum to the new and emerging realities, to lack of indigenous teaching material, to lack of collective effort in projecting the profession in a positive and meaningful manner, to a less than optimal response to many critical issues in the neo liberal and globalised context.

It was against this backdrop, that the Indian Social Work Congress 2013 was organized for the first time in India from the 23rd to the 25th February, 2013 at the University Conference Centre, University of Delhi. It was envisioned to facilitate wide ranging discussions and deliberations on an array of issues related to social work education and practice in India. It was envisaged that deliberations on the issues and challenges in the domain of social work education and practice in India would reveal the important gaps that need to be filled in order to enable the education and practice of social work to occupy their rightful place in the professional context. 'Bridging gaps and building bridges' was not only a notional theme devised for the Social Work Congress, it was essentially the vision and the mission of the Congress. The primary purpose of the Congress was to bring the fraternity of professional social workers together to discuss and deliberate upon issues related to the social work education, practice and research in India. The larger intent of the Congress was aimed at strengthening the social work profession to ensure social justice and human rights for all. It was also envisaged that the forum would enable the social work fraternity to record the response of the profession with regard to various social concerns and to redraw the boundaries that would allow a repositioning of the profession of social work in the contemporary frame. It was, thus, natural that the theme "Social Work Profession in India: Bridging Gaps and Building Bridges" be chosen to denote and depict the overriding concern of the Congress.

The present volume is the outcome of the deliberations of the First Indian Social Work Congress. The present volume encapsulates the papers presented under the cohort of Human Ecology, "Disaster Management and Social Work: Framework for Effective Response." The papers present a diverse set and subsume within themselves an array of themes, all of which have significant potential to inform and impact social work education and practice. Within themselves, they provide a very comprehensive canvas of issues and responses to the concerns in the domain of environment, climate change and disaster management.

Sanjai Bhatt
Neera Agnimitra

Contents

Abbreviations

BEE	Bureau of Energy Efficiency
CC	Community Committee
CBHFA	Community Based Health and First Aid
DRR	Disaster Risk Reduction
DUCKU	Delhi University Karmchari Union
DURA	Delhi University Researchers' Association
DUSU	Delhi University Students' Union
DUTA	Delhi University Teachers' Association
EAA	Earthquake Affected Areas
UNECOSOC	UN Economic and Social Council
FPIC	Free Prior Informed Consent
GEER	Gujarat Ecological Education and Research Foundation
GHGs	Green House Gases
GMOs	Genetically Modified Organisms
GSS	Gram Swaraj Sangh
GT	Gigatonnes
HAC	Human Animal Conflict
HFA	Hyogo Framework of Action
IFSW	International Federation of Social Workers
IJSW	Indian Journal of Social Work
INCCA	India Network for Climate Change Assessment
IEC	Information, Education and Communication
IPCC	Inter-governmental Panel on Climate Change
LFA	Logical Framework Analysis

LRK	Little Rann of Kutch
MDG	Millennium Development Goal
MoEF	Ministry of Environment and Forest
NAPCC	National Action Plan on Climate Change
NASW	National Association of Social Workers
NICRA	National Initiative on Climate Resilient Agriculture
OWG	Open Working Group
PAT	Perform, Achieve and Trade
PDS	Public Distribution System
PRA	Participatory Research Appraisals
PRGF	Partial Risk Guarantee Fund
SAPCC	State Action Plan on Climate Change
SC	Scheduled Castes
ST	Scheduled Tribes
SEC	Specific Energy Consumption
SHG	Self Help Group
SRH	Seismic Resistant Housing
UDAI	University for Development Action and Integrated Learning
UN	United Nations
UNCBD	UN Convention on Biological Diversity
UNCCD	UN Convention against Desertification
UNDRIP	UN Declaration on the Rights of Indigenous Population
UNFCCC	United Nations Framework Convention on Climate Change
UNISDR	United Nations International Strategy for Disaster Reduction
VCFEE	Venture Capital Fund for Energy Efficiency
VRC	Village Reconstruction Centre
VRG	Village Reconstruction Group
WAS	Wild Ass Sanctuary
WCC	World Climate Conference
WCMC	World Conservation Monitoring Centre
WCPA	World Commission for Protected Area
WDR	World Development Report
WMO	World Meteorological Organisation

1

Contextualizing the Environment in Social Work Pedagogy

An Environmental Perspective to Intervention

Sanjai Bhatt and *Neera Agnimitra*

Human beings may be entering very difficult times with the degradation and potential destruction of our sustaining natural world. For more than a decade, there has been an overwhelming presence of significant problems in the earth's ecological domain, and a consequent increase in the concern over such ecological issues. Collectively, we may be facing a fundamental shift in values and approaches towards living on and with this planet. There are indications that society could be in the initial stages of constructing an environmental state as much as we created the welfare state in the last century (Meadowcroft, 2007). The global crisis caused by the ongoing environmental degradation, climate change and depreciation in the natural resources, which constitute the base for subsistence for the critical mass of population over the world, has created a monumental challenge to the survival and well being of the human race. The realisation that the worst negative impact of the environmental problems falls disproportionately on the individuals, groups, communities and societies, who are the most vulnerable, poor and marginalised, both within nation states and across the globe, leads one to contend that the crisis is also grounded in serious concerns with respect to the environmental and social justice. Interest and response to the physical and social aspects of environmental problems is interdisciplinary and has captured the attention of the natural, behavioural and social sciences, with a proliferation of theoretical and application based content in the new and emerging areas of inquiry and action. The dimensions of the deep and intricate consequentiality of environmental well being and human well being have been revealed by an ever expanding body of empirical research across disciplines. Where does social work stand in all this? Have we, the social work professionals, accepted the challenge and the opportunity of engaging with environmental issues and their impact on human well being? Given the humanistic commitment and social justice mandate of social work, can the profession assume a 'neutralist bystander' stance to the critical environmental agenda of our times? In this introductory section, it is our endeavour to initiate a small scale reflection on the erstwhile and the existential response of social work to environmental issues and to the prevailing global ecological crisis. We attempt to locate evidence within the theoretical discourse and the practice parameters to understand the role of social work in understanding and in drawing up a level of response to contribute towards facilitating the planet and its citizens to move towards a sustainable, just and secure future.

It would not be an exaggeration to record that, despite the increasing evidence of the 'ways in which the ecological crisis is impacting human well being and the obvious connections between environmental, ecological and social justice, social work has generally been reluctant to claim or even explore a role in the task of addressing this crisis and finding ways to move forward' (Jones, 2010: 68). Jones (2010) further elaborates that a review of the major social work journals reveals a paucity of literature conjoining social work and the natural environment, and a shortage of courses within social work programmes that link the social and ecological in theory and practice. Well into the present time, social workers have played a largely insignificant role in intermediating with the environment and environmental concerns. However, being a profession that claims to work towards enhancing people's well being, and given the links between the core concerns of social work and the contemporary issues of ecological justice, can social work afford to maintain a premeditated silence on the centrality of environmental issues? Can the social work fraternity even escape its obligation to deal with the problems confronted by the global community and the local constituencies, threatened as they are, by the looming environmental crisis?

As a profession, social work has continued to own a long-standing and declared focus on "person-in-environment", and has consistently worked to establish an adjustment of its clients and client groups within their "environment". However, it is glaringly evident that, right from the beginning of the establishment of the profession, it was the "social" environment that was conceptualised as the pertinent context and setting for the profession. The relationship between the humans and the natural environment was, to a large extent, ignored or excluded from the ecological or the person-in-development models in social work (Coates, 2003). Instead, a conceptualisation of the "environment" evolved that exclusively considered the client's "social" environment and obfuscated any reference to its *natural* counterpart. This "social" environment pertained to the person's relationships with other individuals, groups, communities and organisations, and was hailed by social workers as far back as the 1920s. Mary Richmond (1922) asserted that the physical environment was an important context for social work practice, but that it was subsumed within the social environment and that it 'frequently has its social aspects' (Richmond, 1922: 99). Such an interpretation of acknowledging the "environment" as "social environment", which was primarily understood in social terms and interpreted by 'sociological and economic theory' (Gordon, 1969: 6) continued to remain operational, leading professionals to steer clear of negotiating any agenda with any 'tinge of green'. The ultimate goal of social work was deemed to 'bring about a balance between the realities of a person's capabilities and a person's social situation' (Gordon, 1981: 136). Even from the functional systems perspective, the four basic systems for practice that were proposed were all social and 'the focus of social work was on the interactions between people and systems in the social environment' (Pincus and Minahan, 1973: 3). This meant that social workers were expected to mediate to reinstate or restore that balance or that equilibrium, which existed between the client system and its immediate social systems, in the eventuality of a disruption or an imbalance within the same. The implications of these interpretations led to mainstream social work neglecting the "physical" or the "natural" environment from consideration and from its scope of engagement. It is evident from the above that right from its foundational stage, the 'profession of social work was comfortable using the social science lenses to view the environment rather than perspectives from the physical or natural sciences' (Zapf, 2010: 31).

Some efforts were made intermittently to place environmental issues and concerns centrestage within social work theory and practice. The work of Germain (1979) and Germain and Gitterman (1980) drew focus on interactions between people and their environments within the concerns of an expanded ecological paradigm. Scholars like Weick (1981) contended that the focus of social work on human behaviour had led to a neglect of the physical environment from its ambit and that a dynamic matrix of internal and external environments was integral to the understanding and influencing of human behaviour. The discourse to encourage the profession to reposition itself with regard to its erstwhile *environmental innocuousness* grew in the nineties, and in the subsequent period. Berger and Kelly (1993) advocated the adoption of social work's signature ecological model to be extended to 'a full awareness of human's role in the biological as well as social ecosystems' (Berger and Kelly, 1993: 524). Emphasizing the need to expand the professional horizons of social work, they evolved a '12-point Ecological Credo for Social Workers' (*ibid*: 524-525). Berger (1995) renewed his appeal to the social work fraternity when he professed that the 'Habitat Destruction Syndrome' was leading the human beings to 'collectively engage in practices that damage the environment and ensure our eventual self-destruction' (Berger, 1995; 441) and highlighted the need to 'add environmental activism to social work's list of social welfare concerns' (*ibid*: 443). Between 1992 and 1995, the NASW Journal of Social Work published four articles spelling out a strong case for social work to include the physical environment in its ambit. Hoff and Pollack (1993) also highlighted the social dimensions of the global environmental crisis, and its implications for social work. A book called *The Global Environmental Crisis: Implications for Social Welfare and Social Work* by Hoff and McNutt in 1994 explicated the premise that human and environmental welfare are 'inextricably linked' (1994: 2). They contested that social work, along with other professions, will have to move beyond the largely redundant and oft repeated goals of individual well being and social welfare to adopt new models geared towards protection and sustainability of the environment. Jones (2010) elucidates that many articles in the nineties and the early years of the present century, such as those by Besthorn and McMillan, 2002; Hillman, 2002; Hoff, 1994; Ife, 1997; Marlow and Van Rooyen, 2001; and Park, 1996 argued that 'there were clear and undeniable associations between environmental issues and the traditional social issues with which social work is generally concerned' (Jones, 2010: 70). He further supported the need for social workers to make the environment, physical and social, and the human-environment relationship 'central to our ongoing development of theory and practice' (*ibid*: 71). Coates (2003) in his book titled *Ecology and Social Work: Toward a New Paradigm* supported the same proposition and iterated that 'Social work has the choice of continuing to support a self-defeating social order or recreating itself to work toward a just and sustainable society' (Coates, 2003: 159). As per his recommendation, the major objective for social work at this time is to 'help bring about a transformation of society into one with a vision and mandate that recognizes that we are intimately and symbiotically connected with nature and all people' (*ibid*: 97).

The National Association of Social Workers (2000), in its policy statement strongly upheld the need for social work to add "environment" and "environmental" to its professional mandate when it held that:

> Protecting people and the natural environment through sustainable development is arguably the fullest realization of the person-in-environment perspective. The compatibility of sustainable development and the person-in-environment perspective is a firm theoretical foundation from which to apply macro level social work practice to person-natural environment problems (NASW, 2000: 105).

In a similar vein, an International Policy Statement on Globalisation and the Environment from the International Federation of Social Workers (IFSW, 2004) appealed to social workers and their organizations to:

> Recognize the importance of the natural and built environment to the social environment, to develop environmental responsibility and care for the environment in social work practice and management today and for future generations, to work with other professionals to increase our knowledge and with community groups to develop advocacy skills and strategies to work towards a healthier environment and to ensure that environmental issues gain increased presence in social work education (paragraph 15).

In the more recent context, Zapf (2010) has evolved a new foundation metaphor of *people as place,* which links humans to their natural world and which has great potential in helping to focus on the crucial task of living well on this planet. He goes on to contend that the present day social work practitioners and theoreticians have operated for over thirty years with models of practice based on the paradigm of person-in-environment. However, since then, there have been substantial changes, like the one revealed by the formidable "inconvenient truth" offered by Al Gore in 2006, highlighting the criticality of climate change and other such environmental threats, that were not considered when the existing practice models were created. These models may no longer be adequate for coping with the challenges faced by today's societies and the planet and, therefore, 'it is now past time that social work moves beyond its conventional metaphor of person-in-environment towards a new paradigm, a new understanding of the relationship between people and the physical environment' (Zapf, 2010: 30).

Dewane (2011) has strongly proposed environmentalism in the scope of practice of the profession and has justified her stance based on environmental justice concerns. Calling social work as 'the profession that prides itself on social justice as its foundational principle', she extrapolates the environmental justice premise. She follows this up with the need for social work education to provide opportunity for students to 'explore the nexus between environmentalism and social work' and 'with more community-focused action regarding environmental policy. She has also advocated "Conservation social work" as 'a much-needed interdisciplinary effort for coming to terms with the critical and continual problems that arise when humans interact with animals and nature'. This category of work integrates the relationship between human beings with animals and nature and provides a 'unifying and global approach for addressing problems centring on human-animal, human-nature, and human-human interactions with the vision of promoting well-being for humans, animals, and nature alike' (Dewane, 2011: 20).

In their classic book, *Environmental Social Work,* editors Grey, Coates and Hetherington (2013), also acknowledge the call for 'a paradigm shift within social work in the context of a developing ecological consciousness among social work scholars and practitioners, who see environmental social work as an essential, though underdeveloped area of scholarship and practice' and who argue 'for social work and other professions to break free of their professional silos and work in unison to better understand and respond to the many dimensions of climate change and environmental destruction' (2013: 2). They go on to quote "environment social work scholars", who, in turn, have stated that the predictions of disasters are evidenced to be influenced by climate change affected by human activities, such as globalization, deforestation, pollution, industrial agriculture, habitat destruction, soil and water management problems, species decline and extinction, human population growth and increased per capita incomes, and thereby call upon the society to respond to the symptoms of climate change and environmental degradation. They further articulate the contestation of the environmental social work scholars that 'global warming will not only impact the socio-political, economic and physical environment in which social workers are engaged, but also on the type of work, both mitigating and adaptive that they will be called upon to carry out' (2013: 3). In the preface of the same book, Doherty recommends that social workers can take on the role of attending to the combined natural and human made disasters; and assume work in the field of environmental health, both physical and psychosocial. He also advocates the breaking down of the artificial barriers between "environmental issues", "human health issues" and "social equity issues" to work towards an expanded ecological vision or a "shared" vision (2013: xx).

The latest and perhaps the most influential in the series of environment social work scholars is Dominelli (2012), who has emerged as the most avid proponent of *Green Social Work,* which seeks to strongly argue the case for contemporary social work to engage with environmental issues. She calls her book by the same name as it 'transcends the concerns of ecological social work, which is a system based approach to mainstream social work's preoccupation with... the social environment'. She argues that 'green social work focuses on how responses to environmental crises must both challenge and address poverty, structural inequalities, socio-economic disparities, industrialization processes, consumption patterns... and limited resources' (2012: 3). Dominelli (2012) further states that:

> Given the profession's embeddedness in life enhancing micro practice in everyday routines, I argue that contemporary social work has a vested interest in attending to environmental issues as an integral part of its daily remit if it is to retain its currency in

> contemporary societies, emphasise its relevance to the social issues that people have to resolve in the twenty first century and widen its scope if it is to prevent the haemorrhaging of its activities to related professions [...] I define *Green social work*, as that part of practice that intervenes to protect the environment and enhance people's well being by integrating the interdependencies between people and their socio-cultural, economic and physical environments, and among peoples within an egalitarian framework that addresses prevailing structural inequalities and unequal distribution of power and resources (Dominelli, 2012: 3, 8).

Effectively speaking, in visualizing *Green Social Work*, Dominelli has extended the horizons of social work and has expanded the role of the social worker in key environmental issues of the time–environmental degradation, industrial pollution, overconsumption by a few, climate change, migrations caused by natural disasters and conflicts over water, land and clean air...... in essence what comprises a holistic 'green' agenda, rooted in the interdependency of all people and their socio-cultural, economic and physical environments.

This brief sojourn through the corridors of history has been undertaken to explore and elucidate the status of the environmental commitment of the social work profession over the temporal frame of its existence. Never in this traverse of time was the need to create a vibrant and meaningful environmental presence so strongly felt, as it is now, in the present day context. Within the temporal context, social work has shown an intermediation with environmental issues and problems, albeit in a limited manner. However, given the nature of the environmental crises unfolding around the globe, there is an urgent need for recentring environment in social work practice. The above discussion has also set the stage for the configuration of a series of papers that explore the newly emerging rubric of environmental social work, with its sub components of ecology and social work; social work and climate change and social work and disaster management. The papers attempt to create a tapestry of social work response by weaving in theoretical and practice driven perspectives and interventions to what is truly emerging as the most integral worldview to sustainable ways of reframing people's relationships to their living environments.

The Structure of the Book

The beginning chapter on *Disaster Risk Reduction: A Gender Perspective* by Prof. Santosh Kumar, alludes to the existence of diverse frameworks and tools for addressing issues related with gender and disasters. It elucidates the differential impact of disasters on men and women, and also the need to consider women as a heterogeneous group. It highlights the need to look at inclusive Disaster Risk Reduction in view of the contradictions that exist in society. Discussing the concepts of differential vulnerability and capacity, with special focus on gender, the chapter affirms the need to transform the dominant perception of women as "victims" of disaster to "leaders" and "capacity holders". The author substantiates the practice of gender sensitive community education and the role of women in disaster preparedness and monitoring with early warning systems through exciting case illustrations. He also dwells on the complementary role that men and women can perform in risk reduction and disaster management and discusses the proactive risk management approach, where women's role has been realised and gender analysis has been given priority. The recognition that an increasing number of governments are integrating gender issues in their national DRR reporting to UNISDR, including the Indian government and others in the South Asian region as also that there is an increasing emphasis on policy change in the development discourse for mainstreaming women in DRR has been hailed as significant. The author also discusses the gaps in policy and practice with regard to gender mainstreaming and notes the role of Gujarat post-disaster long term recovery programme and the tsunami relief programme in attempting to change gender relations by making strategic interventions. He also posits the need to analyse and revisit the rules and practices of different social and formal institutions to create a gender just environment and planning for mainstreaming.

In the chapter on *Climate Change and Disaster: Need for a Human Rights Based Approach to Disaster Reduction and Sustainable Development,* Ajay Jha and Sharad Joshi trace the link between runaway climate change and the increasing frequency of disasters. They discuss disaster events across the world and stress the need to halt climate change to reduce the frequency of disasters. The said chapter also looks at the impact of disasters on the marginalized communities and regions. It provides a detailed discussion on the lessons learned from implementation of Hyogo Framework of Action and the role of Conference of Parties in Cancun (2010) on the climate change negotiations associated with disasters. The authors elaborate the position taken in the Conference of Parties in Warsaw, Poland (December, 2013), for the inclusion of the developing countries in disaster and their loss and damage in the future global agreement. According to them, the post 2015 development agenda of the United Nations; the follow up of the Rio+20 Conference and formulation of the Sustainable Development Goals shall undisputedly be the most important future opportunities for mitigating disasters due to COP. The chapter also includes a detailed discussion on India's position in the International negotiations, and presents a critique of the perceptible shift in India's policy and its position in international negotiations (in Copenhagen COP), where India declared that it will reduce its emission intensity by 20-25. The chapter captures an analysis of the National Action Plan on Climate Change and the steps undertaken as part of the National Mission on Enhanced Energy Efficiency, National Water Missions, Mission on Green India, and the National Mission on Sustainable Agriculture. The authors have expressed concern with the snail paced development of State Action Plans on Climate Change and the top-down manner in which most plans have been formulated, without showing any concern for the equity and rights issues. The chapter also discusses the plan of a few states and lays bare the haphazard manner in which some of these plans have been developed. The highlight of the chapter is the presentation of ways to address climate change and disasters in the SDGs.

The chapter authored by Neera Agnimitra on *The Trajectory of Disaster Response: From Relief to Resilience* delineates the significant role that schools of social work can play in creating an opportunity for the student learners to reach out and make a difference in the lives of constituencies, whose lives are suddenly and traumatically interjected from their normal rhythm of life. Disasters, natural and manmade, severely and irreversibly impact and dislocate the lives of the affected communities, and cause havoc in the physical and psycho-social frame of the survivors. The onset of most disasters being sudden, the response is usually delayed, and that adds to the extreme exigencies of the situation. In the given context, the spontaneity of response exhibited by the faculty and students of social work can only add credibility to the vision and mission of the human service profession. It may have lacked the characteristics of a well endowed and institutionalised response drawn up by the humanitarian organisations or the governmental agencies, but it would undoubtedly abound with the throbbing energy of the student youth and their fervent desire to reach out and be there for the masses of people whose sense of existence is shattered by the calamitous event. The author shares with the readers an ethnographic account of engagement with UDAI-II Sahyatri, an initiative of the Department of Social Work, University of Delhi, through which the constituents of this institution extended themselves to the valued aspiration of the profession and to the anguish of its client system. This chapter traces the trajectory of the endeavor and thereby draws lessons for future initiatives. While the process that was assumed transformed as per the needs of the context, the initiative has been instrumental in providing relief and succour to a vast community of affected families on the one hand, and a reinforcement of faith among the social work fraternity in their own commitment and resources for meaningful action, on the other. From its initiation as a spontaneous response to the humongous tragedy of the Kosi floods that befell the people of North Bihar, the journey created opportunities for the team to engage, apply, learn, revalidate and reaffirm all that is taught in the classroom in the domain of Disaster Management and Community Based Disaster Response and Mitigation. It was the desire to pitch in and provide instantaneous solace and succour to the endless number of people ravaged by the fury of the flood that sparked the initiative, which went on to become the mainstay for student and faculty participation in one of the longest and perhaps the most pulsating engagements with the "field".

In a very interesting chapter on *Protected Area and People: Exploring the Role of Social Work Practice,* Digvijoy Phukan and Vinay Kumar explore the synergy and contradictions that permeate the human environment relationship, through the lens of the conservation and livelihood debate. They trace the history and the diversity of perspectives related to the creation and management of the protected areas, and the perception of the local population towards their presence. Rooted in the west during a period when indiscriminate human action threatened to destroy nature, the concept of national parks laid emphasis on maintaining these areas devoid of human presence. The continuing belief that even the activities of the people, who have been living in and around the areas designated as national park, were inimical to the conservation efforts, has been instrumental in ensuring that the history of creation of all the major parks be associated with discontentment among the local population. The adherence to the legacy of exclusive conservation has led to the exclusion of human settlements from the areas where wildlife and habitats were protected. While protected areas have been one of the most important conservation strategies during the last century, their impact on the lives of people living inside and adjacent to them has emerged as a major topic of debate. The efforts towards the creation and management of these areas have been mired by conflicts between the conservationist forces and the people inhabiting the areas. The authors highlight that while the need for ecosystem preservation, provision of environmental services and opportunities for recreation and tourism are major factors driving the establishment of these areas by the governments around the world; the displacement of local people from these areas and the loss of their traditional livelihood strategies put a question mark on the creation of these parks. These approaches simply take away the human face of the conservation strategies. The struggle between local communities and park authorities in most of the protected areas across the country has necessitated the need to gain a comprehensive understanding of the park and people debate in the Indian context. The chapter endeavours to explore the various facets of this debate in the context of the Wild Ass Sanctuary in Little Rann of Kutch (LRK), Gujarat and the Agaria community. While making an effort to ascertain the view of the park officials and local community towards the conflict, the chapter highlights the immense scope of work for social work professionals in such areas. The authors also draw upon the challenges faced by the non-governmental organisations working with the local communities in the LRK, to elucidate the skill base required by social workers engaged with communities living in and around protected areas and threatened by the prospect of being uprooted from their own land.

The chapter by Varun Sharma and Neera Agnimitra titled *Post-Structural Possibilities for Green Social Work: A Brief Review of Literature* is a review of literature but moves much beyond a simply clinical review. Within the social work profession, environmental issues, ecological concerns, and the heedless exploitation of nature, is becoming an increasing concern. Following the stated position of Dominelli (2012) and others, the profession, traditionally concerned with case work and group work, has begun to actively assume green ideological positions. The authors reflect on the Indian context too, where the effort to provide perspectives on varied forms of social activism that emerge out of environmental concerns has predated Dominelli's own work. Work on the categorisation of the social movements relating to the environment and discussion on the classification of ecological movements and protests have found significant scholarly space and recognition, and have contributed to the beginning of a brand of environmental social work in the country. This and other subsequent work notwithstanding, the concern of this chapter may be a little more foundational to the environmental discourse. It is noticed that the three terms "nature", "environment" and "ecology" find simultaneous application, through and through, to the near point of acting as synonyms without even being noticed. Thus, it could be said that a part of this chapter's interest lies in the unique and special meanings that "nature", "environment" and "ecology" invoke – not in laboratories, or as part of textbook learning – but in deliberations and debates of a social and political kind. Without trying to insist that nature, environment and ecology are watertight concepts, this chapter further seeks to address a dismal lack of perspective on such rudimentary terms from a post-structural perspective, particularly in the home context. It is this chapter's enterprise to seek to build a discussion on how professional social work in India can benefit from post-structural perspectives on key terms, which are indispensable for articulating any green ideological position(s), leave alone categorising them. It is important to state that the effort is not to partake in the rhetoric of "nature", "environment" and "ecology", but problematise them using Foucault (1976). It is hoped that such a venture would serve varied purposes. On the one hand, it is bound to give green social workers a critical perspective as regards some foundational terms (nature, environment and ecology), around which we find some very complex discourses to be tightly wrapped. Such an initiative may also dissolve some of the romance involved with the invocation of such terms. On the other hand, this chapter is equally liable to indicate and inform areas of further research that have remained hitherto unexplored. In addition, it is also bound to better verify into the manner in which thinkers and sociologists, particularly in India, have tried to categorize efforts underway to protect the "nature", "environment" and "ecology", without addressing the messy tangle in which such terms present themselves prior to their invocation.

The chapter titled *Community as the Key for Disaster Recovery: A Case of Long Term Intervention in Kanyakumari District* by Subhasis Bhadra portrays the role of social work education in designing models of disaster intervention based on the methods of social work practice. The author introduces the concept of "communities" and articulates a strong need for trained disaster personnel to engage with communities for intervention and for ensuring distribution of benefits at all levels. The author draws from a long-term intervention project on community recovery and presents a case for the engagement of the community as a stakeholder in the recovery process. Using the case study method, he depicts the community empowerment process through a post-disaster intervention programme undertaken by NIMHANS in the communities of Kanyakumari district following the devastating Indian Ocean Tsunami in 2004. The long term integrated community recovery project was aimed at the enhancement of the capacity of the tsunami survivors to recover through community and school based interventions. By drawing in both the sub-systems, the initiative could address both the psychological and the social needs of individuals, families and communities. The highlight of the project was the formation of a representative group in each of the targeted communities. Named as the Community Committee (CC), the group assumed responsibility for various stages of the recovery programme, including planning, implementing and monitoring to ensure the sustainability of the project activities. The need for disaster recovery process to be designed, directed and organised in a fashion that can strengthen the community's capacity for dealing with future uncertainty and the importance of placing value on the cultural sensitivity of the community, its political, economic and social structures, with primacy on its social capital gleans through the description provided by the author. The chapter highlights the significance of a cohesive community, with its reservoir of traditional knowledge about risks and disasters and a pre-existing level of resilience to usher in the overall recovery more effectively and expeditiously. Based on the experience of the study, community organisation has been recommended as the most critical social work method to facilitate post-disaster recovery.

In the following chapter on *Social Work and Human Animal Conflict: Opportunities for Interdisciplinary Practice,* Mayuri Gogoi iterates that the human service profession of social work has largely remained confined to operating within the realms of the social environment, paying inadequate attention to the biophysical environment. Lately, however, there is a new genre of social work practice that is oriented towards addressing environmental concerns and relying on inter disciplinary perspectives. She argues that in the light of these very encouraging developments in social work practice, the theme and interventions in the realm of Human Animal Conflict (HAC) need to be focussed upon. The integration of issues and perspectives of HAC within social work has significant potential to enable practitioners to explore the perspectives of hierarchy, domination, poverty, gender, ethnicity and marginalisation that exacerbate conflict. They also facilitate the formulation of interventions for the development and empowerment of HAC affected communities, along with creating conducive environment for the conservation of animals.

In another chapter on *Disaster Management: An Emerging Field in Social Work Education,* Aruna Gajbhiye and Ravindra Gajbhiye explore the role that social work professionals can be deemed to play in the realm of disaster management. They highlight the increase in the incidence of natural disasters worldwide and the risk of disaster faced by communities across India. Being a multiple disaster prone country, owing to its unique geographical and cultural landscape, the need for an effective and holistic disaster management perspective, structure and approach within the country remains critical. The chapter touches upon the efforts initiated by the Government of India and the impact of disasters on individuals, communities and the economy. The authors present a strong case for the importance of disaster management education in higher education and reaffirm the need for educational institutions of social work to initiate disaster management education through their regular curricula. They trace the long ties between the social work profession and disaster relief and contend that social workers can assume multiple roles to offer multi-level interventions to address the unmet needs of disaster impacted communities. Being a unique and a specialized field, disaster management requires specialized professionals, who can understand human needs, behaviour and cultural aspects, which affect the overall social functioning of the disaster impacted and the disaster vulnerable communities. Social workers are equipped to address and intervene with the social and psychological issues that can block individual and community adjustment in the aftermath of a disaster. Besides discussing in detail the roles of a social worker in disaster management, the authors also contend that it is not only important to work during the disaster situation, but also at the stages of preparedness and mitigation, as these are areas where social workers can prove their credibility and professional expertise. The need to inculcate the culture of safety in the mindset of the people and a major lifestyle transformation in order to minimize the loss of human life, economy, and infrastructure requires social workers to assume the role of change advocates.

The chapter on *Exploring the Climate Change Discourse in India Through the Lens of Social Work Practice* has its authors Vinay Kumar and Digvijoy Phukan discuss one of the most deliberated themes in contemporary times, which is climate change. Climate change has indeed become the nodal global discourse, as it presents one of the most important challenges to the achievement of the goals of sustainable development. India has been identified as a nation, which is among the most vulnerable to the impacts of climate change by the Inter-governmental Panel on Climate Change (IPCC) in its fourth assessment report of 2007. With more than 70 per cent of its population directly reliant on climate sensitive sectors like agriculture, forests and fisheries and natural resources, such as water, forests, land, biodiversity, coasts, and grasslands for their subsistence and livelihood, the country shall face the prospect of declining earnings emanating from the fluctuating climate. Apart from leading to the possibility of food insecurity, the situation shall possibly compel communities to seek alternate livelihood choices, which are outside and away from sectors dependent on the natural resource base. The chapter highlights the nature of pressure that is likely to be generated in the process and that will impinge on other sectors and on the overall socio-economic development of the nation. In the context, an urgency to create and establish strong adaptive and policy measures to adjust and overcome the implications of climate change is emphasized. The chapter explores and analyses the perceptions of lawmakers and the generalised "people" on the issue of climate change in order to derive a convergence of views and perspectives. It analyses the important policies and institutions set up by the Indian government to respond to the threats arising from climate change, as also the governmental stance at the global platform. From the perspective of the profession, the authors suggest potential avenues for social work intervention at the national and local levels to usher in more climate resilient communities.

The chapter on *Social Work Education and Practice in Climate*

Change Adaptation: Realities and Gaps by Nivedita Thapliyal discusses the concept of climate change and underlines its emergence as the greatest challenge for societies in the coming years and also for the future generations. The Intergovernmental Panel on Climate Change states that the adverse change in global climate system is contributed by an unscrupulous and unsustainable consumption pattern of natural resources by mankind. The chapter also takes cognizance of gender as a critical factor in disaggregating the impact and vulnerability of people to climate change, and presents evidence to show that the phenomenon places a heightened burden on women. The author delineates the diversity of roles that a social work professional can play in the realm of climate change, including the facilitation of the development of innovative sustainable agriculture practices; creating and implementing awareness programmes on climate change through the development of resource material in local languages; and adoption of a multidisciplinary approach for conducting practice oriented research and development on issues related to climate change. It is also in the domain of the social worker to support environmental initiatives and movements generated to counter the impact of climate change and facilitating grassroots action to mitigate the negative repercussions of the phenomenon.

The chapter titled *UDAI: A Social Work Response to Managing the Aftermath of a Disaster* by Sanjai Bhatt provides a model for academic institutions keen to design intervention modules while responding to disasters. It espouses the need for such institutional response systems in view of the increased frequency of such situations. The initial section of the chapter discusses in detail the conception of the project, i.e. University for Development Action and Integrated Learning-I (UDAI-I), which originated in response to the earthquake in the Kutchh region of Gujarat in the year 2001 and thereafter traces the subsequent phases of the disaster response. Detailing the extent of damages entailed in the disaster, the ensuing section provides rich insights into the manner in which the objectives of such interventions should be contextualised. It also highlights the role of networking with local organisations for the execution of the disaster rehabilitation project. The chapter underlines four phases of intervention: Preparatory Phase, Action Phase, Consolidation Phase and Termination or Renewal Phase. The author has also provided a lucid presentation of the modus operandi and the activities incorporated within the different phases. The project aimed at contributing in the fields of housing, education, health, psycho-social support, employment generation, environment and legal awareness. It introduced the concept of Village Reconstruction Centre as sites for imparting public awareness for different types of activities undertaken as a part of the project. Highlighting the success of VRCs in Gujarat, the chapter builds a case for the replication of the model in other disaster impacted sites. The paper also underlines the importance of volunteerism and provides a detailed action plan for channelizing the voluntary spirit. It outlines the learning outcomes of the project for the social work student learners, the faculty and the University system and focuses on the extremely significant and exemplary results achieved by the UDAI-I intervention and the team. These outcomes can aid the policy makers designing disaster R&R intervention plans.

References

Berger, R.M. (1995), Habitat Destruction Syndrome. *Social Work*. 40(4), pp. 441-443.

Berger, R.M. and Kelly, J.J. (1993), Social work in the ecological crisis. *Social Work*, 38(5), pp. 521-526.

Besthorn, F. and McMillen, D. (2002), The oppression of women and nature: Eco-feminism as a framework for an expanded ecological social work. *Families in Society*, 83, pp. 221-232.

Coates, J. (2003), *Ecology and Social Work: Toward a new paradigm*. Halifax, NS: Fernwood.

Dewane, C. (2011), Environmentalism and Social Work: The Ultimate Social Justice Issue. *Social Work Today*, Vol.11 No.5, 20, p 20. Retrieved on January 31, 2014 from: http://www.socialworktoday.com/archive/092011p20.shtml.

Foucault, M. (1976), *The History of Sexuality I*. Australia: Penguin.

Germain, C. (ed.) (1979), *Social work practice: People and environments—An ecological perspective*. New York: Columbia University Press.

Germain, C. and Gitterman, A. (1980), *The life model of social work practice*. New York: Columbia University Press.

Gordon, W.E. (1969), Basic concepts for an integrative and generative conception of social work. In G. Hearn (ed.), *The general systems approach: Contributions towards an holistic conception of social work*. New York, NY: Council on Social Work Education, pp. 5-11.

Gordon, W.E. (1981), A natural classification system for social work literature and knowledge. *Social Work*, 26(2), pp 134-138.

Gore, A. (2006), *An inconvenient truth: The planetary emergency of global warming and what we can do about it*. New York, NY: Rodale.

Gray, M., Coates, J. and Hetherington, T. (Eds.) (2012), *Environmental Social Work.* Abingdon: Routledge.

Hillman, M. (2002), Environmental Justice: A crucial link between environmentalism and community development? *Community Development Journal,* 37(4), pp. 349-360.

Hoff, M.D. and Polack, R.J. (1993), Social dimensions of the environmental crisis: Challenges for social work. *Social Work,* 38(2), pp. 204-211.

Hoff, M.D. and McNutt, J.G. (eds.) (1994), *The global environmental crisis: Implications for social welfare and social work.* Aldershot, UK: Ashgate.

Ife, J. (1997), *Community Development: Creating community alternatives– Vision, analysis and practice.* South Melbourne, Australia: Longman.

IFSW. (2004), *International Policy Statement on globalization and the environment.* Retrieved from http://www.ifsw.org

Jones, Peter. (2010), Responding to the ecological crisis: Transformative pathways for social work education. *Journal of Social Work Education,* Vol. 46, No. 1, pp. 67-84.

Marlow, C., and Van Rooyen, C. (2001), How green is the environment in social work? *International Social Work,* 44, pp. 241-254.

Meadowcroft, J. (2007), *Building the environmental state: What the history of social welfare tells us about the future of environmental policy.* Alternatives: Canadian Environmental Ideas & Action, 33(1), pp. 11-17.

National Association of Social Workers (NASW) (2000), *Social work speaks: NASW policy statements.* Washington, DC: NASW Press.

Park, K. (1996), The personal is ecological: Environmentalism of social work. *Social Work,* 41, pp. 320-323.

Pincus, A. and Minahan, A. (1973), *Social work practice: Model and method.* Itasca: Peacock.

Richmond, Mary (1922), *What is social work?* New York, NY: Scribners.

Weick, A. (1981), Reframing the person-in-environment perspective. *Social Work,* 26(2), pp. 140-145.

Zapf, M.K. (2010), Social work and the environment: Understanding people and place. *Critical Social Work,* 2010, Vol. 11, No. 3, pp. 30-46.

2

Disaster Risk Reduction

A Gender Perspective

Santosh Kumar

Much has been said in the past on the subject of Gender and Disasters. Many international agencies, academia, researchers, activists and professionals have put forward frameworks for addressing issues related with gender within the context of disasters. Some of the frameworks are local, while others are national as well as global. Tools to implement frameworks have also been developed by different agencies. It is however important to note that despite the quantum of theoretical work done in this arena; there is disproportionate follow up in the practice realm. There remains a discerning gap between the normative and the actual situation with respect to the consideration of the differential impact of disasters on people segregated by the axis of gender. In the current context, there is a renewed focus on the need for inclusive disaster risk management processes and urgency for ushering in gender mainstreaming and gender justice in disaster management.

Sociologists are perhaps better equipped to theorize about some glaring contradictions emanating out of the 'modern' living of our times. While on the one hand, men and women are discussing and practicing relationships outside the institution of marriage; homosexuality is gaining social acceptance; and there is a campaign to decriminalize it, on the other hand, we are still grappling with the issue of female feticide; lack of protection of the girl child; prejudice with regard to widow remarriage; gender discrimination at all ages and in all spheres of social life; sexual violence; dowry deaths; and domestic violence. Any attempt to building a gender "just" environment must take cognizance of these contradictions so that appropriate interventions can emerge. In the context in which we live, the human rights perspective has permeated our life and living. Constitutional rights have been given to individuals and not to the family (even though it is argued, incorrectly, that attempts to empower women will lead to divisions in the family) and we have to move with the premise that the fundamental rights are a matter of entitlement, not charity. At the same time, we cannot obviate the socio-cultural realities and the entrenched norms, which co-exist with this individual centric, rights-based framework. Needless to mention that, arguments and interventions for inclusive Disaster Risk Reduction (DRR) must also be understood in this perspective.

What is Sex? What is Gender?

Gender, as we know, is not just about women or men; it is about both women and men. Sex, on the one hand refers to the biological difference between men and women, which are genetically determined and cannot be changed naturally. The biological differences between men and women are based on reproductive roles. These differences are common and exist all over the globe, in all cultures, countries, societies and families. Moreover, the biological (natural) differences may be termed as being attributed to the categories 'male and female' rather than to 'men and women'. Gender, on the other hand, is a social construct which is ordained in the social and cultural environment, and is determined by cultural practices, social norms, values, ethics, conduct, behavior, roles, and responsibilities. Its construction varies across cultures, countries, societies and families as these defining parameters are amenable to change. The categories based on gender are therefore socially ordained and these conventional constructions of 'men' and 'women' usually dominate over the biological differences between 'male' and 'female'. It is through gender that male and female centered practices get institutionalized, and it is within the gender discourse that people in their identity and role as men and women become more dominant in the analysis. Hence, studying about men and women is the domain of gender studies.

Gender relations pitch both men and women in relation to one another. The cultural relationships between men and women help to transform the biologically different 'male' and 'female' into culturally defined attributes of masculinity and femininity.

Gender analysis is a process which facilitates the study of the differential impact of the proposed or existing policies, programmes, projects and regulations on men and women. The process recognizes that the realities of men and women's lives are different, and that equal opportunities do not necessarily mean equal results. This analysis recognizes the gendered division of labour, differential access to and control over resources, both tangible and intangible, and differential decision-making capacities. As we are aware, all the fundamental rights in our Constitution are given to individuals, irrespective of their gender, and therefore, legally speaking, both men and women have been given equal rights. However, it is difficult to ignore that the continuing prevalence of moral lessons and codes of conduct for women in the form of do's and don'ts, are typically loaded with patriarchal ideology, belief and practices. This is in spite of the fact that the contemporary discourse is more aligned with the prospect of change; and with the idea that the time has come to change prevalent thinking, ideology, actions and behavior. Considerable legislation has also been enacted in this regard. Despite all this, it is saddening to note that even today, society and its institutions have collectively failed in bringing forth a climate of gender justice, in all spheres of life.

The men with patriarchal mindsets, who listen to debates about gender equality and justice, typecast these as feminist discourses, and claim that the advocates of such ideas are only the 'feminists', who have the fetish for taking centre stage and who are only fond about talking among themselves. By resorting to such a response, these patriarchal ideologues conveniently reject the idea of changing themselves or their behavior. The anger of women in society is undermined or even rejected by typifying it as feminism, a brand to be abhorred. This ensures that there is no breaking of the vicious circle. When media channels invite women to talk about their concerns, they perhaps add to these prevailing notions and mindsets, for they further the belief that issues related to women are women's problem alone. And so more often than not, these get typified as feminist issues, which fall in the line of action of the feminists and their organizations. Such a stance quite naturally favours men, who very easily get away from partaking responsibility to change the nature of things. It is only obvious therefore, that at all levels, instead of limiting such debates to women alone, both men and women should equally participate in them and try to search for sustainable solutions. This has larger implications for inclusive and sustainable development. Gender concerns are legitimate and applicable to both men and women. The debate should not merely linger on the perceived "superiority" of men and the presumed "inferiority" of women, or the other way round. Instead it should focus on a discourse on "who does what" and what set of skills and resources are needed to do the job better. It should amalgamate the reality that exists and address the changes that are required. As in any sphere, the same orientation should also permeate the realm of environment and disaster management. It should lead to the identification of areas that will allow attainment of optimum output and make way for adaptations that need to be necessarily sought to affect the most effective response to mitigate the risk of disasters in the contemporary context.

Gender relations in disasters reflect gender relations prevalent in the society, which are at odds with the legal and constitutional rights of women. Feminists struggle to erase this difference, to challenge patriarchal beliefs and demand a gender just society. This fight is still going on. Different countries, societies and cultures have different kinds of discriminations which get institutionalized and their consequences are reflected in social institutions, like the family, community, market and the state. In this process, resources and power are accessed more by the men, and women are left with lower capacities and power and thus, they become vulnerable. This has deep implications for disaster related vulnerability. Owing to different life experiences and trajectories, women and men experience disasters differently, and respond to and recover from them in gender-specific ways. When disaster strikes, men and women have different abilities and ways of responding, and, in the end, the impacts are different.

Vulnerability and Capacity Approach

Historically speaking, two notable examples from India lend credence to the role women have tended to play within the environment context. The first one, known as Khezari movement, is an illustration from Rajasthan, where in the eighteenth century, more than a thousand women sacrificed their lives while protecting the environment, as they were opposing the order of their ruler to cut down their village forests. The other one is from the twentieth century, where again, women fought tooth and nail to protect their forests being axed by the outside contractors who had been given the decree to undertake tree felling by the government. The latter is none other than the celebrated Chipko Movement, which is known to have heralded a new era of environmental consciousness in India. There are many other such instances at the local levels, where women have been seriously engaged in protecting and regenerating the environment. The symbiotic relationship that women are known to maintain with their environment leads to a reciprocity wherein both nurture each other and ensure each other's survival and well being. In such a context where women's role in the realm of environmental action has been notable, it is surprising to acknowledge that from the time of its genesis to now, formal DRR initiatives have continued to analyse, acknowledge and project women as "victims", and those who are the "most vulnerable" to disasters.

Viewed within the DRR discourse, this representation is not completely incorrect, as under the prevailing context women do stand to lose out much more than men in the event of any disaster, of any nature and magnitude. However, such a representation totally ignores the "effective" persona of women, their individual and collective abilities as leaders, managers and workers, and instances of their path breaking initiatives in the face of disasters. This means that most often formal interventions get designed and implemented with "women as victims" perspective and usually incorporate within them activities addressing the immediate and dominant "needs" of this category. In this process, which is primed towards vulnerability reduction, strategic gender interests are marginalized and empowerment processes are sidelined. Women emerge as a category which is "vulnerable" and deemed to need protection and special assistance, and thereby behest of any significant role in Disaster Risk Reduction and Management.

Before arguing for more responsibilities for women as managers and leaders in the management of ecosystems, environment and DRR, it is worthwhile to spend some more time in unpacking the vulnerability approach. Vulnerability is essentially defined as the capacity of an individual to cope with a stressful situation, and it is the characteristics of the person, the system and environment of which he or she is a part or is exposed to, which makes him or her more or less susceptible to its damaging effects. There are many aspects of vulnerability, which arise out of social, economic, physical, environmental, political and cultural factors and these also vary significantly over a period of time. Vulnerability is not a static concept; it is dynamic and keeps changing as the underlying factors change. The degree of vulnerability varies within the community, family and even among individuals.

Before we proceed, it is necessary to dwell on the question as to whether disasters affect men and women equally or differently? It also needs to be deliberated whether all women suffer the same or similar impact in the eventuality of a disaster. Much experiential data exists to demonstrate that men and women in any society have differential vulnerability and thereby experience differential impacts on account of disaster. It has been widely observed, researched and documented that women are more vulnerable than their male counterparts even within the same social and economic categories, races and age groups, during all phases of a disaster. Gender-based social, economic, religious and cultural constructs marginalize women across all communities and groups; irrespective of class, caste, economic standing, status or age. It would also be fallacious to perceive women as a homogeneous category, which is not the case in reality. Women do not exist as an abstract category, but belong to different castes, cultures, class backgrounds, ages and regional groups. It is again not a hidden fact that it is the women belonging to the poor, vulnerable and marginalized communities who suffer the greatest impact of any disaster.

Effectively speaking, disasters do not discriminate, but people do. Existing socio-economic conditions mean that disasters can lead to different outcomes even for demographically similar communities, inevitably though the most vulnerable groups suffer more than others. Research reveals that disasters reinforce, perpetuate and increase gender inequality, making bad situations worse for women. Gender-based inequalities and vulnerabilities place women at greater degrees of risk to disasters, including less access to early warning systems, to policy and decision-making in disaster management. Disaster situations, which lead to the breakdown of family, community and institutional security and protection, generally make existing gender-based disparities surface to a greater degree than usual, putting already vulnerable groups at a higher risk. Women, in this context, can be identified as among the most vulnerable groups in most societies. In disaster situations, men may not be positioned very satisfactorily, but they are certainly better off in some respects.

It is however significant to note that in some ways men are also impacted by gender-based social expectations, especially in the aftermath of disasters. Socially and culturally, they are expected to deal independently with their own losses and even grieve alone. According to prevailing stereotypes, they are not supposed to cry or 'appear' vulnerable. They do not have adequate means to vent their trauma. Consequently, they may often suffer from post disaster psycho-social trauma. Nonetheless, men's role in the family as breadwinners and resource managers mostly positions them favourably, with the power to take decisions and the power to control other family members. On the other hand, women, in their role as housekeepers have little access to resources and opportunities, and are losers on many occasions. It is important to stress that adopting a gender approach does not imply merely to focus on the needs of women. Rather, it entails ensuring that the different needs of men and women are addressed. For example, the formal aspect of psycho-social support bypasses men, since, according to stereotypical views, they are expected to be strong and face the crisis in a manly manner, but as has been highlighted they are perhaps a significant client group that needs to avail this intervention. Additionally, while there may be specific interventions to help widows and female-headed households to recover, the concerns of widowers, who are left with the responsibility of raising young families, are often not addressed. Furthermore, gender-based social conditioning does not give men the necessary resources to develop skills in domestic chores and care giving and also, they do not undertake such work with pride. This situation often gets overlooked within the gender-blind disaster recovery interventions, and thereby gaps in men's coping capacities in such circumstances can victimize them in the recovery process.

Since in absolute comparison between men and women, women emerge as more vulnerable than men, there is a significant and a real need to focus on women's vulnerabilities. However, such a continuous focus on women has a downside as this promotes the perception of women more as victims, and less as capable and equal actors in the prevention, management and mitigation processes. This contributes to the prevailing situation, wherein men's roles and responsibilities in disaster preparedness, mitigation and management are highly recognized, but women's skills, capabilities and contributions remain sidelined or invisible. As a result, women are disadvantaged on both these counts. The common perception of women as dependent, weak and subordinate acts as a barrier that isolates and excludes them from the planning and decision-making processes. Their skills and life experiences are not identified. They are counted as family, societal and community resources and, are therefore not incorporated into risk reduction and disaster preparedness, relief or recovery efforts. Such a dual disadvantage results in deepened vulnerability and dependency for women, and a denial of opportunities for them to learn, grow, contribute and provide leadership to disaster management initiatives. As a result, the cycle of gender-biased and unequal power relations further intensifies and conditions are created for the perpetuation of a status quo. This situation constitutes a tremendous loss to women in their individual right and a big loss of resource to their families, communities and nations. Meanwhile, the potential contributions that women can offer to the disaster risk reduction imperatives around the world are often overlooked and female leadership in building community resilience to disasters is frequently disregarded. On account of their different role definitions and life experiences, men and women can indeed complement each other when contributing to risk reduction and disaster management. Good practices of gender-inclusive disaster management which have been observed across the globe are evidence of this.

Mainstreaming Gender in Disaster Risk Reduction

To quote the World Development Report (2012) on Gender Equality and Development, "Gender equality is a core development objective in its own right. It is also smart economics. Greater gender equality can enhance productivity, improve development outcomes for the next generation, and make institutions more representative." According to Kofi Annan, the Secretary General of United Nations, "Gender equality is more than a goal in itself. It is a precondition for meeting the challenge of reducing poverty, promoting sustainable development and building good governance." There are new kinds of institutions, incorporating new norms and rules that support equal and just relations between women and men. The WDR has identified and focused on four priority areas for taking forward policy: (i) reducing excess female mortality and closing education gaps where they remain; (ii) improving access to economic opportunities for women; (iii) increasing women's voice and agency in the household and in society; and (iv) limiting the reproduction of gender inequality across generations. The WDR bespeaks of the urgency of mainstreaming gender and gender equality in all realms of life, including disaster management. Coupled with the fact that women demonstrate more vulnerability to disaster impact, yet also possess special capacities to deal with the challenges emanating out of a disaster situation, the need and the urgency to integrate women's participation in all phases of disaster management is only a natural corollary of the discussion.

Regarding mainstreaming gender in DRR, a few questions come to our mind as to what constitutes mainstreaming, what is the basis of mainstreaming and what are the indicators, which will suffice for mainstreaming? In the Disaster Management discourse, the entire process has been classified in four different phases: (i) Disaster Preparedness; (ii) Disaster response and relief; (iii) Disaster Recovery and Reconstruction; and (iv) Disaster Prevention, Mitigation and Risk Reduction. It would be important to look at the gender relations framework in consonance with the disaster risk reduction/management cycle. The challenge is not what to do for gender mainstreaming in DRR, but how to achieve the desired objectives.

UNISDR, (United Nations International Strategy for Disaster Reduction), a committed organization of UN for Disaster Risk Reduction is working for this cause since its inception. UNISDR, as part of the ongoing effort to promote gend er equality in social, cultural and economic development, is determined to increase its efforts to mainstream gender concerns and needs into disaster risk reduction. The Hyogo Framework, which was developed and adopted by member countries in 2005, realized the importance of gender based vulnerability when it emphasized that: "A gender perspective should be integrated into all disaster risk management policies, plans and decision-making processes, including those related to risk assessment, early warning, information management and education and training." It is important to recognize that women and men also have specific needs and vulnerabilities. A project in the Andaman and Nicobar Islands recognized these differences via a Participatory Vulnerability Analysis that gave women space for awareness raising, sharing experiences, and skill-training, together with forming women's groups. Through a Gender-Sensitive Risk Assessment analysis, women expressed their needs and as a result participated in Action Aid supported collective swimming and fishing classes, and training in financial and economic management (UNISDR, 2007).

As per the UNISDR report on gender mainstreaming, an increasing number of governments are recognizing the importance of gender issues in their national DRR reporting to UNISDR, even though the institutionalization of the same in terms of a meaningful progress is far from adequate. Progress in the last five years started from a very low baseline. Successive evaluations made by UNISDR globally to see the gender concerns of government projects, programme and policies found that in 2004, only 19 out of 118 national reports received by UNISDR from governments mentioned gender issues. The reports reflected poor awareness of gender, and a reliance on a disaster response-focused approach that did not factor in gender. In 2007, only 10 out of 62 reports received by UNISDR for the first session of the Global Platform for Disaster Risk Reduction touched upon gender or women's issues. There was overall progress in terms of awareness of the issue; however, most initiatives reported were focused on gender in disaster management, rather than disaster risk reduction. In 2009, 52 out of 62 national reports submitted to UNISDR reported full acknowledgement of gender concerns (UNISDR). The task is not completed yet. There are some initiatives, but there is still a huge gap in terms of actual practice. In the current scenario, although there are numerous policy documents clearly stating political commitment to mainstreaming gender issues into DRR, no tangible or sustainable progress has resulted from this, with the exception of some ad hoc activities. Furthermore, substantial progress has not been made in mobilizing resources for mainstreaming gender perspectives into the disaster risk reduction process.

In recent years, a gradual shift has been observed in the approach; wherein instead of a reactive approach, various governments, and civil societies, with or without the support of UN organizations have taken initiative for proactive risk management. Within the same, women's role has been envisaged and their key role in risk management has been sought to be achieved. The entire framework has been conceived as a mainstreaming effort, where instead of women, gender analysis has been given priority, and both men and women are equally engaged in risk management. Such an approach has begun to yield the much needed positive change in society.

In India, and also in the South Asian region where gender relations are somewhat similar, a lot of emphasis has been given to bringing policy changes to the development discourse for mainstreaming women, and thereby moving forward from a welfare approach to an empowerment approach. However, initiatives undertaken so far have not been as effective as they were intended to be. There has been a huge gap between policy and practice. Dr. Naila Kabeer (1994) has explained this policy practice gap with the logical framework analysis (LFA). She has argued that whenever policy is implemented, it does not lead to the intended outcomes, and also that equal opportunity has not led to equal outcomes. She has also contended that not much emphasis has been given to efforts to address strategic gender interests, which has mostly remained focused on addressing practical gender needs. These largely address the array of issues of women's welfare, but do not focus on the empowerment and inclusive mainstreaming approach, which can ultimately lead to changing the rigidity of the prevailing gender relations. The government of Gujarat did make an exemplary attempt to bring change by making strategic interventions as part of its post-disaster long-term recovery programme. It gave joint ownership of the house in the name of the husband and wife and this actually helped in influencing gender relations. This also gave collateral rights for accessing formal institutions (banks, insurance, cooperative, etc.) in addressing their needs. The tsunami reconstruction programme of 2004 and a few others initiatives have also followed a similar pattern to make for a more inclusive process. Dr. Kabeer suggests three distinct, but inter-related categories of gender disadvantages: (i) gender intensified disadvantage (both suffer, but women suffer in a more intensified form); (ii) gender specific disadvantage (women suffer, by virtue of the fact that they are women); and (iii) bureaucratically imposed disadvantage (little to do with reality, more based on perceptions, biases and prejudices).

Many worthwhile illustrations can be highlighted to lend credence to the role that women are capable of playing in reducing disaster risks. In Bangladesh, a woman named Sahena organized a committee of women to be prepared for floods (UNISDR). This committee teaches women how to build portable clay ovens, elevate their houses, and use radios to learn of possible floods or changes in climate. These efforts have saved many lives and empowered the local women. In India, since the Latur earthquake, women have been supervising, monitoring and undertaking construction, encouraging repairs and verifying if engineers have certified the construction. They participate in the construction of community buildings and model houses, and conduct educational awareness campaigns on earthquake resistant technology. After hurricane Joan, women in Malukutu, Nicaragua, organized to develop plans for disaster preparedness that included all household members. Consequently, Malukutu was better prepared for Hurricane Mitch, and recovered sooner than other similarly affected communities. Unlike many other communities in Honduras, La Masica reported no deaths after Hurricane Mitch in 1998. In response to a disaster agency providing gender-sensitive community education on early warning systems and hazard management six months earlier, women took over from men, the abandoned task of continuously monitoring the early warning system. This enabled a prompt evacuation when the hurricane struck. Women also have a key role to play in village-based disaster-preparedness groups in Bangladesh. The committees use radios to find out about hurricanes and pass on early warning messages. They also make sure that every family has dried food and a portable oven, and a safe place to protect their food and livestock. In the floods of 2007 in Bangladesh, villages with emergency committees were better prepared to deal with the disaster. As primary health care providers in the home, women strive to keep families healthy and teach children about safety and self-protection. These are assets, when communities are severely impacted by a disaster and people face involuntary and unforeseen relocation.

Conclusion

In the larger analysis, women cannot be treated as a homogenous category and, hence, interventions need to be designed with the acknowledgement of their different vulnerabilities and the distinct social cultural realities that they experience. More importantly, there is a discernible need to focus, enhance and tap their capacities, to ensure that women play a significant and pro-active role in the entire process of disaster management. As a first step, the rules and practices of different formal and informal institutions working for community development have to be analyzed and designed appropriately to enable a gender just environment, leading to women's empowerment and altered gender relations. In the discourse of Disaster Risk Reduction, gender based inclusive approach must be adopted. Women should not be looked upon as 'victims' and their wisdom and capacity need to be recognized, and harnessed in disaster risk management.

On the other hand, men should not always be seen as providers, but their disadvantages may also be noted and due interventions should be made. DRR policies, rules, institutions and practices should be revisited to ensure a gender mainstreamed DRR approach. Gender aware, gender-sensitive and gender specific policies and practices for DRR are the need of the hour for creating a gender just society. Needless to state that if we are truly interested in DRR, we will have to radically alter our perspectives and stance, and focus on capitalizing upon women's abilities as leaders and change agents. We will need to change popular perceptions about women from the V&V (victims and vulnerable) approach to thc L&C (leaders and capacity) approach. For the past few decades, we have been investing in the V&V approach, but there is need to revisit the entire approach and invest in a new hypothesis. Only a renewed focus on enhancing the capacities of women to make them effective leaders and disaster risk managers shall create the requisite impetus and the desire for participation by the women themselves, and shall reveal to the world the integral potential of this constituency to partner at each step of the way.

References

Kabeer, N. (1994). *Reversed Realities: Gender Hierarchies in Development Thought*. UK: Verso.

Kabeer, N., and Ramya, S. (eds.) (1999). *Institutions, Relations and Outcomes: A Framework and Case Studies for Gender-aware Planning*. New Delhi: Kali for Women.

UNDP. (2013). *Disaster and Gender Risk Reduction*. New York: UNDP.

UNISDR. (2009). Making Disaster risk reduction gender sensitive – Policy and Practical Guidelines. Geneva: UNISDR, UNDP and IUCN.

3

Climate Change and Disaster

Need for a Human Rights Based Approach to Disaster Reduction and Sustainable Development

Ajay Jha and *Sharad Joshi*

In May 2013, carbon concentration reached 400 parts per million (ppm) at an observatory in Hawaii. Global carbon concentration is supposed to reach 400 ppm soon. It was 315 ppm in 1958, 375 ppm in 2000 (UNEP, 2012). While it increased by 60 ppm in 42 years till 2000, in the last decade, it rose by 25 ppm. The reasons are easy to understand. The global emission was 40 gigatonnes (GT) of carbon dioxide (CO_2)e in 2000, which rose to 50 GT of CO_2 in 2011, rising by 25 per cent in ten years! The current emission levels need to be brought down to 44 GT of CO_2 by 2020, to contain a rise in temperature below 2 degrees Celsius[1] .

Against this rapid increase in climate change, global efforts have been lacklustre. In the business as usual (BAU) scenario, the total emissions in 2020 will be 58 GT. Based on the pledges that have been made by the countries in the United Nations Framework Convention on Climate Change (UNFCCC)[2], and the Kyoto Protocol[3] in the best case scenario, the emissions in 2020 will be 52 GT, in the worst case scenario (low ambition levels), it will be 57 GT. This is only one GT less than business as usual scenario and far above the threshold limit of 44 GT. Obviously, this is not enough to keep the rise in temperature below 2 degrees Celsius. This calls for wartime efforts to reduce the emissions.

Climate Change and Disaster

One of the manifested impacts of runaway climate change has been the increasing frequency of disasters. The World Meteorological

Organization (WMO), in a report released in June, 2013 declared the decade (2001-2010) "a decade of climate extremes," being the warmest decade for both land and ocean temperatures, and in which the rate of increase in global warming has been unprecedented. Every year of the decade, except 2008, was among the ten warmest years. It reported significant loss of Arctic sea ice, decline in the Greenland and Antarctic ice sheets. The global average sea level over the decade was 20 cm higher than that in 1880. The decade was second wettest since 1901 and eastern USA, northern and eastern Canada along with many parts of Europe and Central Asia were particularly wet. Floods were the most frequent climate extreme events with big floods in Eastern Europe, India, Africa, Asia (more than 2000 people died in floods in Pakistan in 2010) and Australia. At the same time, many countries in East Africa, the Amazon basin and Australia were also visited by droughts. The decade saw 511 tropical cyclones, which killed more than 100,000 people and 250 million people were reported to be affected. More than 138,000 people were believed to be killed or missing due to Cyclone Nargis in Myanmar alone in 2008. The decade recorded an astounding 2000 per cent increase in deaths from heat waves (mainly in Europe in 2003 and Russia in 2010) from less than 6000 in 1991-2000 to 136,000 in 2001-2010. According to the data of the Centre for Research on the Epidemiology, a total of more than 370,000 people died due to extreme climate events[4]. In June 2013 itself, Uttarakhand in India witnessed unprecedented damage, by far the worst in the year where flashfloods and landslides killed more than 10,000 people. Cyclone Haiyan also killed an equal number of people in Philippines in November, 2013 and affected almost one million people. It is not only the people in poor countries, who are dying; but the decade has the signature of climate extremes and deaths in all parts of the world.

Global response to Disaster and Disaster Risk Reduction

Over the past 70 years, world's population has risen by 87 per cent. The population living in flood prone river basins has increased by 114 per cent and the population living in cyclone-exposed coastlines has increased by 192 per cent. More than half of the world's population is located in cities lying in huge seismic activity areas.

The economic losses from disasters now stand at $125 billion per year and are rising at the rate of $30 billion per decade (ODI,

2013)[5]. Hydro-meteorological disasters (disasters induced due to climate change impacts) now compose 80 per cent of all disasters and if climate change is not halted, disasters are likely to increase in the near future. It has the potential of reversing the developmental gains achieved over time. Disasters have a tendency to create a class of marginalized communities; the worst affected are poor people in the developing and poor countries and especially the marginalized groups (Scheduled Castes and Scheduled Tribes for instance in India), women, children, aged, disabled and migrants. The experience of disasters in India has revealed discrimination against the indigenous populations and dalits; absence of records of migrants killed due to disasters; significant instances of women compelled to engage in survival sex; and the sale of children to survive[6].

Global response to disasters has been limited to adoption of the Hyogo Framework of Action (HFA) in the World Conference on Disasters (2005), which was adopted as a response to the Asian Tsunami and with the commitment to reduce risk from disasters. HFA has been adopted by more than 168 countries since its adoption in 2005. The first phase comes to an end in 2015, and a lot of discussions on the successor of the Hyogo Framework of Action (HFA 2) have already taken place. While the achievements during the period have been significant in terms of adoption of policies, legislations and institutions by the countries, and increase in the coverage of people by fiscal instruments/insurance; the challenges have been equally significant.

Experience and Lessons Learnt from Implementation of Hyogo Framework of Action

The implementation of the HFA has shown that despite an increasing number of countries adopting HFA and creating national frameworks to disaster reduction, disaster reduction is yet to be recognized as a core development policy. It often ends up at a losing end in competition of the larger development goals, such as poverty reduction, economic growth, health and food security concerns. Some of the lessons learnt are listed below:

(i) Challenges of translation of priority areas of HFA into targets internationally and into national programmes.
(ii) Focus on *ex post* responses, rather than *ex ante* measures.
(iii) Lack of capacity for assessment, preparedness and responses and lack of data.

(iv) Lack of role for communities in preparedness and responses and lack of community based institutions, which are generally the first to come to the rescue of affected populations.

Some of the overarching concerns arising from the experience of almost a decade of HFA are as below:

(i) It is only the disaster communities, which become relevant for HFA, it's not owned by countries or international community, and therefore, action has been limited to creating a national platform for disaster reduction, without essential priorities of HFA being woven into the DRR framework. It must address power imbalances and political dynamics within the communities and countries, and has to be seen in the context of stronger accountability framework.

(ii) HFA looks only into the environmental/hazard impact, while social, economic and psycho-social aspects remain unaddressed. Experiences show that 90 per cent of the losses in disasters arise out of low intensity high frequency events, which underlines that social, economic and psycho-social aspects need to be addressed in an adequate manner.

(iii) Disasters have been mainly addressed to reduce development/economic losses, while the current paradigm of development continues to create unacceptable levels of risk and exposure.

Scope and Opportunities

In the last few years, there has been an increasing discussion on disasters in the context of increased risk from climate change impacts. This has formed a significant part of the discussion in the climate change negotiations since the Conference of Parties in Cancun (2010), which adopted the Cancun Adaptation Framework (composed of an adaptation committee, an adaptation fund and a work programme on loss and damage from climate change induced disasters). The recent Conference of Parties in Warsaw, Poland (December, 2013) reiterated that loss and damage is an integral part of climate change adaptation and resolved to set up a mechanism to look into loss and damage. The developing countries are increasingly asking for a prominent place for disaster loss and damage in the future global agreement, which is supposed to be ready by the year 2015.

There has been significant discussion on the successor of HFA in the World Conference of Disasters, the Global Platform on Disaster Risk Reduction (2009) as well as in report of the like Commission on Climate Change and Development (CCD, 2009) and the special report Intergovernmental Panel on Climate Change (IPCC) on managing the risk of extreme events and disasters to advance climate change adaptation (IPCC 2009). However, the biggest opportunity lies in the series of discussions and responses in the post 2015 development agenda of the United Nations; the follow up of the Rio+20 Conference; and formulation of the Sustainable Development Goals. The report of the High Level Panel of Eminent Persons[7], which was commissioned by the United Nations Secretary General to look into the post 2015 development agenda of the United Nations, recognized "Sustainable Development at Core" as one of the major transformational shifts desired. It also recognized climate change as one of the global challenges and reiterated the link between climate change and sustainability, poverty, and inclusion. The Open Working Group on Sustainable Development Goals[8] (OWG) set up to follow up on the outcomes of the Rio+20 Conference looks at climate change and disasters as one of the important areas for discussion in the context of the sustainable development goals. The OWG is aiming to include goals, targets and indicators to address climate change and disasters within the sustainable development goals. The current proposals on the table include either having a stand-alone goal on climate change and disasters, or having specific targets related to climate change and disaster woven within the larger development goals, such as economic growth, poverty reduction, gender empowerment, education, etc. Yet another proposal concerns an integration of climate change, energy and disasters.

A Reflection on India's Climate Politics

International negotiations on climate change face continued bottlenecks. The Conference of Parties, the annual high level meetings of the United Nations Framework Convention on Climate Change (1993), which is the only international treaty to ensure global cooperation towards climate stabilization and the meetings of Kyoto Protocol, which laid down the science based targets for the developed countries emission reduction, have failed to lead to adequate mitigation efforts by the developed countries. The Conference of Parties at Durban decided to have a new framework of international cooperation where going beyond Kyoto Protocol, all developed and developing countries are likely to contribute to mitigation and adaptation. Without going into the details of this proposed transformation, it is highly unlikely that the new treaty will provide the transformational shift, which is required to keep the rise in global temperature below 2 degrees Celsius and 400 ppm of carbon concentration in the atmosphere.

In the face of an impending global impasse, national and sub national policies on climate change are becoming increasingly important. A number of developed and developing countries have adopted policies and legislations at the national and sub-national levels to reduce emissions and emission intensity. It is encouraging to see that the developing countries have taken a lead in adopting these national and sub-national policies.

India's Position in International Negotiations

India has been one of the important countries to have acknowledged the importance of having development strategies integrated with objectives of environmental and social protection. Mrs. Indira Gandhi participated in the famous Stockholm Conference (1972), which for the first time brought environment on the global political agenda. The Rio Conference on Earth and Development (UNCED, 1992) reiterated this global intention by listing impressive outcomes in the UN Convention on Biological Diversity (UNCBD), UN Convention against Desertification (UNCCD), UN Framework Convention on Climate Change (UNFCCC), and Agenda 21. India has also played a significant role in shaping the global environmental policies. Nationally too, India has enacted a slew of legislations for the protection of the environment, biodiversity, water and ambient air, among others. However, over the period, there has been a significant and perceptible shift in India's policy and its position in international negotiations, which has raised international curiosity and has also been subject to scathing criticism at home. Having the advantage of low per capita emission of the GHG (1.6 per ton of carbon emission per capita, as opposed to 20 tons of the US, and a global average of 4 tons), India initially harped on the per capita principle (right of countries to atmospheric space should be determined on per capita emission basis) and refused to acknowledge any role for developing countries in the climate stabilization efforts. Mr. Manmohan Singh declared in 2008 that India's per capita emission will never surpass that of the developed countries. However, gradually, India could understand that this position has led to its isolation in the international community, and a shift has been necessitated to maintain its leadership role globally and among developing countries. Preceding the Copenhagen COP Meeting (2009), India declared in the Major Economies Forum Meeting at L' Aquila that India will reduce its emission intensity (emission per unit of the GDP). In Copenhagen COP, following China's declaration, India declared that it will reduce its emission intensity by 20-25 per cent (on a 2005 baseline) by 2020. Since then India has steadfastly guarded its position and India's domestic policies have also targeted a 20-25 per cent reduction in emission intensity, which have been essentially based on India's international pledge. The scope of the current paper does not allow us to go deeper to explore whether this target is ambitious enough, however, it will suffice to say that many countries have understood that having ambitious climate policies is in their national interest, and therefore, they have gone beyond their international pledges and adopted more ambitious national and sub-national policies.

India's National Action Plan on Climate Change and Recent Developments

The Prime Minister of India declared a National Action Plan on Climate Change (NAPCC) on 30th June 2008.

The NAPCC has laid down the following eight Missions:

1. National Mission on Solar Energy, launched as Jawaharlal Nehru Solar Mission in 2010, with targets of generating 20,000 MW from solar energy, (including 2000 MW of off grid) by 2022, and achieving 15 per cent of RE in the total energy mix.
2. National Mission on Enhanced Energy Efficiency, objective of saving about INR 75,000 crores worth of transactions in energy efficiency. In doing so, it will, by 2015, help save about five per cent of the annual energy consumption, and nearly 100 million tons of carbon dioxide every year.
3. National Water Mission, to ensure water use efficiency of about 20 per cent.

4. Green India Mission, with the goal of increasing forest cover by ten million ha and enhancing the quality of forests in another 10 million ha.
5. National Mission on Sustainable Agriculture, to introduce climate resilience (no specific target).
6. National Mission on Sustainable Habitat (no specific target).
7. National Mission on Sustaining Himalayan Ecosystem (no specific target).
8. National Mission on Strategic Knowledge (no specific target).

The NAPCC was declared without any public consultation and PM's council on climate change (with no member from the public, and having only one member from outside Delhi) was charged with the implementation of the NAPCC. This lack of consultation was decried by the civil society and the experts alike. The MoEF which is the nodal ministry for climate change efforts, assured that detailed public consultations will take place at the time of the formulation of the Missions. Another major allegation that NAPCC faced was the lack of clear targets, timelines, sources and modalities for implementation. It was dubbed as a "wish list without any roadmap". Even after five years of being launched, there has been no review or assessment of the NAPCC by the government. An informal stocktaking of the NAPCC, in late 2011, summed up the developments as "many of the missions except solar mission, energy efficiency, green India and water mission have failed to take off due to lack of clarity of targets at the operational level." The Planning Commission Working Group, while formulating the 12th FYP suggested merging many missions and scrapping a few, for the lack of financial resources and implementability. An assessment done by the IIT Chennai and IIT Mumbai groups (2011-12) reiterated the lack of clarity on targets, timelines, modalities and financial resources as major constraints hampering the implementation of the NAPCC. As a matter of fact, only a few missions of the NAPCC have moved forward as expected. The solar mission has registered an impressive growth, and has achieved the target of generating 1000 MW of solar PV in the first phase (2010-2013). However, the progress on off grid and solar thermal has remained limited with solar thermal capacity creation of only 5.5 MW against the target of 470 MW. However, the achievements have been marred by gaps in policy and regulatory lapses. Lanco cornered one-third of the projects (235 MW) in the first phase by operating through many front companies of dubious credentials, while the target was to limit the participation to 20 MW-40 MW, so as to prevent monopolistic practices in the solar sector. Flawed policies and lack of emphasis on domestic content requirement (DCR) also resulted in most capacity creation through imports rather than enhancing domestic capacity. The three most expensive solar programmes of the world (which require 2 lakh crore of investment of public money) remain severely challenged by the US and Chinese competition.

The National Mission on Enhanced Energy Efficiency has also witnessed major progress. Partial Risk Guarantee Fund (PRGF) and the Venture Capital Fund for Energy Efficiency (VCFEE) set up and Perform, Achieve and Trade (PAT) were launched. Under the PAT, specific energy consumption (SEC) targets have been identified for designated consumer (DC) companies across eight sectors with targets to be achieved by 2014-2015. The Bureau of Energy Efficiency (BEE) has also framed labeling standards for a number of home appliances. However, it also remains beset with many problems; viz. focus on EE without integration with R&D; and poor coordination with states. PAT is available only for big companies, not SMEs, while the Indian industry is dominated by the SMEs.

The National Water Mission seeks to introduce water use efficiency of 20 per cent. However, it is largely focused on mountain watersheds and wetlands, with little concerns for water demand management and irrigation. The mission continues with the age old model of centralized water resource development projects, long distance water transfers and canal irrigation. Emphasis could have been laid more on developing and strengthening local authorities for management of water resources. The mission also reveals poor inter-disciplinary coordination and fails to capture the complexity of the domain. The only benefit that the mission provides to the people is that it promises to put all data related to water use in public domain. There has been little progress besides release of some policy documents. The National Water Mission; restructuring of central water commission; and draft guidelines for development of water use efficiency in rural, urban, industrial and irrigation sectors; and web enabled water resources information system of India (India-WRIS) are a few things that the Mission could achieve till now.

The Mission on Green India has progressed faster than the NAPCC, because of lure of international funding that India looks forward to seek from REDD+Programme. However, the achievements have been limited on the ground. Three advisories have been issued till January 2012 and they focus on: (i) selecting landscape and operational units; (ii) operations to be undertaken after short listing landscapes/sub units; and (iii) funding of the Green India Mission. The states were supposed to provide bridge plans (by the end of 2011) and five to ten years perspective plans (by February 2012), which they are yet to submit. The state governments are also supposed to identify land and seek funding. A fund of INR 4,500 crore per annum has been earmarked for the GIM, any additional support required is planned to be met from external funding. The Ministry of Finance has allocated INR 500 crore from the national clean energy fund for the bridge plan and for the GIM. The Union Budget 2011-2012 announced INR 200 crore as the take off fund for the GIM. However, recent developments suggest fast movement and MOEF is organizing one workshop in each state every month on REDD+preparedness. All the SAPCCs are also focussed on earning money from REDD+Programme.

The National Mission on Sustainable Agriculture seeks to mainstream mitigation and adaptation in agriculture through a number of centrally sponsored schemes, namely, NFSM, NHM, RKVY. However, till the Mission was launched as part of the 12th Five Year Plan, there were limited efforts. The Indian Council of Agricultural Research undertook a National Initiative on Climate Resilient Agriculture (NICRA) to promote strategic research and technology demonstration in 100 vulnerable districts with a budget of rupees 350 crores. The National Mission on Sustainable Agriculture was launched with the 12th FYP. The mission is highly technology driven and promotes GMOs, Bio-fuel, and no till agriculture, which are not in consonance with the reality of the small and marginal farmers. There is very little support for adaptation, risk insurance and coverage. Also, there has been little coordination between the centre and the states with the centre having no control over state projects and priorities. Besides these missions, there has been almost no development in the rest of the missions.

State Action Plan on Climate Change

The MoEF asked the states of formulate State Action Plan on Climate Change (SAPCC) to support the NAPCC. States started reluctantly to formulate the SAPCCs after flunking many deadlines. By now over 20 states are in the various stages of formulation and submission. Five SAPCCs (MP, Rajasthan, Sikkim, Tripura, Arunachal Pradesh) have been approved by National Steering Committee on Climate Change and six SAPCCs (Andhra Pradesh, Assam, Mizoram, Meghalaya, Odisha, West Bengal) are under consideration by the Expert Committee. Many coastal states like Gujarat, Tamil Nadu and Kerala, and Maharashtra. Gujarat and Bihar are yet to submit their plans. Most of the Plans based on the framework of the NAPCC, have a very wide sweep and include energy, agriculture, water, forests, urban development, health, animal husbandry and energy efficiency.

A peep into the SAPCCs manifests that it is highly secretive and top down. Not all plans are in the public domain. No information is available even with the MOEF regarding the process and timeline. It has been essentially a consultant driven and bureaucratic exercise, with no ownership of the states. Except in the Madhya Pradesh, nowhere have meaningful consultations with experts, impacted communities and civil society taken place. There is no deadline and no clarity till when and how plans will be finalized, what is the basis. There is also huge amount of hankering over finances to implement the plans.

Most of the plans have no concern for equity, rights of people and gender. Plans do not talk at all about increasing access and equity in energy, water or natural resources. They also remain equally insensitive to gender concerns in climate change. None of them even mention the UN Declaration on the Rights of Indigenous Population (UNDRIP). Many of the states are being helped by World Bank, UNDP, DFID, GIZ, etc. and have clear imprints of international negotiations rather than local concerns and priorities. Most of the states have actually developed these plans without any mapping, vulnerability assessment of regions or sectors. States do not possess much vision in missions on energy efficiency, industries, health, livelihoods and urban planning. No plan shows real affinity with the people who are being affected due to climate change impacts.

Most of these plans pay lip service to agriculture and food security. While most of the states acknowledge the importance of agriculture, many of them propose actions which will harm agriculture and endanger food security. The Manipur Plan talks about "modern scientific agriculture" and proposes a set of actions to improve agriculture, including "modernization of agriculture:

biotechnology, seed replacement increased use of fertilizers...." West Bengal and Rajasthan propose "zero tillage agriculture" and Rajasthan includes "exploring carbon sequestration potential of carbon deficient soil" and "increased use of biotechnology". Odisha has also given extensive treatment to agriculture in the plan, however, it failed to allocate a single Rupee to agriculture in the first draft! As far as agriculture is concerned, it is "more of the same" except for some research proposed for vulnerability mapping for specific agro-climatic zones and crops. The actions suggested will harm small holder farmers and endanger food security rather than enhancing it.

Recommendations on Fundamental Principles in Addressing Climate Change and Disaster in the SDGs

While the proposals are still being vetted, it is important that the OWG goes beyond having climate change and disaster in the narrative. Formulated in any manner, it is extremely important that some important principles arising from the overarching concerns in the implementation of the HFA are woven into the proposed framework. These include:

- Recognition of goal of keeping rise in temperature below 2 degrees Celsius and to progressively reduce this target to 1.5 degrees Celsius.
- Recognition of Common but Differentiated Responsibility based on Respective Capability (CBDR-RC) and equity as foundational principles in climate change responses.
- Reduce risk and exposure (besides economic losses) and significantly increase resilience of communities through strategies integrating poverty reduction, employment and livelihoods, education, health, urban development, transport and human security with climate change adaptation and disaster.
- Recognition of disaster reduction as a development policy, removing conflict between development policies and disaster reduction.
- Incorporation of human rights based approach in disaster reduction, and focus on marginalized populations, IDPs, physically disabled, women and children, poor and migrants.
- Recognition of the fact that people in disaster have same rights as citizens and human beings and measures are

needed to remove discrimination in disaster responses; state should have the primary responsibility to protect, promote and respect rights of affected people and assist them in rehabilitation and reconstruction; affected people must be able to access information related to disaster risk; improvement of early warning systems and coverage of people with insurance. Rebuilding should be looked as an opportunity to remove discrimination and promote rights and equity.

- Focus on preparedness and *ex ante* measures.
- Convergence of climate change adaptation and disaster reduction strategies as sustainable development practices.
- Strengthening community based disaster reduction approaches, with involvement of communities and vulnerable populations in all phases of disasters including preparedness, response, prolonged displacement and relocation and recovery and reconstruction.
- Increased policy and budgetary support to facilitate rights based disaster risk reduction frameworks.

Incorporation of these principles in the SDGs will create a mutually reinforcing agenda and integration of human rights dimensions in climate change adaptation, disaster risk reduction and sustainable development. However, this would not be achieved without a robust global cooperation framework on climate change and disaster.

References

1. All data based on the UNEP's "Emission Gap Report 2012" available at http://www.unep.org/publications/ebooks/emissionsgap2012/, last accessed on 13 November 2013
2. UNFCCC is the only global treaty to stabilize climate and has membership of 193 countries.
3. Kyoto Protocol obliges developed and industrial countries to reduce their emissions, however, top emitters like US and Australia have renounced KP, and China, by virtue of being a developing country, is exempted from compulsory emission reduction.
4. All data are based on the WMO report released in July, 2013 titled "2001-1020; A Decade of Climate Extremes" available athttp://www.wmo.int/pages /mediacentre/press_releases/pr_976_en.html, last accessed on 13 November 2013.

5. http://www.odi.org.uk/sites/odi.org.uk/files/odi-assets/publications-opinion-files/8358.pdf
6. The organization making the submission has worked extensively in Kosi Floods in Bihar (2008) and Flashfloods and landslides in Uttarakhand (2013), and have come across many stories cited in the experiences.
7. In July 2012, Secretary-General Ban Ki-moon announced the 27 members of a High-level Panel to advise on the global development framework beyond 2015, the target date for the Millennium Development Goals (MDGs). The Panel was co-chaired by President Susilo Bambang Yudhoyono of Indonesia, President Ellen Johnson Sirleaf of Liberia, and Prime Minister David Cameron of the United Kingdom, and it includes leaders from civil society, private sector and government. The Panel submitted its report on 30 May 2013.
8. The Open Working Group was established on 22nd of January 2013 by decision 67/555 (*see* A/67/L.48/rev.1) of the General Assembly. The 30-member OWG of the General Assembly is tasked with preparing a proposal on the SDGs and will submit its report by the end of the 68th session (September 2014) of the United Nations General Assembly.

4

The Trajectory of Disaster Response

From Relief to Resilience

Neera Agnimitra

UDAI-II – *Sahyatri* has indeed meant co-travel... co-travel with the trajectory of the disaster, and with the communities which became the unfortunate victims of the disaster. It also entailed a shared journey of the faculty and the students of the Department of Social Work, University of Delhi, the team at the project site that was adopted by the Department, and the communities. The co-travel has lucidly demonstrated the emergence and the sustenance of meaningful relationship between an academic institution imparting knowledge and competencies to its learners to engage with disasters and disaster management and, the communities, who were impacted by a disaster of significant magnitude and dimensions. The co-travel has been arduous, fraught with uncertainty, trepidatious, challenging, and agonizing, for it has meant, sharing in the trauma of the impacted people and yet, it has been engaging, meaningful, exciting, gratifying, inspiring, insightful, and emotionally satiating, as it has provided an opportunity to engage with praxis. It enabled the Department to integrate the theoretical knowledge, skills and the rich experience that it had garnered in engaging with erstwhile disasters like the Gujarat Earthquake in the year 2001, to assuage the havoc that the flood in the Kosi river wreaked in the lives of thousands of people who had build a life on its banks, and even beyond.

In engaging with the disaster, the team traversed from a phase where immediate relief was the most spontaneous response to the humongous tragedy that had befallen the people, to the after phase, in which the people needed more than just a stop gap arrangement of supplies and services. The fact that the disrupted lives had to be rebuilt and the ruptured sense of existence had to be consolidated, led the team to extend its journey into the recovery phase of the disaster. The journey has not ended... it is ongoing, as is the experiential learning that has come as a consequence of the engagement. The journey has enabled the team to explore and innovate with a range of interventions to assist the communities to recover and to develop a level of resilience to deal with a disaster of the nature that it experienced in August 2008. In many ways, *Sahyatri* has become an integral part of a professional, and indeed, personal traverse of the team with the lives of the people who became its *Sahyatris*. In more ways than one, the co-travel truly enabled its valued team members to understand the meaning and ramifications of being comrades in arms and participants in action, and this is indeed an integral premise and the basis of all communitarian practice.

The trajectory of the disaster response originated in August 2008 and traversed the temporal frame to reach the present. Having become an integral part of the *Sahyatris*, it is a journey without an end. While the journey has been 'seamless', as it negotiated an almost reflective engagement with the field and the people, it can be arranged in terms of certain distinct phases that any disaster intervention naturally alludes to in its paradigmatic form. The distinct phases presented their inherent issues, concerns, and challenges, in terms of the criticality of the needs and problems experienced by the impacted communities, and offered opportunities to the team to apply itself to the same, in conventional and non-conventional ways. The journey also provided the team with rich insights about the multiple ways in which communities engage with and cope with a disaster, and about the role that a school of social work can play in mitigating the impact of the disaster and in facilitating recovery.

A Personal Trail.... Within the Journey

From its initiation as a spontaneous response to the great tragedy that befell the people of Supaul, Madhepura, Araria, Saharsa and Purnea districts in Northern Bihar, when the Kosi River breached its embankment and decided to alter its course, to the present, the journey has been wrought with multifarious challenges and has been replete with multiple lessons that were learnt. It created opportunities for each member of the Core Team and each participant to fit their efforts, attributes and competencies into the larger initiative. The initiative came to life, almost as unprompted as the river was when it chose to permeate into the lives of the people who inhabited its plains. For the author, conjoining with the initiative was a very natural outcome of her association with disasters and disaster management. As the course teacher teaching this *hugely in demand* optional course on 'Social Work and Disaster Management' offered by the Department of Social Work, the urge to respond to the tragedy of the Kosi flood disaster was a natural one, and as she sees it now, her association with UDAI-II, *Sahyatri* gave her the unprecedented opportunity to personally engage with, apply, learn, revalidate and reaffirm all that she has been teaching in her classroom interface with her students.

The author distinctly feels that all those of us who teach social work, do discern a strong sense of incompleteness within ourselves, if we have not quite had the opportunity to procure a 'hands on' experience in the chosen domain of our teaching. Quite naturally therefore, her own urge to work and contribute to interventions of disaster management and mitigation has been incessant, and the desire to plunge into available opportunities compelling. It is her belief that justifiably so, the students, who are expected to listen, absorb and apply all of that she has to offer in the theoretical domain, also look up to her to help them translate into practice, at least a few out of the array of issues, problems and interventions that she elucidates, dissects, and theorizes in the classroom. And so, apart from her own wanderlust for engaging with praxis, it is the occasional questioning look in their eyes that sets in her a kind of a quest to seek meaningful action to support the sense of unstinted commitment to the profession that she attempts to integrate in them, in her more than occasional imploring to them to be true to their calling, the one that has brought them to the ramparts of the social work profession. The author needs to add here that, the hugely transformed context in which the students of the present generation have been socialized does not provide them with much conviction or temptation to blindly accept and imbibe the core values of social work, merely on the insistence of a teacher who vouches for the same. Having been in close quarters with students for the past more than twenty five years, the author has no hesitation in saying that the credibility of the words of the teacher is tested against the credibility of the work that supports such claims. Besides, it is her unflinching conviction that the passion for work that she so earnestly wants to instill in her students has to emanate from within her, and that it should stimulate in them either their own natural urge to act, or induce them to respond to her prompting. More than anything else, it is also her conviction that the onus to validate some of the eternal truths that we the faculty, as a collective body present before our learners, ultimately does to a considerable extent rest on us.

So, the author's personal trail within the journey of *Sahyatri* began with the earnest yearning to reach out to the vast humanity of people who seemed to have been jostled out of their ordinary everyday existence in a way that they had never envisaged, and by a river that they had construed as a lifeline. It was tinged with a desire to test whether all the disaster contextualised knowledge that she had gathered in the multiple conferences, seminars, and core committees of which she has been an integral part, could help deliver respite and relief to at least a miniscule of those on behalf of whom she has discussed, deliberated and recommended.

The journey for her has been all of this and more. It has enabled her to apply some of that which she teaches and wishes to demonstrate, and also revise some of what she holds as integral to the practice of social work. By virtue of working with a team that steadfastly stood by what it believed, the journey has indeed been inspiring. Despite the umpteen hurdles that threatened to interrupt, like the occasional resource crunch and episodic delay on account of the bureaucratic structures that prevail, and the maze of paperwork that quite naturally becomes an inherent part of any action that emanates from a mammoth, homogenized structure which supports such action, the journey continues. Indeed, it has come to acquire a meaning and a significance that could not have been sensed or imagined at its 'flagging off' stage.

Mobilising Mandate, Manpower, and Materials... the Genesis of the Journey

The UDAI-II (University for Development Action and Integrated Learning-II) was initiated with two fold objectives. While the first one was to facilitate the relief and rehabilitation of the flood impacted persons, the second objective was to bring back experiences of learning into the knowledge system of the Department. Within the first broad objective, the aim was to assist in the relief distribution at the most impacted sites and to the most marginalised families; contribute to a streamlining of the relief initiatives of agencies working at the disaster sites; and identify the most urgent needs and requirements of the affected populace, with the ultimate objective of accomplishment of the same. At the time of initiation, the commitment to partnering with the communities to enable them to transit into a more stable recovery and rehabilitation phase was undoubtedly present, but the same was expected to emerge from the ground reality, as it was to be experienced, both by the team and the communities of people who were to be *hand held* in their struggle for survival.

Within the ambit of the second objective, it was envisaged that the UDAI-II intervention would demonstrate and consolidate the concept of *University beyond classroom* and a *campus which is alive to critical social realities.* The attempt to create experiential learning and indigenous teaching learning material also incentivised the team to commit to the engagement. It was also envisaged that the student volunteers would procure the opportunity to act, learn, reflect and share their experiences with the wider student body, leading to a consolidation of the much 'talked about' praxis.

In accordance with the priorities of the contingency at hand, the journey began with an army swift action to garner relief for the flood impacted. The aim of any emergency response in a disaster is to maintain life, promote safety and provide sustenance to the impacted populace to overcome the contingency. Such assistance may range from rescue and evacuation; provision of aid, in the form of food, water; medicines; medical assistance and temporary shelter. This phase may also entail restoration of the damaged infrastructure. The focus of the response and relief phase is on meeting the basic needs of the people until more permanent and organised arrangements can be ushered. An array of humanitarian organisations usually steps in to play a role in this immediate post disaster phase. The first 72 hours are recognised as the critical hours as they mean the *difference between life and death* for the disaster struck. Although the distance, the process of seeking permission from the University, and the anticipated entanglement with the machinery to get the team and its resources going did not really create this ideal situation of prompt disaster response, but at least at the level of commitment to join forces, the Department was in unison and prepared to take an instantaneous plunge.

Almost as soon as the Department decided to take the lead in engaging with the disaster impacted communities in Bihar, the first requirement was to organise the much needed relief materials. Frenzied efforts to mobilize the most urgently sought after articles of need were launched by the student volunteers, who assumed an almost unbelievable metamorphosis from fledgling field workers to a disciplined and focused team of *movers and shakers*. It was an immensely gratifying experience to see an element of transition in even the most laidback of the students, who took their place within the rank and file of the brigade. The precision with which they embarked upon the task of mobilising relief materials from individuals, groups and institutions was a sight to behold. It initiated the faculty to the immense potential and the pulsating raw energy that the student learners possessed and confirmed our steadfast belief that learners could be depended upon to rise to the occasion, when the situation so demanded. It also substantiated our faith that students do look up to their teachers to assume the position of a role model, and with that having transpired, they walk that extra mile effortlessly and manage to keep pace with their mentors. The Department, with the steadfast support of the University was thereby able to embark upon the most genuine and innovative disaster response.

The initial phase of mobilisation of relief exemplified the most tremendous outpouring of support to the Department's request for relief materials. The stockpiling of relief materials of diverse kinds demonstrated the goodwill that the Department has built with its partner agencies and communities. The phase was also beset with many problems, some surmountable, others unnerving! The realisation that many donors used the opportunity to dispose off and rid themselves of the clutter within their houses was an eye opener and a letdown. The idea that even in charity people do indulge in the most uncharitable action was distressing in itself, as was the realization that the condescending among the donors unflinchingly treat the disaster impacted persons as deserving of any largesse, even if it comprised of the most lowly and subhuman of help that could be offered to them at their most vulnerable phase in life. So while the team garnered many articles of immense utility, they were also confronted with heaps of torn, damaged and tattered clothes and unusable materials that created an unnecessary and onerous responsibility on the members to dispose them off appropriately. Sorting, packing and labeling materials in cartons and dispatching them to the disaster sites was also a monumental task, made more difficult by the unwillingness of the great Indian Railways to cart them with the same sense of urgency as was exhibited by the team.

The greatest learning that was gleaned from this phase of work which was spread over more than a month was that *learning by doing* is the most significant and long lasting learning that can be garnered by the budding professionals. The high level of collaboration, coordination, trust and networking that was established among the students group, faculty, staff and the relief providers (individuals, groups, agencies) was instrumental in the successful accomplishment of the objectives of this phase. The natural progression of work demanded that tasks and responsibilities be assumed by distinct committees like those constituted for:

1. Public Relations: networked with the potential relief providers and the media; prepared information and publicity material and manned the helpline.
2. Fund Raising: networked with agencies for fund raising and relief mobilisation.
3. Procurement and Packaging: procured relief material from donors, maintained stock and inventory; and packaged relief for dispatch to site.
4. Volunteer Management: networked with institutions for volunteers; coordinated volunteer teams and their participation/work allocation.
5. Base Camp Reinforcement: maintained volunteer database; ensured coordinated movement of volunteers; and dispatch of relief materials; and
6. Finance Management: maintained financial accounts, disbursed cash and kept records.

All of the above were coordinated by the Central Coordination Committee, which maintained a liaison with the University for funds and support; and with the 'On' site team; and provided regular updates and feedback with regard to the progress of the intervention. It was significant to note that the overwhelming impact of the disaster and the challenge that the situation presented spontaneously channelized the energies of the students into avenues which suited their individualized aptitudes and capabilities. Without any effort to seek them out and coalescing their participation into the different committees, they quite naturally aligned themselves with the work that they were naturally inclined into, and came together to contribute to a smoothened process of relief mobilization. A consistent assessment of the ground situation; a timely alignment with the requirements of the 'site'; and the establishment of a suitable data base all yielded an optimal grounding to the *Sahyatri* initiative.

The human chain constituted by the student volunteers to cart the bulky relief cartons from the Department to the railway station, and further to the trains was meant to overcome the shortage of staff and the disinclination of the administration to transfer the relief from its origin to its destination at the relevant locales in Bihar. Here again, the administration once again stalled efforts to distribute the materials to their rightful claimants. The magnitude of mobilization of relief was so monumental that it reinforced the confidence of the team in the skills and competencies of the volunteers to organise, innovate, coordinate, collate and mobilise all the articles that seemed to be needed at the disaster site. The initiative exemplified the diehard spirit of the students, their team work, leadership, initiative, determination, self-application, and ability to rise to the occasion when the situation so demanded.

The Deliverance of Relief... and Solace to the Survivors

Disaster response, includes all actions taken just before, during, or just after a disaster to reduce casualties and damage, and is the most dramatic and time-sensitive part of the disaster cycle (Pampel, 2010). It involves the individuals, families and communities doing what they can do to protect themselves and their property, as the disaster affected need to rely first on their own resources and ability to stay safe. Governments and disaster organisations have an integral role to play, as do the first responders like the emergency medical personnel, the army, the police, the local administration, and the private and voluntary organisations. Spontaneous volunteer activity from within the community and outside also emerges after the disaster, and the response of the Department could be categorised as thus. Voluntarism arises spontaneously, as tragedies heighten the solidarity of community members, and in the case of severe disasters, they evoke a sense of civic responsibility in people across the country and across the world.

The first team of volunteers who took the plunge to travel to the uncertain destination comprised of faculty members, members of the staff and a student brigade. Apart from ferrying the first stock of basic supplies, they were also expected to undertake a reconnaissance of the area and the people who had been affected by the flood. The volunteers trudged within and along the raging waters of the Kosi for an umpteen number of hours and kilometers. They were undeterred by the multiple challenges that came their way as they covered destination after destination to assess the situation at ground zero. Multiple sites ranging from Bhutahi to Kataiya to Majhoua, to Deenapatti to Patarghat, prompted the team to note, with anguish, the calamitous impact that the breached river had wrought on the life and livelihood of the poor and the marginalized communities who were the unfortunate inhabitants of the flood affected spaces. Unlike any usual flood that had previously shown the audacity to rampage the area, the violent outburst of the river this time, had created a 'death dance' and an unprecedented spate of destruction. It seemed as if the Kosi had really lived up to its name *Sorrow of Bihar,* in the right earnest.

Most of the sites were grossly under resourced and were only being 'served' by one or two brave heart private agencies and voluntary organisations. The children, the elderly, the physically challenged and the homeless were thronging these sites, yet were the most unattended constituencies of any institutionalised disaster response, even after the critical 72 hours of the emergency. The sheer inadequacy and the lethargy of the state administration to respond to the plight of the people was distressing to register, as was its unwillingness to loosen its bureaucratic rigmarole to assuage the suffering and the plight of its ill fated citizens in a timely and sensitive manner. Despite the tall claims of the government, site after site visited by the team enabled the members to see for themselves the zenith of insensitivity and the nadir of ineffectiveness to relocate, and/or resurrect the present and the future of its constituents.

Having set up its base camp at Saharsa, the team worked tirelessly to sustain the physical well being of as many people as it could reach out to. Disbursal of relief is the most important component of the immediate disaster response, and despite the clamour of the media about the unprecedented emotional response that the calamitous event was drawing from across the nation, the scene of concern exhibited a contrast, as it was evident that the much solicited and basic items of daily living had not reached the different sites, even days after the disaster had struck. It was evident that the much acclaimed institutional disaster management system at the level of the district was 'in place' only in the policy documents and the manuals, but was conspicuous by its absence in the reality context. This led to inert governance which negatively impinged on the access of the affected communities to procure the containers of relief material that had been mobilised by humanitarian organisations, but which remained piled up at the railway stations or at the district headquarters.

Needless to say, 'the post disaster environment is a period requiring intense decision-making based on limited information, about complex issues with very powerful and long term impacts.... Additionally a large influx of resources need to be coordinated, allocated and tracked, while all the time ensuring minimal waste and maximal sustainability... and within such a context, governance is the overall process by which affected governments, organisations and populations determine decisions and their implementation' (UNISDR, 2010a: 2). What the team witnessed at the disaster sites was a lack of coordination among the state agencies, donor bodies and the community responders; a lack of concerted action and willingness of the officials to step up the supply of relief initiatives even to the critical sites, which were languishing in extreme shortages. In such a context, the relief material garnered by the team was much in demand and despite the struggle to keep the supply lines open, was proving to be less than required.

The students, staff and the faculty of the Department stood out among the rest of the responders, as they were the only team which responded to the specificity of the need for the specificity of the victims. The requisitions were communicated back to the supply link and the more generalist relief acquisition campaigns were quickly adjusted to the emerging needs of women, children and the elderly. The need for tinned baby milk powder, torches, umbrellas, mosquito repellents, chlorine tablets and medicines led the Delhi based counterparts to mobilise these articles in larger quantum. This sensitivity of response did not go unnoticed and found appreciation in and among the compatriots from other organisations that were also tending to the disaster impacted families in familiar and unfamiliar ways. Networking with governmental and non governmental agencies is yet another forte with social workers, and capitalising on the same, the team was able to fill up the inevitable gaps that kept propping up when resources and rightful claims seem to be placed at the most disparate of ends.

Apart from the seriousness of providing physical support, there was a discernible need for providing solace to the devastated families, all of whom seemed to have lost someone or something precious. There was a need to listen and hear out the lived experiences of the people, right from the time the disaster suddenly and ominously hit them, and the ways in which it totally transformed their world for them. It needs to be highlighted that most assistance that is offered in the initial phase of response seems to be driven with the urgency of providing physical support to help the 'body' survive the odds, but not much attention is attributed to the 'mind'. Psychosocial and mental health issues are often not addressed even in pre-disaster planning efforts within most countries. It is well recognised that the psychosocial impact of a disaster is harder to see than the physical effect, yet recovery from it often takes longer. Disasters being as sudden and often as catastrophic as they are, they bring with them grave emotional reactions. Normal responses to a traumatic event include: intense and unpredictable feelings; mood swings; unprecedented anxiety, nervousness and depression; traumatic flashbacks; psycho somatic reactions like rapid heartbeats or sweating; disrupted sleep and eating patterns; strained inter-personal relationships; and even survivor's guilt (UNISDR, 2010b). At such times, the traditional coping abilities and mechanisms of the individual and the community are paralysed, and people experience serious incapacities in coping with the loss that the disaster inherently brings within their lives. Coping and dealing with this sense of loss and acute helplessness often curtails their desire to seek even physical help, and this enhances the risk of losing out on the survivors of the disaster too.

It was therefore quite natural that the team was also overwhelmed by the responses and the reactions of the disaster survivors. People manifesting reactions relating to severe anxiety, restlessness, and panic, incessant crying, sleep disturbances, nightmares, and recollection of the traumatic episodes of the flood continued to pour in. There were also people who were finding it difficult to communicate and articulate their grief and sense of shock, and those who even seemed withdrawn or 'cut off' from the living world. In such a context, the need to provide psycho-social help and support to the disaster affected individuals presented itself as the most vital priority, almost at par with the need to provide materials for physical survival. It needs to be spelled out that the need for trained mental health professional/

s and a basic training to the student volunteers on handling the psycho-social ramifications of a disaster was gravely felt, and that constituted one of the most important lessons for the *Sahyatri* team.

Although at that initial phase of engagement, the team did not have the support of such a mental health professional with them, members were able to discuss and evolve a basic approach to handling this challenging, yet critical task of providing psycho-social support. It is noteworthy that the subsequent teams who stepped into the frame and took over from the first team were provided with a basic orientation to the psycho-social impact of a disaster and guided about skills/competencies and procedures required to offer a basic level of psycho-social support to the people to deal with all the serious changes and the trauma that the disaster had heaped on them. This was done at the Department itself, and thereby a more sustained approach to the provisioning of this input could be integrated. At that time of initial contact, the team decided to capitalise on 'empathetic listening' as that is one of the most valuable assets that social workers possess, to bond and facilitate a catharsis and an outlet for the array of traumatizing emotions that the people seemed to be manifesting. The members of the team opted to listen unobtrusively; showed by their actions and words that they cared; and most importantly provided practical help in dealing with the disaster. Social workers as a creed are adept at establishing an 'empathetic' bond; creating a 'sensitive' atmosphere and providing a 'non judgmental' space to all those who needed to share and catharsize.

The immediate need of the situation notwithstanding, the reality of the immense havoc caused by the flood became evident only after the flood waters had receded, for it was only then that the mammoth dimensions of what needed to be done to rebuild the shattered lives of the people really became discernible. The imperative of now creating more need based interventions to counteract the ominous impact of encounter that had befallen their fate and to appropriately respond to the impassioned appeals of the populace emerged. The team noted with great concern the escalating toll that the disaster was taking in terms of mortality, and also the heavy morbidity emanating from the near epidemic dimensions of some diseases accosted by the communities. The hordes of *saviours* who seemed to have inundated the disaster scene, acknowledged that they found it challenging to provide more than food, medicines, blankets, clothes and tarpaulin sheets to the survivors. Not undermining the immense value associated with the provision of such life saving imperatives, it goes without saying that rebuilding lives has much more to it than mere provisioning of daily rations and a temporary shelter at a relief camp site to cope with the severe rigours of daily living thrust upon the people by a flood.

As the team started weaving the future initiative together, the need to focus on the community as a unit of engagement was obvious, as was the determination not to lose sight of the most vulnerable constituencies among the disaster impacted. The vulnerability of people to any disaster emanates from the way in which certain social, economic and political forces influence the extent to which various people and communities experience the impact of the disaster, in direct and indirect ways. Examining disasters through the lens of vulnerability confers real insights. Vulnerability is the key to understanding of risk that attempts to break from the all-too-technocratic attitudes that have characterised relationships between human societies and their environments (Hewit, 1983). Instead of conceptualising disasters as purely physical occurrences, requiring largely technological solutions, such events are better viewed primarily as the result of human actions – as the 'actualisation of social vulnerability' (Lewis, 1999: 8). Social processes generate unequal exposure to risk by making some people more prone to disaster than others, and these inequalities are largely a function of the power relations operative in every society. Critical to discerning the nature of disasters, then, is an appreciation of the ways in which human systems place people at risk in relation to each other and to their environment – a relationship that can be best understood as an individual's, a household's, a community's, or a society's vulnerability. The determination of vulnerability is a 'complex characteristic produced by a combination of factors derived especially (but not entirely) from class, gender and ethnicity' (Cannon, 1994: 14-19). Piers Blaikie *et al.* (1994) offer a working definition that states that vulnerability is... *the characteristics of a person or group in terms of their capacity to anticipate, cope with, resist, and recover from the impact of a natural hazard. It involves a combination of factors that determine the degree to which someone's life and livelihood is put at risk by a discrete and identifiable event in nature or in society.* The vulnerability of people refers to a certain level of exposure to hazard that derives from the social or economic condition of the individual, family or community concerned. It was this critical of vulnerability that provided the guiding perspective to the team to connect with sites and constituencies that had gone unnoticed and maybe even, knowingly unrecognised, on account of their particularly vulnerable status within the larger socio-economic construct. There are 'groups of individuals in every society whose unique needs and circumstances make them more vulnerable to the impacts of a disaster than others. This group of 'special needs' populations include children, pregnant and/or nursing mothers, individuals with disabilities and the elderly, to name a few' (UNISDR, 2010c: 4). They also include those that are segregated by the virtue of caste or religion or even economic parameters.

The volunteer task force established an interface with the inhabitants of the Bhutahi-Dafarka-Kosi colony, who comprised the most vulnerable and marginalised among their peers in other flood impacted zones and with whom no state agency had established any contact. Even the local religio-political organisations had a marginal presence in their frame, and they were placed in the most precarious position as far as disaster impact was concerned. It was the proclaimed commitment of the UDAI team to reach to the weakest in the link and the most marginal in the catchment of the disaster that guided members to set up post in Dafarka in Triveniganj in Supaul. Mostly belonging to the Musahar community, they faced the double whammy of being one of the most backward 'Dalit' communities, and tugged all the other disadvantages of being a minority community as well. They became the prime recipients of the *Sahyatri* intervention, not only in terms of provisioning for them the invaluable articles of daily living, but also in terms of capturing their agonies, anxieties and stories of trauma. They were thus placed at the centre stage of the reckoning of the response. Focusing on the infants, children, elderly, women, Dalits, Muslims, and the extremely backward class communities, the intervention derived the unique distinction of being the only one which engaged with the narratives of those who remained on the peripheries and were almost 'invisibilised' in the larger canvas of the disaster. Listening patiently and endlessly to the tragic travails of the people was integral to the daily context of each team member, as an outlet to their agonising experiences provided the sufferers with the much needed catharsis to negotiate the pain and trauma of the loss that they had incurred.

From August 28, 2008 to the end of January, 2009, eighteen teams of students, faculty and staff from the Department, Aditi Mahavidyalaya, B.R. Ambedkar College, as also other colleges of the University of Delhi formed a chain of human professionals, who toiled and persevered to reconstruct the lives and the spirit of the Kosi impacted. As one team tapered off its engagement, the subsequent one stood empowered to resume the process without a gap or even a kink. As a teacher, the author was literally awe struck to see for herself, the near surreal integration of all that she had taught in the classroom translate so beautifully into practice. The creation of the 'process' that appears so very challenging to the most seasoned of community practitioners arose so spontaneously... that it was a joy to behold. The entire rank and file of the University performed in such synchronised manner that the author's faith in her students and in *social work* as a *profession with a conscience* was reaffirmed multiple times over.

Hamara Aspatal **(Our Hospital) and** ***Hamari Pathshala*** **(*Our School*)....** ***Small*** **Steps, yet** ***Big*** **Results for Recovery**

In the eventuality of a disaster, the mortality risk associated with age is a U-shaped curve with higher mortality amongst the young (under 15 years old) and the senior (above 50 years old) cohorts. Results of research and experience also show that there exists a heightened risk for women that could be attributed to a combination of factors including biological, physical and cultural differences. Apart from this, the presence of small, dependent children and the inability to swim also mars their chances of survival in hydrological disasters (Guha & Parry *et al.*, 2006). Although the exact dimensions of the mortality associated with this calamity were not known, the fact that a large number of elderly, children and women had perished, or were missing was an inescapable reality. Most of the sites were also witnessing deaths on account of the near epidemic situation which prevailed in the immediate post disaster time. The health scenario for the disaster impacted villages was very precarious, as cases of viral infections, water borne diseases and skin infections were rampant. The health infrastructure was dilapidated, and with no recourse to any health provider or facility, there seemed to be no solace or respite to the spiralling number of medical exigencies that were emerging.

The threat of epidemics was real and the administration seemed to be faltering in responding to the criticality of the situation. With just a level of professional expertise in the matter of public health, but with great ingenuity, the members of the team were quick to realize that they needed to pitch in and contribute in any way in which they could. Dafarka, Bhutahi Baandh came across as a site where the health indices were very grim for the people, especially the elderly, children and the pregnant women. *Twenty bamboo poles and tarpaulin sheets* were all that were required by the team for what was to become the most efficacious health facility in the area! What began as a temporary structure for the disbursement of basic health care and medicines evolved as a nodal health resource for the local populace for a long time to come! *Hamara Aspatal* (our hospital) was created with minimal material due to the limited resources that the team from the University had at its behest, yet what was inadequate in terms of a resourceful structure was compensated for, by the love, care and personal touch of the carers... the students who opened their hearts to all those who came with the hope of receiving help. Those initial few days of work were so immensely arduous, yet so gratifying for the team that members seemed to have grown manifold in the eyes of their peers and co-professionals.

Having an extraordinary capacity to convince, coordinate and motivate, the team was extremely expeditious in locating the pool of expertise and in gathering it in a meaningful manner, to make it available for the people in a usable format. Doctors from different collaborating institutions were mobilized to work towards provisioning medical care at *Hamara Aspatal*. Without the overtones of any complicated systems in place, it was a place where all who came got something to notch up their health and sense of well being, and that is what made the people establish the *connect* with the team. Warm words of solace and comfort and a willingness to listen were more resplendent than costly medicines and procedures, but these seemed to work almost miraculously in the context in which the team found itself. Having been gifted with an ambulance, the team was also able to translate into reality, its desire to create a mobile health service to cater to a largely un-accessed area lying between Patarghat in Sonbarsa to Majhoua and Kattaiya in Raghpur.

During the initial phase of the rescue and relief assessment and support endeavour in villages of Supaul, Saharsa, and Madhepura, each doctor associated with the team attended to an average of almost two hundred and fifty patients in a day. The team, comprising of faculty, students and doctors reached out to people at diverse rescue points and shelter relief centres, and provided medical and material help. The team ensured that the helpline numbers set up by it, were adequately publicized and this yielded rich dividends in the form of the fruition of many medical camps all over the devastated area. Each medical mobile camp became instrumental in providing help to 200-300 people, and out of them a majority was women, elderly, infants and children. This experience with patients brought along rich learning about health components, and members were able to become more equipped to deal with the wide range of problems that people approached them for. Even the inventory of medicines became more distinct and segregated, so as to cater to more ailments than the team was able to target in the preliminary phase.

Knowing that more hands would be required, and realizing that the need to capacitate the local volunteers to gradually assume charge would emerge, the team readily roped in the traditional birth attendants (the *dais*), the ASHA workers, and the anganwadi workers to become partners in the engagement. Reproductive health interventions were also mandated, keeping in view the management of incoming and forthcoming deliveries that were slated to happen. All in all, the health interventions of *Sahyatri* became a rallying point for its initial foray into the lives of the people struggling to cope with disaster devastation.

It is unfortunate that not much credence is given to the children who experience a disaster situation, as they are expected, and often perceived to be the most non-impacted categories when dealing with the impact of a disaster. Rosenfeld and Caye have elucidated the urgent need to focus on the harmful effects of disasters on children and the need to create children specific intervention strategies (Rosenfeld, Caye, *et al.*, 2005). While all individuals involved in a disaster are impacted by it, children are particularly impacted because they have a difficult time explaining their fears and anxieties. This is particularly so when planning for longer term recovery and rehabilitation intervention is being considered. Parents and the generalized others often ignore, or are unaware about the unspoken and unarticulated fears and anxieties that originate within the children's experiences of the disaster and then embed themselves in their impressionable hearts and minds. These have great potential to leave permanent scars on children and wreak havoc with their abilities to deal with contexts and issues in their later life. Within the context of the team's engagement with people, the opportunity of keeping children in the central frame was not missed. The *lesser* narratives of the children were mesmerizingly real and were duly captured by the student volunteers. Thus, it was not per chance that children became the central theme for a significant part of the interventions of *Sahyatri*, in all phases of its work in Bihar.

In the context in which the team was working, it did not take members very long to realize that the families (from twelve villages and two panchayats), who had set up shelter on the Bhutahi Baandh, which essentially comprised of two flanks of a canal surrounded by flood waters were living a very precarious life. Most at risk were the children, who were the most vulnerable to the fury of the water in the canal, and this fear came true when two children drowned in the canal. The tragedy shook up each and every member of the initiative and forewarned them about the intimidating possibility of more such tragedies just waiting to happen. The child centric approach that was being contemplated from the very beginning of the engagement was immediately fast forwarded, and a second instance of *bamboo poles joined together with tarpaulin sheets* created what it took to create a *pathshala* (school) for embarking upon a meaningful and stimulating interaction with the vast constituency of the children. In many ways, the many children who were being met during the course of the day seemed to be unperturbed by the tragedy, and were almost happy with the prospect of school closure. Yet the susceptibility of them being unattended, while the adults in their family struggled with building up life from whatever remnants the flood had left them with, was very real. The unfortunate death of the two children sounded alarm bells in the cognisance of the team, in terms of the responsibility that members needed to partake with regard to this fragile constituency in the disaster frame.

In mainstream parlance, the literal translation of the term *pathshala is* 'the place of learning' and usually connotes a school. However, the *pathshalas,* as they were envisioned and as they evolved were exact reversals of what any mainstream school *is or does*! It not only represented an unlimited space for *unbridled learning* for the children, it also metamorphosised into a 'school' for the team. The journey of *Hamari Pathshsla* from its genesis to the present context enabled the learning of many new lessons and coerced the team into 'un' learning many of those that it had traditionally been acclimatised to accepting unquestioningly. The space that was nomenclatured as the 'school' was really an open ended abstraction that derived body and shape, as the team traversed its journey within the setting. It took on more specific, yet unconventional contours as members 'experienced' the world of children from their perspective, and from an 'unfolding' of their gradually 'unfolding' aspirations.

The first *pathshala* was envisaged with a more limited perspective of safely engaging children, thereby liberating the parents from worrying about them as they went about restoring the fabric of their lives. However, as the *Sahyatri* sojourn went along, these spaces changed their dimensions and became novel centres for innovative learning. From singing songs, painting, conversing, storytelling and numerous other stimulating engagements as a starting point in the first *pathshala*, to the creation of twenty such innovative schools all over the adopted locale of work of the *Sahyatris*, it became a very memorable and fulfilling passage, in more ways than one. These twenty non-formal remedial and alternate education centres, all rolled into one, are *uniqueness personified*! From evolving new paradigms about learning content and pedagogies to redrawing the traditionally segregating lines between government schools and non-governmental initiatives, the *pathshalas* have proved to be such an exceptionally inventive educational excursions, that they have surpassed even the team's own vision and expectations.

Restoring Lives and Building Social Capital

In many ways the journey of the team meandered just as the river that stemmed this journey did. From a relief response to the longing to provide more than temporary succour and from an instantaneous reaction to a planned and deliberated response, the yearning and the compulsion to be there for the people in the direness of their need was writ large in the hearts and the minds of the core team. There was a realization that the umpteen number of crusaders and *knights in shining armour*, who seemed to have surfaced in the initial hours and phases of the disaster would slowly but surely melt away, and would leave behind a huge gap of unfulfilled needs, unmet expectations and feeling of frustration among people... frustration to the incompleteness of response and even the falsehood of promises made by some of them, wishing to grab attention, accolades and media coverage.

The narratives of the hundreds of stranded families substantiated the strongly held belief and assertion that it is really the erstwhile vulnerability of the people that forms the basis of their future travails as the worst incumbents of a disaster. As it is consistently highlighted, through text and experience, the vulnerability of the people to any disaster does not stem from the disaster itself. It is in fact, a part and parcel of their daily life and living. Vulnerability pertains to the way in which certain social, economic, cultural and political forces influence the nature and extent to which certain people and communities experience the impact of disaster. A growing body of research demonstrates how various attributes such as poverty, caste, class, religion, age, health, physical ability, and gender make certain constituencies more pre-disposed to a higher susceptibility to become the undiscerning victims of a disaster, and expose certain people more than the others to the forsaking of the most adverse consequences of disaster. These vulnerability 'criticals' are integrally linked with and operate through the structural mechanisms of unequal access to social, economic and political resources and the decision-making structures that govern them. The occurrence of a disaster merely washes away the covering and exposes the true nature and extent of their vulnerability in the most ghastly of ways. It is therefore a myth and a misgiving to treat disaster vulnerability as distinct from the generalised vulnerability that many people and communities face even in the non disaster context. Disaster risk is socially distributed in ways that reflect the social divisions/ cleavages that already exist in society. Disasters simply interact with the pre disaster socio-economic and cultural context, not only to expose what really exists, but also to contribute towards exacerbating the plight of those already on the margins of society and despair.

Therefore, while in the context in which work was being undertaken, doling the families out of the disaster was the immediate and impending task before the team and yet, the imperative of the intervention needed to be essentially geared towards catapulting them out of the disaster risk situation in which they found themselves in, time and again. The reality of their life was woven around the presence of the many 'real' hazards, lurking in their frame and those which threatened to disrupt their tranquility, every time the river decided to alter its tranquil persona or the rain gods opted to play 'truant' or 'over benevolent', as the case may be. Towards that end, the recognition that efforts needed to be made to help them surmount the socio-economic and political deprivations that shaped their existence, even in the non-disaster time frame of their lives emerged, in a very strong and convincing way.

Having said that, there is also a myth and a mindset that needs to be dispelled/altered, and that pertains to an overwhelming image of the disaster impacted individuals, groups and communities as 'victims' and as 'objects' of charity and mercy, for there cannot be any greater disservice to their cause than an acknowledgement of the same. That the community is an entity that possesses a repertoire of capabilities and capacities, which exist, but may come into play in the eventuality of a crisis or a calamity is largely undermined and relegated to the background, both when post disaster interventions are being organised and when pre disaster mitigation plans are being discussed. This folly is premised in the reality that not much is written or generated about this persona of the community in a significantly convincing manner. The media too plays a part when it focuses on stories of the several *messiahs* who enter the scene and perform great service in helping the community and the people in 'picking up the threads of their life'. Therefore, the need to identify, codify and perpetuate the story of the community in working towards writing and rewriting its own story is vital, as that asserts the real strength of the people, their ingenuity, their social capital and their resilience. It represents something that is theirs, that is time tested and is culturally approved, accepted and even assimilated for overcoming other odds that may knock on their door in their future. Ultimately, the risk that an individual or the community reflects is interplay between vulnerability on the one hand, and capacities on the other. This realization shaped the later trajectory of response and created avenues for the core team to further negotiate with the disaster, after the initial shock of the flood fury had settled down in some measure, both in the physical terrain and, in the lives of the people.

The phase immediately following the relief and evacuation and the immediate resettlement of the flood impacted brought forth the need to integrate and perhaps facilitate the transition of the communities into becoming less vulnerable and more disaster resilient. This was by no means an easy task in that, the deconstruction of this most generally used but most often misused term "community"... used to refer to the aggregate of people inhabiting the Kosi banks was in itself a matter of much reflection and deliberation. Within the broader ambit of the disaster impacted populace, who were our chosen stakeholders and our critical prospective partners, the ones who really needed to be enrolled in the longer term process, with deliberation and determination? This was indeed a question that that we were unsure about right from the time of the inception, but having chosen to thrust ourselves headlong into any work that deserved our attention in the troubled context of the communities, this question largely remained in the peripheral zone and did not occupy centre stage till now.

However, when the core team was contemplating settling down into the reconstructive phase of engagement, members were compelled to reframe the context and action from the newly emerging reality of the time that the effort was placed in. While the community remained the over arching client and partner, the imperative to work with the women and the youth as distinct categories emerged more as a recognition of the fact that they comprised the more vulnerable of groups within the larger context of the community, and also because they represented those who demonstrated greater potential as the repositories of capacity, perhaps latent at that point, but awaiting manifestation.

There is no discounting the fact that women are often portrayed as the weaker sex, who are unable to squarely handle contingency, given their frail physical structure and 'untrained' and 'undeveloped' mental faculties. Images of women as hapless victims of disasters undermine their involvement in disaster response (Enarson and Morrow, 1998). The media too plays a mammoth role in projecting women as the 'inconsolable' face of any disaster, leaving women to be perceived as objects of mercy. Current experience and research show that the majority of relief and recovery initiatives, even in the present reflect traditional gender stereotypes that distinctly prioritise the needs and contributions of men. *Male biased perspectives dominate policies and intervention processes, often excluding women from equitable compensation and assistance and subsequently placing them at even greater risk of future harm of hazards and disasters. Damage, needs and vulnerability assessments too fail to capture the different impact of disasters and disaster response on men and women. The immense contributions women make to recovery too often go unrecognized, while the marginalization of their skills and knowledge limits their opportunities to play a greater role in building back better* (UNISDR, 2010d: 7). The fact that the formal system of disaster response and mitigation obviates their presence is nothing but a surreal construction of a distorted frame that has been perpetuated by a system grossly tilted in favour of the stronger sex.

The feminist theoretical perspective squarely demonstrates that gender serves as the primary organizing principle of all societies and is an essential lens through which to view the experience of disaster. Indeed, disasters and their aftermaths mirror the pre existing social inequalities of caste, class, ethnicity, disability and age with gender cutting across all of them. This should perforce have led to a situation wherein, a disaggregation of the disaster "impacted" became the norm and the defining principle of all disaster related work. However, even in the broader international context, the differential impact of disasters on men/ boys and women/girls is hardly, if at all, taken into account while responding to a disaster situation, and the integration of the gendered dimensions in planning to mitigate the ramifications of impending disasters still remains a distant dream. Resource distribution, in a post disaster scenario, which is intended for the entire community/population of a disaster-affected area, relies on the existing structures of distribution that reflect the patriarchal system of society, leaving women and girls marginalized in their access to such resources. In the post relief frame, these constituencies are once again sidelined in all initiatives to foster rehabilitation, recovery and resilience building. Tragically, in such a milieu, the immensely significant contributions that the females of the species can offer to disaster risk reduction are often undervalued, undermined or mostly overlooked. Their unique role in building community resilience to disasters is hardly acknowledged or contemplated. This is clearly gleaned in the lack of availability of any viable platforms that women are able to employ for sharing their needs, experiences and reality. Gender stereotypes come into full play in placing stress on men to assume larger than life roles and responsibilities aligned to the gendered norms and expectations. All this categorically obviates the need to dwell on the differential needs, vulnerabilities as also the capacities and competencies of women as critical stakeholders in community based disaster risk reduction or community resilience building.

In recognition of the above, it was an avowed objective of the entire intervention, spanning the relief, recovery and rehabilitation components, that a focus on women's needs and a role for the women in the different phases of work would be omnipresent. Active partnerships with women, as also youth were forged when the team was in the midst of tapering the relief centric phase, and were bound towards identifying avenues for a more long term role to support the recovery of the flood impacted families in the catchment area of UDAI-II. Recapitulating the process as it unfurled itself; it was after the termination of active participation of the students, towards the end of January, 2009, that the core team, together with an empowered brigade of local volunteers ventured forth into the recovery phase of disaster work. Faced with the reality of being a small, yet significant part of a University, and not having the freedom to mobilise funds beyond what the University offered to us, the team could not visualise a capital intensive intervention for the *Sahyatris.* However, it could most certainly draw up a plan that could be *people intensive* and which could enable the *Sahyatris* to demonstrate the worth of community based interventions in disaster landscapes. With almost sixty local boys and girls working as volunteers, the team set about embarking on a mission to explore new parameters of engagement.

Based on the magnitude of loss, and devastation, and the quantum of the need base, the team set about selecting villages for the second phase of work. The modus operandi that evolved, almost spontaneously, entailed holding of *Baithaks* (meetings) within the *tolas* of the villages. Primarily and deliberately mobilizing the youth and the women, these meetings were initiated with a dialogue on the situation as it pertained to them in the post disaster context, and culminated in the constitution of a local committee to spearhead prospective work. Relying on a transparent and democratic framework of functioning, an election ascertained membership to this body. The initial focal point of engagement within the village remained on youth mobilization, and once the youth volunteers were ready to participate, women's groups were constituted. In the ten villages initially selected as priority work sites, these groups, which came to be known as the *Sakhi Sangi* and *Hum Yuva,* emerged as capacitated pressure groups that showed an extraordinary determination and ability to participate and mobilise for social action and advocacy initiatives, some details of which shall be elucidated in this section a little later. At each step of the way, the socio-economic topography of the site of engagement formed the basis of selection of participants in the *Sakhi Sangi* and *Hum Yuva* groups. The community biographies of the twenty villages selected for intervention revealed the predominance of vulnerable groups who had been bypassed by the development process and seemed to be maintaining a peripheral existence. The basic premise underlying the group formation was a conscious integration of diversity, and a representation of the poorest and the most socially vulnerable families. As the initiative took flight, there were vociferous demands from the adjoining and even distant villages to coerce the *Sahyatris* into including them in the ambit, but a realistic resource check constrained the team to spread beyond the twenty villages.

Exploring avenues to facilitate disaster resilience among the communities, and analysing the perspectives of their constituencies, it was realised that much of the vulnerability that was faced by the people, especially those belonging to the most marginalized groups stemmed out of the almost total lack of awareness about the schemes and their entitlements within the same. As a result, they were totally on their own in times of disaster as also outside of the same. As is the usual case, the programmes of the government are usually manned by many such functionaries who ensure that the programme benefits do not reach their rightful claimants, leaving them untouched and incapacitated. Even the flagship poverty alleviation schemes of the government like the MNREGA, NHRM, SSA/RMSA, NBA, NSAP and others have continued to remain beyond the cognition and reach of most people. Whether it was the Public Distribution System, or the Old Age/Widow Pension Scheme, there seemed to be a gaping disconnect between the programmes and the people. This was the favoured situation for the multitude of the vested interests that were blissfully appropriating the programme benefits, while the vast majority of the populace remained oblivious to their existence. Moreover, the health infrastructure and education system as they existed were a far cry from those claimed in the text and discourses of the governmental agenda. This for the *Sahyatris* represented a vast ground to cover, for if they could stimulate a wave of awareness and agitation to arouse the people into claiming what was essentially theirs, it would most certainly make a notable difference to their 'ability' to negotiate a decent life in all circumstances, including those created by the vagaries of nature. This could be a basic first step towards reducing vulnerability and enhancing capacity.

Stimulating discontent and then channelizing it into meaningful agenda with achievable goals, to be achieved by the community is ordained as a function of the profession and the team was unanimous in charting this course of action within the interventions that were being devised. The advantages that weighed in favour of this proposition were: one, that this would require us to align our work in the tradition of peoples power; two, that it would ascertain that we begin with the lowest common denominator of ensuring for the people what exists, and exists as a 'right'; three, it would entail an immersion of our 'selves' into the process, instead of relying on outside experts and agents; four, that it would offer the exciting possibility of capacitating indigenous personnel and empowered groups to stimulate action; and five, it would enable us to course over the resource limitations that we were confronted with, yet ensure full capitalization of the strength of our methods and skills of community work and social action.

The process began in December, 2009, with the facilitation of the formation and the consolidation of the two categories of groups, the women's groups or the *Sakhi Sangis* and the youth groups or the *Hum Yuva*. Regular visits by the *Sahyatri* team and their focussed interaction enabled the community to relate to the initiative. The goodwill of Delhi University provided the team with a distinct stamp of credibility, trust and assurance of the people. Cluster based training for women on a multiplicity of issues concerning their lives, ranging from child survival, first aid, safe birth practices, utilisation of RTI, immunization, nutrition, team building, and other issues that required urgent attention were organised, and these instilled an urge and an inclination among the women to join in as *Sakhi Sangis*. Awareness Campaigns on Reproductive Health and Early Childhood Care were launched in the entirety of the project area. Intensive engagement with the concept and practice of Community Based Disaster Preparedness/ Management formed the core of the initiative, but it was different in that it was built around indigenous practices and traditions of the people, instead of being transplanted from a textbook or a disaster management manual of a foreign funder or an international expert body.

Intensive awareness building workshops on the programmes/ schemes of the government and nongovernmental agencies were held, as also capacity building sessions on the use of the RTI to procure information on the provisions, current status and beneficiaries of the programmes. Six cluster in-charges were trained to spearhead the initiatives in the twenty villages, with other local volunteers and peoples' participation. A minimum of two meetings per month were organised every month, both by the *Sakhi Sangi* and the *Hum Yuva* groups to plan, consolidate and review action. Joint meetings were also held on convergent issues and plans. The overall structure of the *Sahyatri* has been very broad based, open and inclusive. It relies on the strength of volunteering and has thrown up leaders, both men and women. There are six active cluster in-charges, eighteen educators and a band of volunteers, headed by a core team. Members belong to both sexes and represent all castes and communities.

Traversing the Stretch... of Time and Space

The change that has been brought in the process has been humongous and unimaginable, given the modest financial resources that have been invested in the initiative, from then till now. The lack of monetary investment has been more than compensated for, by the investment of 'renewable' energies of the team, the volunteers and the communities. It has proved the often verbalised (but less applied) version that conviction and determination to achieve a mission; the sincerity of purpose that one displays in the mobilisation of the initiative; and the faith that one reposes in the enterprise and vision of the local actors are undoubtedly the overriding determinants of longer term and irreversible change.

The organization of the youth and women's groups in the twenty villages has led to a significant mobilization within the communities. The *Sakhi Sangi* and the *Hum Yuva groups* have really taken on the mantle of *change agents,* in that they are facilitating a churning... *a manthan,* as they call it, within the communities. The latter seem to be aroused from stupor and are keenly seeking stimulus from the core team and spearheading social action in their locales. The groups in villages like Bishanpur, Heeranagar, Chatgaon, Barahkurba, Laxmania, Hemantganj, Vidyanagar, Sripur, Mayurva, and Medhia are truly empowered and striving to create change in many ways. Long standing issues like dysfunctional village schools, lack of satisfaction with the local anganwadis serving less than optimal quality of mid day meals, seized job cards of the Panchayat Rozgar Sewa, and other critical issues are beginning to attract the attention and stimulation of action by the peoples' organizations. The *Sakhi Sangi* and *Hum Yuva* groups in the twenty villages which constitute our core area are working with an integrated perspective and an important change that has been ushered is an enhanced awareness of the Panchayat Rozgar Yojana under the MNREGA, and about the yet (deliberately) concealed nuances related to the job cards of eligible and participating persons covered by the programme. This has led to many more people becoming active participants in seeking entitlements under the programme. The term *entitlement* is not being used loosely here, as the processes unleashed in the communities at hand made a strong point for seeking the provisions of the schemes and programmes as a right rather than as a benefit or a dole from the provisioning authority. A case in point is that of village Laxmania, where the job cards of beneficiaries were in possession with the contractors and the post office personnel, who used to forcibly take their signatures from them without confirming whether due and timely payment of wages was being deposited in their accounts. The village groups were apprised of the exploitation meted out to the beneficiaries and in response, an action movement was spearheaded in the community. The people were apprised of the provisions of the scheme, their entitlements and rights. They were also enlightened about the malpractices adopted by the vested interests to exploit the beneficiaries and the need to unite against them. As a consequence, the beneficiaries refused to sign the job cards without ascertaining the reason for the signatures and claimed their job cards back. The core team persevered to fight against the long standing exploitation, despite threats from the strong contractor lobby and others involved in the wrong doings.

In a few villages like Hemantganj, the Public Distribution System (PDS) was being used by the suppliers to eke profits by fooling the community. The ration supplies were not delivered on time and were dispersed in quantities less than stipulated. Yet, the coupons were taken from the beneficiaries to show a fully functional and 'upright' system of delivery. The *Sakhi Sangi* group of the community took up this core issue and spread awareness about the programme benefits, stipulations and beneficiary rights. The community was facilitated to become vigilant against people wresting their due rights and as a result, the ration shops were left with no option but to confirm to the mandated time schedules, quantum and procedures. In another instance within the same community, the *Hum Yuva* group was called upon to resolve a caste dispute that arose when the school teacher used derogatory language for a child. Through the intervention of the youth group, the teacher not only apologised, but also volunteered to seek a transfer from the specific school.

In Heeranagar, alcoholism was rampant and the women were extremely agitated with this development. The women's group spearheaded a campaign to force men of the village to shed this habit through motivation, followed by strong coercion and even penalisation. In the Sikiyahi village community, *Hamari Pathshala* functions in the madarsa. The local masjid was not fully constructed there, and the *Hum Yuva* team mobilized voluntary labour and money to complete the construction. In the same community, *Hum Yuva* mobilized families to seek admission of their children in local government schools, where parents were refused the same in the first instance. The quota for admission of children from Dalit families was enforced, to enable this group to seek schooling for their wards. In Chatgaon, the primary school was running in the open, at a site where the ground was at a lower elevation, which caused frequent flooding and regular closure of the school. In consonance with the panchayat, the groups mobilized voluntary labour to raise the ground level and initiate the construction of the school building. In Mayurva, a bout of chicken pox among twenty five children of the village was enough to prompt the youth group to almost forcibly bring government doctors to the scene, and to organise health interventions to treat and contain the infection.

In Vidyanagar, there was a precedent of the post office functionaries taking money from the community to open their account under the post office scheme, which was unwarranted. The youth group mobilized the villagers to protest and give a representation to the Collector and the Commissioner. An investigation was ordered and consequently the money charged was deposited in the accounts of the persons concerned. Within the same community, the school also remained closed and no mid day meal was provided. Acting on a call given by the women's group, a complaint was forwarded to the DEO and the BEO and the matter was resolved permanently. Still further, the widows within this village were deliberately misguided about the provision of widow and elderly women's pension. They were made to fill up the forms, but deprived of the entitlement, which seemed to be diverted to some other account. At the behest of the women's group and the youth group, complaints were filed against the erring officials and lists of persons eligible for the different schemes were rectified. Disputes pertaining to other entitlements were also redressed. Right to Information is readily relied upon to seek information about government schemes and to facilitate full utilization of these by the eligible persons.

The village communities have become vigilant about health, hygiene and education related issues and provisions. They keep a check on the work undertaken by the ASHA workers and the school teachers. During village meetings, the best performing teachers are acknowledged and awarded. With regard to other issues, women's groups now take the lead and update the cluster in-charges, who then direct them to organise self participatory action, and even confrontation with the erring persons/officials, forcing them to reform and straighten up. Even when the educators of *Hamari Pathshalas* are late in reporting for work, the villagers call up the Sahyatri team and complain. Schools are prompted to provide stipends, uniform and books as per stipulated norms and within the given time frame. Any lapse is duly reported and action sought using the grievance redressal mechanisms available to the community. This alertness and newly found confidence in people, has shown exemplary results, as the government machinery is falling in line and the *Sahyatri* villages are showing a more optimal utilisation of programmes and their entitlements.

Early marriage was prevalent in many villages, but a campaign by the groups has led to the practice almost dying out in the area. A family was arrested during the organization of such a marriage, and this instance was converted into an example to coerce those people who were not deterred otherwise. Meetings with children to influence them to refuse to such pressure by the families were organised. Campaigns to prevent the incurring of unnecessary expenditure during marriage ceremonies were also launched with good results. Construction of community toilets also formed the agenda of the groups, and community mobilization ensured that the community managed with internal resources in most cases.

Many voluntary organisations like Christian Aid Fund have relied upon *Sahyatri* support to work on their agenda for livelihood promotion. Experiencing a lack of participation from the people, it requested the team to offer to them their network with the local people to usher in their programme. Another voluntary organisation which had even procured funds for housing for the disaster stricken families from the World Bank also had to seek the cooperation of *Sahyatris* to forge a rapport with its prospective client base. The *Sahyatri* ambulance service is a prized service for the locals and its utilisation is determined by the *Hum Yuva* members themselves. It is they who decide which patients shall be facilitated and how much payment shall be collected from them to enable the service to finance itself. The local leaders including the ward members, pradhans, block pramukhs, and even MLAs are aligned with the initiatives and lend whole hearted support from time to time.

The performance of *Hamari Pathshalas* in all the twenty villages is exemplary and has been instrumental in the spreading the name and fame of UDAI *Sahyatri* far and wide. In fact, so novel is this concept that there is a huge clamour for starting this programme in many other villages too. Another unusual, yet very welcome aspect pertains to the extremely amicable relationship that these centres maintain with the local government schools. There is an unwritten rule that all the families shall continue to hold children in government schools and the children would come to *our pathshalas* in non-school timings. Alongside, it is also accepted that children from all communities, especially those belonging to the most vulnerable families would be integrated within the group. The timing of the *pathshalas* has been aligned with the timing of the government schools and based on their time table; the *pathshalas* engage the children before the regular school hours of government schools. The schools in fact continue to request the *Sahyatri* educators and cluster in-charges to visit their schools; to organise innovative programmes for their students and interact with the parents' body to encourage them to retain their wards in school. A door to door visit is undertaken by representatives of the groups to motivate parents of non-school going children to enroll them into the school. Following a fluid and pioneering format, the educators and the cluster in-charges amalgamate academic inputs with co-curricular ones and enable the children to discover themselves in a facilitative environment. They find themselves immersed in activities that are innovative, and which allow their childishness to flourish, while they acquire the competency to read, write, calculate, recite, draw, enact, dance and sing.

The little *Sahyatris* embolden the confidence that the community reposes in our work, and deepens the bonds that we have forged over these many years. An engagement with the children's group during the yearly Foundation Day that is celebrated in Triveniganj, as also through their participation in the Annual Day celebrations of the Department leaves one spell bound and amazed, for the volume of confidence, talent, humility, exuberance and the sensitivity to social issues that they manifest, makes them stand out even among the city bred children of today.

Towards a New Beginning...

The dream of the Core team to empower the local team into assuming full ownership of the vision and mission of UDAI *Sahyatri* has been realized. The ongoing team building and organisational development endeavour has culminated in the evolution of an empowered community based organisation,

Sahyatri (Co-traveller), which is committed to an onward journey. Sharing in the turbulences presented by the disaster and the challenges confronted in the post disaster phase has bonded the young team into cohesive camaraderie and a spirited group, which is demonstrating commendable momentum, despite constraints of resources. The energy and the enthusiasm of the team have enabled the intervention to not only gain acceptance but also to spread over a wide locale. The goodwill generated for the Department and for the University is phenomenal. The *Sahyatris* have gained the confidence and the inspiration to pave their own way ahead, and to enlist the companionship of many more *Sahyatris* along the way.

The transition from the 'relief' phase, where the community was construed as a 'victim' of one of the worst disasters to a stage of 'resilience', wherein it is accumulating the capacity to transforming its own lived reality has been unique in that it has not traced a stereotypical path encapsulated by the regular 'Disaster Management Cycle'. Instead it has created its own distinct path by amalgamating the issues and problems that have been found to curtail people's access, entitlement and rights. The approach is grounded in the premise that resilience can be integrated if the community is able to strive to claim what rightfully belongs to it. This may not be in line with the path prescribed by disaster experts, but it definitely works towards preparing the community to develop self-help skills and capacities and to become more resilient to the vagaries of nature and the vagaries of governance.

The move to form Self Help Groups among the villages has been initiated and women's own ideas to determine sustainable livelihood options are being garnered. The idea of promoting sustainable livelihoods in the disaster risk areas has caught the imagination of people and a consensus on the adoption of weaving; to produce baskets, fans and other locally utilised articles with indigenous raw materials seems to be emerging, together with another very original idea to generate income for the women's groups. This relates to evolving a corpus for the groups to purchase tents, gas stoves, utensils and other accompanying material, which can then be rented out at reasonable rates within the village itself, for marriage and other ceremonies, thus yielding a continuous income for the women's collective. The reality of the possibility of sustainable livelihood generation for the village constituencies is immensely incentivising, but the challenge to ensure this goal remains arduous. If achieved, it shall facilitate the mitigation of disaster risk and vulnerability in a significant manner.

The noteworthy lessons learnt during the trajectory of the disaster and its management entailed:

1. UDAI-II *Sahyatri* has provided strong credibility to the idea of *University beyond classroom* and the possibility of *a campus that is alive to critical social realities.* It is the strong contention of the team that education needs to move beyond the narrow confines of the classroom and a structured syllabus, and conjoin with the lived reality of people. Working towards the creation of a campus that is the seedbed of a diversity of ideas and perspectives, and one that is alive and attuned to reflection and action is the only way to generate citizens who are sensitive and 'engaged' with the critical social realities, and who show a proclivity to side with the huge constituency of the vulnerable and the marginalized in the country.
2. A focus on garnering a partnership and a sense of ownership from amongst the local people themselves for long term engagement in responding and mitigating the risk of disasters is the surest way of building resilient communities. Long term sustainability of the intervention has been successfully ensured due to dependence on local energies, leadership and enterprise. Right from the beginning of the endeavour, the ownership of the initiative was reposed in the local volunteers and communities. The approach enabled the UDAI team to hand over the functioning of the programme to a community based organisation, which is now steering it forward.
3. A disaster context provides a natural laboratory for the social work fraternity to test its competency and the commitment to spontaneously participate and contribute to a situation of monumental human crisis. The Kosi disaster response tested the tenacity of the Department to assume the challenge of reaching out and persisting in providing the much needed shoulder of support to the most 'un-provided for' communities of people. It enabled the participants to persevere with the several odds and to approach the disaster challenge in many unique ways. The emergent response assumed structure and functions based on ground realities and the needs of the affected

populace and in doing so were able to contribute in a manner which we in social work describe as truly 'contextual'.

4. The process of engagement with the disaster not only demonstrated to its participants the physical fragility of vast human settlements to a consistently calamitous existence on account of their location in the area of influence of a natural hazard, it also validated the overwhelming presence of a socio-economic fragility that remains integral to people's overall vulnerability and peripheral status. Vast communities of people manifest a predisposition to enhanced disaster impact on account of their accentuated marginality and social segregation in human settlements. They confront gross disadvantage which emanates from their social and economic positioning, and which impinges on them even in the normal, 'non' disaster context, and which translates into an almost total lack of resilience in the eventuality of a disaster situation. The vulnerability of these constituencies of people was not only seen and assessed; it was also 'experienced' by the team. It revealed that many people are rendered vulnerable by the development process itself, by virtue of it invisibilizing their presence and thereby, passing them by. It brought to fore the fact that disasters do not occur out of context, they are embedded in the political structures, economic systems and social orders of the societies in which they take place (Bankoff, 2006). It also brought into cognizance the imperative of disaggregating disaster impact, risk, vulnerability and resilience, and the need to build short term and long term disaster responses on these disaggregated profiles of the disaster impacted.
5. The engagement lucidly corroborated the truism that the concept of vulnerability needs to be unpacked, in theoretical terms and in practice contexts too, in order to uncover its underlying ecological, political, and economic and socio-cultural implications. This is important for social work practice, as what is understood merely as an environmental calamity is much more than that...it has 'socio-cultural and political economic underpinnings' (Bankoff, 2006: 11) that need to be understood and woven in the interventions for relief, recovery, reconstruction and

rehabilitation. That is the difference that social work can make to its series of disaster engagements.

6. People's interface with disasters provides them with ways in which they can cope with the effects of the disasters. People who live with the frequent threat of disaster frequently evolve strategies or coping mechanisms for dealing with the same, and these are often quite effective. Recognising their worth and significance can be critical and can lead to empowering the local people to assume an active role in their management.
7. Government systems or institutionalised structures in charge of addressing disasters through facilitating preparedness, prevention, and mitigation have not assumed an effective edge, which can be attributed to a lack of political will and lack of faith in the pre disaster phases of disaster management. While the paradigmatic shift in disaster management from a reactive to a preventive and proactive stance is recognised beyond doubt, the same is yet to find expression in action. Within the context of the UN International Decade for Disaster Reduction during the nineties, the prevention of disasters and risk management was the fundamental strategy for sustainable development, but the same has not found its due place in the formulation of prevention and mitigation activities, especially with communities in the lead. Even in the response and aid phase, the government machinery was found to be unwieldy, slow and disconnected to the needs of the critical masses of people who seemed to be struggling under the burden of rebuilding their lives after the disaster.
8. There was also evidenced a politics in the provision of relief, and support for reconstruction, recovery and rehabilitation in favour of certain constituencies and in disfavour of certain others, and which was accepted without any misgiving. This was assumed to be a natural outcome of a hegemonic discourse propagated by the privileged to appropriate the largest share of the benefits and entitlements.
9. Inadequate resources and infrastructure do not make or break interventions. Non conventional and field driven approaches can lead to successful outcomes. A synergised engagement of the teams of student volunteers and the

local volunteers, who formed a chain of disaster responders could create an effective, ongoing, constantly evolving, need based, and phase centric intervention.

10. A process of recovery through building and renewing social capital is the surest way of creating resilience. Developing people's organisations, social support mechanisms and networks can empower the community to be the first and the ultimate responder to all the hazards which translate into disasters for them. The community becomes the key factor in this process of scaling up disaster resilience. Building the capacities and the confidence of the community to acquire rights, entitlements and resources is an effective and achievable way of consolidating the resilience of the community to confront the challenges arising out of the hazards and even the pressures of daily living.
11. A synergy of Departmental goals and the needs, expectations and aspirations of the community enabled a successful and enduring partnership between the *Sahyatris.*

The Core team is committed to support the strengthening and consolidating of UDAI *Sahyatri* as a community based NGO for the local people and is proud to proclaim that it has at its behest, a fully empowered and charged band of workers to carry the work forward.

The road that the Sahyatris have made by walking together is strong, yet incomplete... and the journey to resilience is never ending... the author has been fortunate to be a part of this co-travel, for it has given her unbounded joy; a lifelong relationship with her team, the volunteers and the constituencies; the renewal of conviction in the ability of her students to create change; a reaffirmation of faith in the tenacity of people; and above all the pride of being a SAHYATRI.

References

Bankoff, G., Frerks, G., and Hilhorst, D. (eds.) (2006). *Mapping Vulnerability: Disasters, Development and People.* London, Sterling, VA: Earthscan.

Blaikie, P., Cannon, T., Davis, I. and Wisner, B. (1994). *At Risk: Natural Hazards, People's Vulnerability and Disasters,* London and New York: Routledge.

Cannon, T. (1994). Vulnerability Analysis and the Explanation of "Natural" Disasters in A. Varley (ed.) *Disasters, Development and Environment*. Chichester, New York, Brisbane: John Wiley and Sons.

Enarson, E. and Morrow, B.N. (eds.) (1998). *The Gendered Terrain of Disaster: Through Women's Eyes*. Westport, Conn: Praeger.

Guha-Sapir, D., Parry, L.V., Deggome, O., Joshi, P.C., Saulina, Arnold J.P. (2006). *Risk Factors for Mortality and Injury: Post Tsunami Epidemiological Findings from Tamil Nadu*. CRED.

Hewitt, K. (ed.) (1983). *Interpretations of Calamity from the Viewpoint of Human Ecology*. London and Sydney: Allen and Unwin Inc.

Lewis, J. (1999). *Development in Disaster Prone Places: Studies in Vulnerability*. London: Intermediate Technology Publications.

Pampel, Fred. C. (2010). *Disaster Response*. New Delhi: Viva Books.

Rosenfeld, Lawrence B., Caye, Joane S., Ofra Ayalon, and Mooli Lahad. (2005). *When Their World Falls Apart: Helping Families and Children Manage the Effects of Disasters*. Washington D.C: National Association of Social Workers.

United Nations International Strategy for Disaster Reduction (2010a). *Guidance Note on Recovery: Governance*. Kobe: International Recovery Platform Secretariat.

United Nations International Strategy for Disaster Reduction (2010b). *Guidance Note on Recovery: Psychosocial*. Kobe: International Recovery Platform Secretariat.

United Nations International Strategy for Disaster Reduction (2010c). *Guidance Note on Recovery: Health*. Kobe: International Recovery Platform Secretariat.

United Nations International Strategy for Disaster Reduction (2010d). *Guidance Note on Recovery: Gender*. Kobe: International Recovery Platform Secretariat.

5

Protected Area and People

Exploring the Role of Social Work Practice

Digvijoy Phukan and *Vinay Kumar*

The relationship shared by humans with nature has been the focus of intense debate, discussion and deliberation. Elders of the Agaria community living adjacent to the Little Rann of Kachchh (LRK) for centuries narrate tales of how they were chosen as the protectors of the 'nanu' (little) Rann, a unique ecosystem on this earth. They claim that it is their duty to protect the area from plunderers from outside and in return they have the right to make 'mithu' (salt) from the brine below the surface of the Rann to earn their livelihood. Salt is the gift that mother earth had bestowed upon Agarias for guarding the territory. The efforts of the government and conservation groups to protect the uniqueness of LRK, on the other hand view the presence of the Agarias, the people who feel that the duty to protect the area has been entrusted upon them, as detrimental to the survival of animal and plant species in the LRK. Salt making by the Agarias has been pointed out as inimical towards the fragile ecosystem of the area. The notification of the area as the Wild Ass Sanctuary (WAS) in 1973 is a landmark which marked the beginning of feelings of alienation and dissatisfaction that permeate the air in the area.

The claims of community elders in Kharaghoda that Agarias have been entrusted with the task of protection of the Rann and the efforts of the conservationists share some common ground, albeit for entirely different purposes and by the adoption of dissimilar measures. Both stress upon the fact that there is a need to protect and to conserve the bounties of nature around them. The idea of conservation is embedded in the description of the Rann by Agarias and highlighted in bold through the words used on signboards posted across the boundary of the Rann by the forest officials, to welcome and warn the visitors to the Rann. Reflecting at its core specific values individuals and societies hold about nature and human-nature relationships, conservation marks this common ground (McNeely and Mainka, 2009). Originating in U.S., the creation of protected areas has been a major strategy for conservation across the countries of the world. The history of the protected areas can be traced back to the 1864 federal transfer of Yosemite Valley to the state of California for use as a park and the subsequent establishment of the Yellowstone National Park in U.S. in 1872. The efforts of the international conservation organisations like IUCN had led to the establishment of protected areas around the world in the 1960s. The passing of the Wilderness Act in the U.S. in 1964 further promoted the idea of maintaining nature in its pristineness. Almost a decade after the passing of the act in America, LRK was declared as a sanctuary in 1973. The notification of the sanctuary can be seen as part of the global trend of establishing protected areas through legislation as a major conservation strategy.

Conte (2007) has stated that the task of carving out protected areas was carried out by twentieth century colonial governments after the nineteenth century naturalists had identified the wilderness areas. According to Sarkar (2005), the designation of national parks until 1940s was entirely based on the exquisiteness and appeal to the visitor. The selection of sites for the early national parks attested to this point. These were the places of sublime beauty. The wary humans could visit these spots and enjoy nature in all her glory. Adams (2004) has opined that it was in Africa that the American concept of a national park matched the belief of the conservationists in search of a newer and permanent concept to replace the game reserves, which due to their permeability could offer only temporary solutions to the challenges of conservation. He has added that for the colonial governments the major lure of national parks was their 'permanence as such sanctuaries' (p. 77). Undoubtedly, protected areas have been the most important conservation strategy during the last century. In 1902, British hunter turned conservationist and President of SPWFE, Edward North Buxton had written of Africa 'the maintenance of reserves, or sanctuaries, is the first essential for the preservation of various species' (as quoted in Adams, 2004; p. 4). Beinart and Hughes (2007) have stated that the trend to establish permanent national parks through legislation started after the Second World War and replaced the reserves established by proclamation and decree.

The strategy of formation of protected areas through legislations has gained impetus after the establishment of IUCN. According to McCormick, IUCN is an 'unusual network of states and non-governmental organisations' which looks into the implementation of environmental treaties, acts as a link between the UN and the non-governmental organisations and arranges funds for the establishment of parks (McCormick, 1989; as cited in O'Neill 1996; p. 524). The preparation of a 'World List of National Parks and Equivalent Reserves' by IUCN's newly formed protected areas commission, renamed the World Commission for Protected Area (WCPA), in response to the 1959 UN Economic and Social Council (ECOSOC) recognition of national parks and equivalent reserves as major factors for the judicious use of natural resources has been discussed by Phillips (2008). This further showcases the involvement of IUCN in strengthening the protected area movements globally after the Second World War. The IUCN definition of protected area, revised in 2008 highlighted the importance of legal mechanisms in the formation of these areas. It defines a protected area as:

> "A clearly defined geographical space, recognised, dedicated and managed, through legal or other effective means, to achieve the long-term conservation of nature with associated ecosystem services and cultural values" (Dudley, 2008; p. 8).

The protected areas around the world have been designated different names in different countries of the world during the period of the conference in 1933. The confusion which arose out of such diverse terminologies was highlighted in 1962 by C.F. Brockman at the First World Conference on National Parks, held in Seattle, U.S. (Phillips, 2008). It was in 1994 that IUCN adopted the present system of classification of protected areas into six categories based on their 'management objectives' (Francis; 2008; p. 20). These categories have been listed in Table 5.1. According to Philips, the guidelines intended to bring uniformity in classification of these areas and pointed out the need for creation of these areas to the governments around the world.

In light of the rapid economic developments, World Bank has stated that the protected areas have provided society with many benefits in terms of ecosystem preservation, provision of

Table 5.1: IUCN Categories of Protected Areas

S. N.	*Category*	*Description*	*Examples*
1.	I a	Strict nature reserve	Boheman Bird Sanctuary, Norway Wolong Nature Reserve, China
2.	I b	Wilderness area	Apache Creek Wilderness, U.S. Imfolozi Wilderness Area, South Africa
3.	II	National park	Huerquehue National Park, Chile Yellowstone National Park, U.S.
4.	III	Natural monument or feature	Bosques Petrificados National Monument, Monterrico Multiple Use Area, Guatemala
5.	IV	Habitat/species management area	Central Kalahari Game Reserve, Botswana Dja Faunal Reserve, Cameroon
6.	V	Protected landscape/ seascape	Brecon Beacons National Park, UK Fuji-Hakone-Izu National Park, Japan
7.	VI	Protected area with sustainable use of natural resources	Annapurna Conservation Area, Nepal Wudangshan Scenic Area, China

Source: Lausche (2011, p. 27)

environmental services and opportunities for recreation and tourism (Sobrevila, 2008). Adams (2004) has noted that the website for the Fifth World Parks Congress described protected areas as 'a cornerstone of global conservation efforts' (p. 4). The importance laid on protected areas as a conservation strategy can be gauged by its role as an indicator of the UN Millennium Development Goals (MDG). The ratio of protected area to surface area has been considered as an indicator (26) of the target (9) to integrate the principles of sustainable development and reverse loss of environmental resources under MDG goal (7), which intends to measure environmental sustainability (Brockington, Duffy, and Igoe, 2008). Neumann (1998) has held the view that ecological validations for the establishment of protected areas around the world have increased since the days of creation of the world's first national parks in America. He has viewed tropical deforestation and species extinction to be the major factors accelerating the establishment of the protected areas. While protected areas have been declared as cornerstones of national and international conservation strategies, their impact on the lives of people living inside and adjacent to them remains a major topic of debate.

Protected Areas as Sites of Livelihood and Conservation Conflict

A glimpse into the history of conservation would tell us that the efforts towards the creation of areas of wilderness have been mired by conflicts between the conservationist forces and the people inhabiting the areas. The establishment of the earliest national parks in the US saw the forced removal of Indians from their territory and their history being systematically wiped out from the memory of the later Americans to create the myth of an isolated area of wilderness established through legislation (Adams, 2004; Sarkar, 2005). The Yosemite nation was excluded from Yosemite, the Crow, the Shoshone and the Bannock from Yellowstone (Sarkar, 2005 p. 40; Sobrevila, 2008; Higgins-Zogib, Dudley, and Kothari, 2010). The adoption of 'Yellowstone model' has been promoted all over the world as this model provided a means to the powerful organisations of mainstream conservation to decipher the world (Brockington *et al.*, 2008; Sobrevila, 2008). The 'conservationist impulses' (Beinart and Hughes, 2007; p. 289) of the imperial expansion also chose the American national parks as models for their conservation strategy. They have further argued that in the colonies the legacy of exclusive conservation was adhered to leading to the exclusion of human settlements from the areas where wildlife and habitats were protected.

It has to be highlighted that the international bodies working on issues related to conservation through protected areas have chosen to ignore the history and the narratives of the communities displaced or in conflict with the protected areas. The IUCN maintained WDPA provides exhaustive geographical and ecological information on the worldwide protected areas, however the database does not offer any information on the communities living near these areas. The conflicts have been systematically swept inside the mat to create an image of a peaceful, protected and pristine area. The documents of IUCN illustrate cases of success in efforts concerning the involvement of the communities around the protected areas while carefully avoiding the tales of the people whose livelihood has been disrupted and those who have been displaced from the land of their ancestors. Neumann (1998) has aptly stated:

> "National parks are treated as threatened by land-hungry populations rather than as being historically complicit in the creation of conditions of land and resource scarcity" (p. 8).

The conflicts arising out of the establishment of protected areas and the subsequent imposition of restrictions on the access to resources by the local communities emanated from several issues. Discussing the case of Arusha National Park in Tanzania, Neumann (1998) has highlighted that for people associated with conservation, the conflicts are centred around issues related to livestock trespass, illegal hunting and wood theft, whereas for the local communities issues of land access, resource uses and agricultural loss due to wildlife are the sources of conflict. It can be inferred that the theme of conflict differed based on the side of the fence where one was situated. Conte (2007) has lamented the fact that the global acceptance of the American model of a national park has also disseminated the preservationist spirit of establishing spaces without human presence. He has added that the first World Conference on National Parks held in U.S. in 1962 was a landmark step on the part of the international conservation organisations' tireless attempts to promote the concept of protected areas around the world. The IUCN categorisation of the protected areas based on management goals have brought to fore the emphasis laid by these agencies in the creation of exclusive spaces for wildlife. This categorisation has focused on restrictions imposed upon human activities in and around the different categories of protected areas. Further this prescription for the survival of wildlife has formed the basis of protected area legislations by the governments around the world. These restrictions have directly impacted the livelihood of the local communities and triggered people and park conflicts. As commented by Norton (2004), the protection of biodiversity often implied handling of humans, rather than management of wildlife.

Bokil (1999) based on his study with people living near the Koyna Sanctuary in Maharashtra has showed how restrictions on the access to the resources inside the sanctuary on which they depend cause adverse effect on the traditional lifestyle, besides impacting their livelihood activities and freedom of movement. Conservation initiatives have adversely impacted local livelihoods almost everywhere and have at times involved the use of violence against people and property as in the case of Lake Mburo National Park in Uganda and forced resettlement leading to long term deterioration of living standards, as in Mkomazi Game Reserve in Tanzania (Hulme and Murphree, 1999). Nightingale (2003) while looking at community forestry initiatives in Nepal has opined that the establishment of protected areas has led to two fold impact on the lives of the local people, on one hand it has denied them access to the natural resources on which they have been depended and on the other they have not been provided with any new options to earn their livelihood.

Protected Areas in India and Local Communities

The turn of the century saw the establishment of national parks around the world and India did not remain untouched by this model of nature preservation that was initiated in America and implemented widely across Africa (Rangarajan, 2005). The first sanctuary was established in Kaziranga, Assam for the preservation of the Indian rhinoceros (*Rhinoceros unicornis*) in 1908. Shrestha (2009) has argued that the establishment of the sanctuaries in India should be seen in the context of the situation where the area under cultivation was extending, population was expanding and forest cover was reducing, making it difficult for the laws alone to ensure protection to animals. According to her, the rigid segregation of land for game preservation and crop production was the British strategy to protect the wildlife in the emerging scenario. Independent India retained the structure established by the British in India for conservation of nature. The onus of conserving India's forests and its wildlife remained with the forest department and its foresters who focussed their activities on the control of hunting, protection of large animals, and creation of national parks (Saberwal, Rangarajan & Kothari, 2001; Rangarajan, 2005).

The emphasis on establishment of protected areas has also been a key government strategy to conserve wildlife in India. It has been a part of the government policy since the second five year plan (1956-1961) and is an important action point of the National Wildlife Action Plan (2002-2016). Saberwal *et al.*, (2001) have rightly commented that this strategy of implementation of protected areas is rooted in the doctrine of 'natural wilderness areas' that considered human land use to be detrimental for ecosystem (p. 44). Guha (2005) has added that the management of national parks in the third world nations has been fashioned in the pattern adopted in America. He has stated two axioms pertaining to the national parks: the axioms of 'giganticism and hands off nature' (p. 151). According to him, the idea behind stopping human activity in entirety was flawed as biodiversity levels are highest in areas where intervention exists in some form.

The case of Keoladeo Ghana National Park in Rajasthan, India, where prohibition of buffalo grazing in the long term affected the wetland species and the richness of species diversity noted in the Quitovac oasis on the Mexican side of the Sonoran desert where traditional use was continued as compared to the low diversity in the oasis on the American side which was included in the Organ Pipe Cactus Natural Monument support the above argument (Sarkar, 2005; Dudley, 2008).

Almost every community living on the fringe of a protected area in India is struggling for its traditional rights over the land sustaining them for centuries. The issue of conflict between livelihood of the locals and conservation of wildlife gains strength as 56 per cent of national parks and 72 per cent of sanctuaries in India have people residing in them and 60 per cent of the national parks and 92 per cent of the sanctuaries in India have not received legal status (Hosetti, 2005; p. 21). Rangarajan (2001) alluding to the tension between residents living in the periphery of the protected areas and authorities has stated that in the 1980s one in five protected areas reported clashes between authorities and the residents. The conflict has stemmed out of the state policy to exclude local people traditionally living near the areas demarcated for wildlife under the 'Yellowstone model' of conservation. The exclusion as described by the Agarias has been not only from the physical space but also from the matters of policy formulation and implementation. Saberwal *et al.*, (2001) while questioning this segregation have opined that the denial of the rights to resources on which communities have been dependent for centuries result in protests by the local people.

The history of Indian protected areas is also marred with conflicts like its counterparts across the world. Guha (2005) has cited the examples of conservation induced displacement in Rajaji National Park in Uttarakhand, Simlipal National Park in Orissa and Kanha National Park in Madhya Pradesh to argue that the advocates of human free parks pay scant regard to the interests of local people who are traditionally dependent on the areas. According to Shahabuddin (2010), the efforts to link the protected areas and the local economies have not made any head start. She has viewed the promulgation of Scheduled Tribes and Other Traditional Forest Dwellers (Recognition of Forest Rights) Act, 2006 as a major step towards the realisation of rights of the traditional dwellers but has lamented the fact that several protected areas have not settled the rights leading to the final notification. It is ironic that while the website of the ministry entrusted with the task to preserve wildlife proudly highlights its achievements, thousands of people have either lost or are on the verge of being displaced and losing their livelihood in the name of conservation. Unless the benefits of conservation are shared by locals who have been traditionally living near these areas the claims of the government will remain hollow.

Livelihood and Conservation Conflict in the Context of Agarias of Little Rann of Kachchh

Like most other communities across the country, the notification of a sanctuary has touched the lives of the Agarias of Little Rann of Kachchh (LRK). Remoteness from mainstream society has ensured that the Agarias are not only unorganised but also unrecognised and their role in providing society with one of its most important requirement is largely unnoticed. It has to be noted that the term Agaria includes both salt workers in the LRK and those in the coastal regions of Gujarat. The primary difference between the two is that the Agarias of LRK are dependent on sub-soil brine whereas those working in the coastal belt utilise the seawater for salt making. The villages of Agarias involved in the production of inland salt are located in the five peripheral districts of LRK namely, Surendranagar, Kachchh, Patan, Rajkot and Banaskantha. Agarias from these districts migrate to LRK every season to produce salt from sub-soil brine. This paper attempts to explore the lives of the Agarias of LRK also referred to as the inland salt workers of Gujarat as they struggle to fight for their rights to make salt inside the LRK. It is based on the in-depth interviews conducted with Agarias engaged in inland salt prodution inside LRK, NGO professionals working with the Agarias and the 'Conservationists'; a term applied to those involved in and advocating for people free protected areas.

Majority of Agarias involved in the production of salt from inland brine belong to the Chunvalia Koli community. Chunvalia Kolis constitute 60 per cent of the inland salt workers while 35 per cent is composed of the Sandhi and Miyana Muslims and communities like Darbars, Ahirs, Bharwads and Dalits constitute the remaining five per cent of Agarias (Yadava, Mukherjee, and Munde, 2006; Bharwada and Mahajan, 2008). Singh (1998) has stated that Chunvalia Kolis in Gujarat are distributed in the Surendranagar and Junagadh districts and derive their name from their homeland Chunvalpradesh, located near north-east of Viramgram. He has added that the name originated from the existence of forty-four (chummalis) villages in the area. According to Singh, another view is that they are descendants of Jhala Rajputs. They belong to the Makvana tribe of Kolis and have features similar to the Bhils (GoG, 1977; p. 189).

Malekar (2009) based on his interview with Ambubhai Patel, a local historian-writer from Kharaghoda and also a key informant of the researcher, has stated that Agarias have always remained the unsung beasts of burden of the salt industry. Agarias claim that their ancestors have been migrating to the LRK to produce salt from sub-soil brine since time immemorial. Agariya Heet Rakshak Manch (AHRM), an Ahmedabad based organisation formed to advocate for the rights of the Agarias are in possession of a *firman* (an official order) issued by the Mughal Emperor Aurangzeb in the year 1669-70. Agarwal (1956) has also referred to this order, which according to him, established the hereditary rights of the Rulers of Dhrangadhra to make salt in Kuda (p. 233). Based on the reference to the 'salt pits' in the *firman*, it has been argued that organised inland salt production has been undertaken since that period.

The dynamics of the salt trade in India has added an interesting dimension to this livelihood and conservation debate. Unlike most communities living near sanctuaries, Agarias of LRK have been part of a major revenue earning industry. India is the third largest producer of salt in the world after China and the U.S. (GoI, 2011). However, the deplorable working and living conditions of the Agarias of LRK is indicative of the fact that the gains of the industry have not benefitted them. Shah (2008) has pointed out that the Agarias of LRK are at the lowest end of the salt industry in India getting only ten per cent of the market price towards their labour. Inspite of being perennially in debt and exploited by the persons controlling the inland salt trade, producing salt under extremely harsh conditions of the Rann has been their sole livelihood activity. The notification of the LRK as the Wild Ass Sanctuary (WAS) has threatened their livelihood of producing inland salt.

In tune with the government objective of establishment of 'human-free' protected areas as a major conservation strategy, Wild Ass Sanctuary (WAS) was notified in 1973 under sections 20 and 21 of the Gujarat Wild Animals and Wild Birds Protection Act, 1963. The sanctuary is distributed over the districts of

Kachchh, Banaskatha, Patan, Rajkot and Surendranagar districts. Though LRK is internationally famous for the endangered Asiatic Wild Ass (*Equus hemionus khur*), it has been stated in the exhaustive report on the biodiversity of the LRK published by Gujarat Ecological Education and Research Foundation (GEER) that it is also an abode of variety of other mammals, birds, reptiles, amphibians, fish, micro and macro invertebrates and plants (Singh *et al.*, 1999). The sanctuary is internationally famous as the site where the endangered Indian wild asses are found. Locally known as *Ghurkhad*, the wild asses belong to the order Perissodactyla of the family Equidae. According to Srivastav and Nigam (2010), wild asses in the LRK occupy the saline mudflats, grassland, *bets* and the fringes where natural vegetation is interspersed with croplands, are active during night to maximise resource utilisation at the interface between natural vegetation and agriculture and breed predominantly during monsoon.

The conflict between livelihood and conservation in the area surrounding the LRK stems from the presence of 52,634 households in the 108 villages spread across five districts of Gujarat (GoI, 2009). Conservationists are of the opinion that wild asses of LRK are threatened by anthropogenic activities inside the Rann, including inland salt production, livestock grazing, army firing, charcoal making, etc. (Singh *et al.*, 1999; Feh *et al.*, 2002). They have also highlighted the impact of the invasion of *Prosopis juliflora*, an exotic plant species on the habitat of the wild asses. The efforts to scientifically conserve the wild ass have been lauded by the conservationists. They repeatedly stated during their interviews that they are not against communities inhabiting areas bordering the WAS. Conservationists are also unified in their stand that humans and their activities inside the sanctuary are the greatest threat to plants and animals of LRK. They believe that only 'fences' can protect the biodiversity of the Rann. They think that it is essential to stop salt production and other anthropogenic activities inside the sanctuary which are inimical to conservation initiatives. Conservationists stated that Agarias are unaware of the ecological significance of the region. Many of them said that prior to the declaration of the area as a biosphere reserve they had proposed the declaration of the LRK region as a national park. This would have imposed further restrictions on human activities inside the sanctuary. A senior official in Gandhinagar pronounced with an air of authority, *'it is an established fact that activities related to salt pans and livestock grazing are the biggest threat to species inside the*

Rann...to ensure that our efforts do not go down the drain we have to keep the area free from these activities...it is the duty of every citizen of the country to protect the voiceless animals.'

Agarias are convinced that there is no need to transform the Rann into a sanctuary. They denied the charges that salt production damages the ecology of the Rann. They said that the salt pans are always located away from the Bets and routes taken by animals inside the Rann. For the Agarias, the Rann is a sacred place. They are also certain that the Rann is endowed with human attributes. They perceive the Rann as someone who has sustained their community. This role ascribed to the Rann is evident from the description of their association with the Rann during successive stages of salt production. They also possess extensive knowledge regarding the economic value and medicinal properties of various plants in the region. NGO professionals strongly believe that the traditional knowledge associated with inland salt production will enable the Agarias to claim their rights over the Rann under the Scheduled Tribes and Other Forest Dwellers (Recognition of Forest Rights) Act, 2006. Efforts have been undertaken by NGOs to systematically document this knowledge possessed by the community to strengthen their arguments for the recognition of rights under this act. In light of the decision taken by the forest department in 2007 to recognise the rights to continue prawn fishing and fishing inside the Rann, the NGOs have hardened their stand that the rights of the Agarias should also be recognised. Few NGO officials added that Agarias should also be allowed to make salt inside the Rann as per sub-section 24(2)(c) of the 1991 amendment to the WLPA (1972) which empowers the collector to allow, in consultation with the chief wildlife warden, the continuation of any right of any person in or over any land within limits of the sanctuary.

Agarias who are aware of the notification of the sanctuary said that it only causes problems in their lives. They were unanimous in their opinion that notification of the sanctuary has worsened their plight. The adverse impacts of the notification of the sanctuary as perceived by Agarias were gauged based on the factors identified by Colchester (2004) on impact of protected areas on people. The analysis of results reveals that the illegality imposed upon them for undertaking their livelihood activities inside the Rann, fissures in their symbolic ties with the Rann and the weakening of their cultural identity are the major impact of the notification on their lives at present. Respondents were afraid of losing their right to produce salt inside the Rann, complete rupture of their ties with Rann and the possibility of leaving their villages due to the protected area in future. It has been argued by Knudsen (1999) that securing livelihood options for people is essential for furthering the objectives of conservation. The lack of benefits or proper compensation to local communities around protected areas have resulted in giving rise to feelings of suspicion and hostility among local communities associated with these sites Kothari (2008). Though sanctuary officials have not stopped Agarias from entering the Rann to produce salt, yet the looming threat of losing their livelihood due to notification of the sanctuary and declaration of the area as Kachchh Biosphere Reserve in 2008 has forced many Agarias to migrate to areas where the sea salt industry is flourishing. Agarias are grieved at the portrayal of the 'friend' as the 'foe' by those who have never lived in the area. They are convinced that their livelihood activity of salt production does not harm the biodiversity of Rann. For the Agarias, their annual migration to Rann for salt production is their right.

Park and People Conflict: Scope for Social Workers

The tremendous worldwide growth of protected areas over recent decades has been pointed out by Lausche (2011). Based on the figures collected from UNEP-World Conservation Monitoring Centre (WCMC), she has stated that in 1962 there were 9,214 sites covering 2.4 million km^2. By 1992, these figures had grown to 48,388 protected areas covering 12.3 million km^2. The 2011 UN List contained 1,30,709 national protected areas covering more than 24.2 million km^2 (IUCN and UNEP, 2009a). Emphasising upon the need to extend the global coverage of protected areas to meet the target set by CBD, 2010 UNEP-WCMC indicator factsheet on Biodiversity Indicator Partnership (BIP) has noted that 12.2 per cent of the planet's total land area and nearly one per cent of the planet's total sea area designated as protected areas (IUCN and UNEP, 2009b).

As noted by Kaus (1993), there is an urgent need to shift the thinking from looking at the role of people in protected area to that of protected area in the lives of local people to ensure success of the conservation initiatives. Based on their work with the Maasai Pastoralists in the Ngorongoro Conservation Area, Homewood and Rodgers (1991) in their book 'Maasailand Ecology' have highlighted the lopsided sharing of benefits derived from the establishment of a protected area. In the context of the eviction of the Maasai pastoralists, they have stated that the aesthetic experience and the scientific opportunities are enjoyed by the foreign visitor by paying minimal financial costs, the national prestige and international political leverage gained by the national government balance the political and financial costs. Besides the government and the private sector share the revenue earned from tourism. The authors have opined that the original inhabitants of the area who have traditionally relied on the resources of the area for their survival are forced to bear only losses, which according to them, include denial of access to resources, land alienation, damage to land and property and emotional loss.

The case of the Agarias of LRK highlights the manner in which the livelihood of people living adjacent to and inside the protected area for centuries is threatened by the expanding network of protected areas in India. It also underlines the need to secure livelihoods for people living adjacent to the protected areas to ensure success of the conservation strategies. There is also the need to involve the local community in the management strategies of the protected areas. This involvement of community necessitates an in-depth understanding of the views of local people regarding nature, the conservation initiatives of the government and integration of their traditional wisdom pertaining to resource use with the conservation strategies. In this emerging scenario, working with communities caught in this livelihood and conservation debate offers a new avenue of work for social workers. Social workers can play a pivotal role in ameliorating the lives of Agarias and members of other communities caught in the park and people conflict.

The social workers working with such communities caught in park and people conflict should at the outset assess the stage of livelihood and conservation conflict. This should be based on the legal position of the protected area, status of implementation of the legislative provisions for creation and maintenance of protected areas and execution of the legislations protecting the rights of the local people in and around the protected areas. This should be followed by an assessment of the awareness among the community about the conservation initiatives and their legal rights. Simultaneously, a social impact assessment and an ecological assessment should be undertaken. Social worker can also play a key role in the implementation of the programmes specifically designed and aimed at promoting alternative livelihood options for the local communities traditionally dependent on the protected area for their livelihood. S/he can also be a key player in the promotion of eco-tourism initiatives which develop following the creation of protected areas. Social workers will have to also ensure the development of the skills of local communities to derive benefit from them. Another key role of a social worker working with such communities is to generate awareness regarding the traditional rights of the community and the ecological significance of the protected area. The skills of community organisation acquired by the social workers shall give them an advantage over professionals from other disciplines in engaging with local communities in and around the protected area. It is important for social workers to design and implement strategies which will safeguard the long-term sustainability of species and ecosystems and are acceptable to local communities and the government. The formulation of policies aimed at the integration of the dual objectives calls for an extensive understanding of various issues involving the local communities affected by the protected areas. It also demands that the social worker relies on her/his knowledge and skill base to mitigate the conflict between protected area and people living in and around it.

References

Adams, W.M. (2004). *Against Extinction: The Story of Conservation*. London: Earthscan.

Agarwal, S.C. (1956). *Salt Industry in India* (Vol. I). New Delhi: Government of India Press.

Beinart, W., and Hughes, L. (2007). *Environment and Empire*. Oxford: Oxford University Press.

Bharwada, C., and Mahajan, V. (2008). *Yet to be Freed: Agariayas' Lives and Struggles for Survival in the Little Rann of Kutch*. Ahmedabad: SANDARBH.

Bokil, M.S. (1999). People in Protected Areas Koyna Sanctuary in Maharashtra. *Economic and Political Weekly*, 293-299.

Brockington, D., Duffy, R., and Igoe, J. (2008). *Nature Unbound: Conservation, Capitalism and the Future of Protected Areas*. London: Earthscan.

Colchester, M. (2004). Conservation Policy and Indigenous Peoples. *Cultural Survival Quarterly*, *28*(1), 17-22.

Conte, C. (2007). Creating Wild Places form Domesticated Landscapes: The Internationalization of the American Wildernes Concept. In M.

Lewis (Ed.), *American Wilderness: A New History*. pp. 223-242, New York: Oxford University Press.

Dudley, N. (2008). *Guidelines for Applying Protected Area Management Categories*. Gland: IUCN.

Feh, C., Shah, N., Rowen, M., Reading, R., and Goyal, S.P. (2002). Status and Action Plan for the Asiatic Wild Ass (Equus hemionus). In P.D. Moehlman (ed.), *Equids: Zebras, Asses and Horses. Status Survey and Conservation Action Plan*. Gland: IUCN.

Francis, G. (2008). Evolution of Contexts for Protected Areas Governance. In K.S. Hanna, D.A. Clark, and D. Slocombe (Eds.), *Transforming Parks and Protected Areas: Policy and Governance in a Changing World*. pp. 15-38. New York: Routledge.

Government of Gujarat. (1977). *Gujarat State Gazetteers: Surendranagar District*. Ahmedabad: Government Printing, Stationery and Publications.

Government of India. (2009). *Environmental and Social Management Framework in Biodiversity Conservation and Rural Livelihood Improvement Project*. New Delhi: Ministry of Environment and Forests. Retrieved September 18, 2011, from http://moef.nic.in/pt/BCRLIP_ESMF.pdf

_______, (2011). *Annual Report 2010-11*. Jaipur: Salt Department, Ministry of Commerce & Industry, GoI.

Guha, R. (2005). The Authoritarian Biologist and the Arrogance of Anti-humanism: Wildlife Conservation in the Third World. In V.K. Saberwal, and M. Rangarajan (eds.), *Battles Over Nature: Science and Politics of Conservation* (pp. 118-139). New Delhi: Permanent Black.

Higgins-Zogib, L., Dudley, N., and Kothari, A. (2010). Living Traditions: Protected Areas and Cultural Diversity. In S. Stolton, and N. Dudley (eds.), *Arguments for Protected Areas: Multiple Benefits for Conservation and Use*. pp. 165-179. London: Earthscan.

Homewood, K.M., and Rodgers, W.A. (1991). *Maasailand Ecology: Pastoralist Development and Wildlife Conservation in Ngorongoro, Tanzania*. Cambridge: Cambridge University Press.

Hosetti, B.B. (2005). *Concepts in Wildlife Management*. Delhi: Daya Publishing House.

Hulme, D., and Murphree, M. (1999). Communities, Wildlife and the 'New Conservation' in Africa. *Journal of International Development, 11*, 277-285.

IUCN, and UNEP. (2009a). *Growth in Global Number of Protected Areas (1911-2011)*. The World Database on Protected Areas (WDPA). Cambridge: UNEP-WCMC. Retrieved March 5, 2012, from World Database on Protected Area: http://www.wdpa. org/Statistics.aspx

_______, (2009b). *Protected Area Overlays with Biodiversity*. The World Database on Protected Areas (WDPA). Cambridge: UNEP-WCMC. Retrieved December 4, 2012, from World Database on Protected Areas: http://www.wdpa.org/resources/statistics/2010BIP_Factsheet_Protected_Area_Overlays_with_Biodiversity.pdf

Kaus, A. (1993). Environmental Perceptions and Social Relations in the Mapimi Biosphere Reserve. *Conservation Biology, 7*(2), 398-406.

Knudsen, A. (1999). Conservation and Controversy in the Karakoram: Khunjerab National Park, Pakistan. *Journal of Political Ecology, 56,* 1-30.

Kothari, A. (2008). Diversifyig Protected Area Governance: Ecological, Social and Economic Benefits. In *Protected Areas in Today's World: Their Values and Benefits for the Welfare of the Planet* (Technical Series No. 36), pp. 57-66. Montreal: Secretariat of the Convention on Biological Diversity.

Lausche, B. (2011). *Guidelines for Protected Areas Legislation.* Gland: IUCN.

Malekar, A. (2009). *Salt Pains.* Retrieved August 9, 2009, from Info Change: http://infochangeindia.org/Agenda/Occupational-safety-and-health/Salt-pains.html

McNeely, J.A., and Mainka, S.A. (2009). *Conservation for a New Era.* Gland: IUCN.

Neumann, R.P. (1998). *Imposing Wilderness: Struggles over Livelihood and Nature Preservation in Africa.* California: University of California Press.

Nightingale, A. (2003). Nature-Society and Development: Social, Cultural and Ecological Change in Nepal. *Geoforum, 34,* 525-540.

Norton, B.G. (2004). *Searching for Sustainability: Interdisciplinary Essays in the Philosophy of Conservation Biology.* Cambridge: Cambridge University Press.

O'Neill, K.M. (1996). The International Politics of National Parks. *Human Ecology, 24*(4), 521-539.

Phillips, A. (2008). A Short History of the International System of Protected Areas Management. In N. Dudley, and S. Stolton (eds.), *Defining Protected Areas: An International Conference in Almeria, Spain,* pp. 13-17. Gland: IUCN.

Rangarajan, M. (2001). *India's Wildlife History: An Introduction.* Delhi: Permanent Black.

_______, (2005). The politics of Ecology: The Debate on Wildlife and People in India, 1970-95. In V.K. Saberwal, and M. Rangarajan (eds.), *Battles Over Nature-Science and the Politics of Conservation,* pp. 159-189. New Delhi: Permananet Black.

Saberwal, V., Rangarajan, M., and Kothari, A. (2001). *People, Parks and Wildlife: Towards Coexistence.* New Delhi: Orient Longman Private Limited.

Sarkar, S. (2005). *Biodiversity and Environmental Philosophy: An Introduction.* Cambridge: Cambridge University Press.

Shah, R. (2008). *A Pinch of Salt: A Study of Salt Workers of Kutch, Patan, Rajkot and Surendranagar District of Gujarat.* Ahmedabad: SAVE.

Shahabuddin, G. (2010). *Conservation at the Crossroads—Science, Soceity and the Future of India's Wildlife.* New Delhi: Permanent Black.

Shresth, S. (2009). *Sahibs and Shikar: Colonial Hunting and Wildlife in British India, 1800-1935.* Duke University.

Singh, H.S. (2000). Status of Indian Wild Ass (Equus hemionus khur) in the Little Rann of Kutch. *Zoos' Print Journal, 15*(5), 253-256.

_______, Patel, B.H., Pravez, R., Soni, V.C., Shah, N., Tatu, K., and Patel, D. (1999). *Ecological Study of the Wild Ass Sanctuary.* Gandhi Nagar: Gujarat Ecological Education and Research Foundation.

Singh, K.S. (1998). *People of India: India's Communities (H-M)* (Vol. V). Delhi: Oxford University Press.

Sobrevila, C. (2008). *The Role of Indigenous Peoples in Biodiversity Conservation: The Natural but often Forgotten Partners.* Washington DC: World Bank.

Srivastav, A., and Nigam, P. (2010). *National Studbook of Indian Wild Ass (Equus hemionus khur).* Dehradun and New Delhi: Wildlife Institute of India and Central Zoo Authority.

Yadava, Y.S., Mukherjee, R., and Munde, R. (2006). *Socio-Economic Status of Workers in the Salt Industry in India: A Report.* Chennai: Bay of Bengal Programme Inter-Governmental Organisation.

6

Post-Structural Possibilities in Green Social Work

A Brief Review of Literature

Varun Sharma and *Neera Agnimitra*

Considering Nature, Environment and Ecology

This is a review of literature and something more at the same time. Within the social work profession, environmental issues, ecological concerns, and the heedless exploitation of nature, is becoming an increasing concern. Lena Dominelli's (2012) recent contribution, *Green Social Work*, stands in simple testament to the same, where one may wonder what this profession, traditionally concerned with case and group work, has to do with green ideological positions. However, in India the effort to provide perspectives on varied forms of social activism that emerge out of environmental concerns predates Dominelli's own work. Andharia and Sengupta (1998) writing in the *Indian Journal of Social Work* (IJSW), have submitted eight categories under which social movements relating to the environment can be clubbed. In a discussion on the classification of ecological movements and protests, we can scarcely omit the efforts undertaken by Gadgil and Guha (1998). In their article, 'Towards a Perspective on Environmental Movements in India' they submit 'crusading Gandhians', 'ecological Marxists', 'appropriate technologists', 'scientific conservation' and 'wilderness enthusiasts' to be some of the chief categories of efforts underway to protect nature. In more recent times Rangarajan (2003) has argued that 'constructive work', 'urban intelligentsia' and 'rural activists' make for three categories which 'help to tease out the rich and complex processes at work' without necessarily being 'ideal types' of any kind.

Notwithstanding the validity of such categories, the concern of this paper may be a little more perverse. The three terms 'nature', 'environment' and 'ecology' find simultaneous application, through and through, to the near point of acting as synonyms without even being noticed (a thing that already stands demonstrated in the opening lines of this very introduction!). Thus, it could be said that a part of this paper's interest lies in the unique and special meanings that 'nature', 'environment' and 'ecology' invoke—not in laboratories, or as part of textbook learning—but in deliberations and debates of a social and political kind. Without trying to insist that nature, environment and ecology are watertight concepts, this paper further seeks to address a dire lack of perspective on such rudimentary terms from a post-structural perspective, particularly in our home context. It is this paper's enterprise to seek to build a discussion on how professional social work in India can benefit from post-structural perspectives on key terms, which are indispensible for articulating any green ideological position(s), leave alone categorising them.

Post-structuralism, on its part, has been described by Giddens (1987) in a rather formal manner as a 'peculiar concern with the nature of writing and therefore textual materials, and interest in the character of temporality as somehow constitutive with the nature of objects and events'. What we are concerned with over here, however, is post-structuralism of the order of Michel Foucault. It is indeed true that very little of Foucault's work was directly concerned with the environment, leave alone social work. He remains more famous for making that pith connection, by now so famous among social historians and political scientists, between knowledge and power: 'Power produces knowledge (and not simply by encouraging it, because it serves power, or applying it because it is useful); [but] power and knowledge directly imply one and another' (Foucault, 1977). Eric Darrier (1999) in *Discourses of the Environment* reminds us as to how Foucault was to once state that he had his 'back turned to it' (i.e. the environment), meaning he had little interest in deliberating upon the subject. But even though the environment (or ecology and nature, for that matter) do not constitute the philosopher's oeuvre, it has not stopped a number of thinkers and scholars concerned with the environmental problematique to use a barrage of Foucauldian concepts and ideas. Instead of presenting the philosopher's work separately, an effort has been made to weave key Foucauldian ideas into the main text of the paper, making it a part of the review itself.

It is important to state that the effort is not to partake in the rhetorics of 'nature', 'environment' and 'ecology', but problematize them using Foucault. It is hoped that such a venture would serve varied purposes. On the one hand it is bound to give green social workers a critical perspective as regards some foundational terms (nature, environment and ecology) around which we find some very complex discourses to be tightly wrapped. Such an initiative may also dissolve some of the romance involved with the invocation of such terms. On the other hand, this paper is equally liable to indicate and inform areas of further research that have remained hitherto unexplored. In addition, it is also bound to better verify into the manner in which thinkers and sociologists, in India in particular, have tried to categorize efforts underway to protect the 'nature', 'environment' and 'ecology', without addressing the messy tangle in which such terms present themselves prior to their invocation. It is imperative to state that this paper does not attempt to untie any knots; in fact this paper itself is encumbered with the tendency to use the three terms of our reckoning in a relational manner. With this caveat, it can be said that the prime intention of this paper, then, is to render visible that relatively inconspicuous morass, in which the terms of 'nature', 'environment' and 'ecology' are intertwined, and upon which classifications as submitted by Andharia (1998), Guha (1998) and Rangarajan (2003) are substantiated. We try to compass this task through three sections, namely, Ecology: the essence of science; Environment: the essence of government; and Nature: the essence of the timeless. In trying to canvas a vast area, this paper can be accused of some (sweeping) generalizations.

Ecology: The Essence of Science

As noted earlier, eminent scholars Gadgil and Guha (1998) have provided a lucid yet broad summary of efforts underway to address ecological and environmental issues in India. For them the 'ideological preferences of the various stands of the Indian environmental movement' comprises of 'crusading Gandhians', 'ecological Marxists', 'appropriate technologists', 'scientific conservation' and 'wilderness enthusiasts'. But from the categories presented, it is quite apparent that no hard and fast line is drawn in sand or stone between what constitutes and differentiates the environment from the ecology. This ambiguity is replete in more than one work by the scholars. It is equally interesting to note that a number of non-governmental agencies working in India, a host of which dot India's forested areas, explain and justify their efforts through an intermixture of both the terms. Though there is justifiably nothing inappropriate about it, it is important to recognize that scholars, researchers and thinkers elsewhere have indeed made efforts to distinguish the two terms of environment and ecology. Perhaps, a clarificatory note as regards the same could help steer the discussion in the direction of what is coming to be recognised as the arena of 'post-structural political ecology' (Peet and Watts, 1996), and in addition go to address the prevailing ambiguity as regards the way in which both the terms 'environment' and 'ecology' are employed synonymously.

A common view about the innate departures between the concept of environment and ecology are encapsulated, somewhat historically, by scholars such as Sterling (1991). Stephen Sterling offers a typical understanding of the evolution of ecological thought out of the limitations of 'environment', which is differentiated as an older concept. In his article 'Towards an Ecological Worldview', Sterling (1991) traces some of the dilemmas that environmental thought had encountered in days passed, and how these dilemmas forced us to seek recourse in what is recognised as ecology. Sterling shares that the mechanistic conception of environment is an 'offshoot of the western world view'. According to Sterling, 'the Western world view developed directly from the scientific revolution of the seventeenth and eighteenth centuries. The work of key figures such as Galileo, Bacon, Descartes, and Newton stimulated changes in thought on a scale that eventually eclipsed the earlier world view of medieval Christendom'. In congruence with Carolyn Merchant (1996), the author of *Ecology: Key Concepts in Critical Theory*, Sterling contends that the likes of Bacon advocated extending the dominion of man over the entire universe through an experimental science that sought to put nature on the rack. It is for these reasons that, there exists for Sterling (1991), 'a bias in favour of thought over feeling, reason over emotion, fact over value, intellect over intuition, analysis over synthesis, instrumental over intrinsic goals, and quantity over qualitative factors'.

Ostensibly, Murray Bookchin (1996) condemns the common practice of using the two terms interchangeably, and highlights a crucial point of difference in his article *The Concept of Socio-Ecology*. Bookchin (1996) states that:

> [...] the environment is a mechanistic, instrumental outlook that sees nature as a passive habitat composed of "objects" such as animals, plants, minerals, and the like, which must merely be rendered more serviceable for human use. Given my use of the term, "environmentalism" tends to reduce nature to a storage bin of "natural resources" or "raw materials" ... Environmentalism does not question the most basic premise of the present society, notably, that humanity must dominate nature; rather, it seeks to facilitate that notion by developing techniques for diminishing the hazards caused by the reckless despoliation of the environment. (Bookchin, 1996: 154-155)

On the other hand, for Bookchin, ecology is described as a science that deals with:

> [...] the dynamic balance of nature, with the interdependence of living and non living things. Since nature also includes human beings, the science must include humanity's role in the natural world—specifically the character, form and structure of humanity's relationship with other species and with the inorganic substrate of the biotic environment. (Bookchin, 1996: 155)[1]

Likewise, Dobson's (1990) *Green Political Thought* is an important reading if one wishes to comprehend the distinctions laid out by Bookchin in greater detail. Here Dobson distinguishes between 'environmentalism' and its corollary of 'ecologism'. Dobson's distinction between environmentalism and ecologism according to John Barry (1999), the author of *Rethinking Green Politics: Nature, Virtue and Progress* was largely motivated by a concern to explore the 'real' or 'true' green ideological position. Ecologism is deemed to be the true green political viewpoint, in compare to environmentalism. It is held to be superior on account of its marked radicalism, 'which is made up of, inter alia, an acceptance of the limit to growth hypothesis, an eco-anarchist critique of present political and economic arrangements, a particular vision of the future 'sustainable society', a moral critique of anthropocentricism and an endorsement of eco-centricism'. But from Barry's (1999) added statements, we can deduce that the terrain between ecology and environment, though distinguishable from a sociological point of view, is necessarily a contested one. Barry (1999) gives voice to a growing concern by arguing that 'true' and 'false' accounts provided by scholars such as Bookchin and Dobson proliferate 'binary ideological accounts' that are unnecessarily restrictive to the evolution of the subject. 'Ecological thought does not have a monopoly on defining the scope, principles or values of green politics' (*Ibid*).

Barry (1999) argues that, 'ecocentric demands are premised on an over hasty dismissal of anthropocentrism, which recedes recognition of the positive resources within anthropocentrism for developing an appropriate moral idiom to cover social-environmental interaction'—this is powerfully stated. Thus for the many ways in which the terms environment and ecology are bundled together, one finds it is available to various permutations and combinations—at one extreme, ecology tries to shirk aside environmental thought, on the other, it is compelled to admit that anthropocentricism (as innate to environmental thought) cannot be wished away. Interestingly, the oft-questioned divide between the concepts of environment and ecology is not an issue for (pure) science alone, but a concern that is complicated by the role of social and political thinking as well. Haila (1999), arching back to the early modern period, provides an added dimension in *Ecology, Domination, Solidarity* by positing that, 'the English 'natural rights' tradition and Rousseau's 'social contract' were attempts to define in a coherent way human culture and society as distinct from nature' (Haila, 1999).

It is in this very regard that Sachs (1992) provides a telling critique of ecology, which shows how in its grossest form, ecology becomes the very same thing as that which environmentalism tries to distinguish itself from. Sachs claims that ecology is a 'hybrid mix of computer modeling, political action and scientific discipline'. It is hybrid for the additional reason that it has been able to draw from 'the arts', 'organicism', 'the glory of nature', and a 'transcendental creed', just the same. The concept of ecology joins two different worlds for Sachs—protest movements across the globe that rely on the evidence allegedly offered by the scientific discipline, on the one hand, and the science itself which studies relationships between organisms and their environment, on the other. Clearly, Sachs' understanding resonates with certain post-structural ideas, which we undertake in greater detail in the later parts of this section. Engaging with

Sachs makes it possible for us to question the work of science, and the 'truth-making' it entails.

For Sachs, the early emphasis of ecology was on competitive/cooperative relations between organisms in a given environment (this was under the influence of Darwin) and their adaptive change through time (which Darwin called natural selection). But this anti-reductionist attitude was doomed after the Second World War when ecology became ripe for a restructuration along the lines of positivist methodology. 'The ensuing search for general laws implied concentration on a minimum of elements, which are common to the overwhelming variety of settings' (Ibid). The calorie thus became a cross-cutting unit of measurement for it permitted description of both organic and the inorganic worlds as two aspects of the same reality (Ibid). 'Biology', Sachs (1992) claims was 'reduced to energetic[s]', while rather contradictory ecology began to speak a language of holism.

Notwithstanding, it seems that these ruptures hidden in a past have acquired a different form now. Sachs (1992) shares as to how ecology has assumed the form of a discourse: an 'ecocratic discourse', which is as much about bureaucracy and technocracy as it is about ecology. Needless to state, it was Foucault (1976) who was early in stating that it is in discourse that 'power and knowledge' are joined. We are told that the ecocratic discourse since the 1990s forms the conceptual marriage of environment and development, and for this purpose it finds its cognitive base in ecosystems theory, and aims to attain new levels of administrative monitoring and control. This discourse, Sachs points out, is unwilling to reconsider the logic of competitive productivism, which is at the root of the planet's ecological plight. 'It reduces ecology to a set of managerial strategies aiming at resource efficiency and risk management'. With the rise of ecocracy, however, the fundamental debate that is needed on issues of public morality—like how society should live or how much and in what ways it should produce and consume—falls into oblivion. Instead western aspirations are implicitly taken for granted. With this we find that the votaries of ecology, seeking to distinguish themselves from the more traditional thematic of the environment, for necessity betray, bend and re-connect with the latter in a slightly circular way. One would, still, like to wish it is a spiral and not a circle.

However, socio-ecology and other interdisciplinary methods, as being championed by a number of NGOs representing ecological issues and interests, fail to discern how both the social and ecological sciences are already wedded in the murky bid to distinguish themselves from the purportedly earlier concept of the environment. In failing to discern this, they do something easier, and that is treat the terms synonymously. Both the terms, ecology and environment have been imported from the west by Indian scholars without much heed or concern for the dynamics they entail. The 'true green position', is perhaps, bound to remain helplessly trapped in such musings unless they are approached in a more fruitful way. This is where the expositions of Michel Foucault can be of relevance. If ecology is touted as a superior science it seems pointless to argue against it, but it is better to verify into its mechanics by tracking what Foucault had called the 'hazardous career of truth'. We could directly quote Foucault here as stating:

> Since Nietzsche this question of truth has been transformed. It is no longer, 'What is the surest path to Truth?', but what is the hazardous career Truth has followed?' That was Nietzsche's question, Husserl's as well, in *The Crisis of the European Sciences*. Science, the constraint to truth, the obligation of truth, and ritualised procedures for its production have traversed absolutely the whole of Western society for millennia and are now so universalised as to become the general law for all civilizations. What is the history of this 'will to truth'? What are its effects? How all this is interwoven with relations of power? (Foucault, 1980:66)

One can truly ask as to what purpose such a perspective can offer. But this can be explained through instances from our own context that raises serious doubts and questions for the work of science. For instance the typification of India's national animal, the tiger as an 'indicator species' of the health of an ecosystem is truly puzzling, since it was the work of science itself that previously categorised the same animal as a 'dangerous beast' that was meant to be exterminated in colonial India (Rangarajan, 1996). Does not this 'career of truth' merit a careful consideration on the part of green social workers who are unanimously engaged in the one pointed project of saving the species? Could not this project have something to do with relations of power, when seen historically?

The winding journey of truth can perhaps be discerned better, if we resort to Donna Haraway's suggestions on the matter. Post-structural in her bearings, Haraway (1989, 1992) engages with the profound transformations brought about by new computer technologies and biotechnology, which are advancing in the core countries of the capitalist system. Taking Simone de Beauvoir's declaration that 'one is not born a woman' into the post-modern domain of late twentieth century, Haraway (1992) argues that, 'If organisms are natural objects, it is crucial to remember that organisms are not born; *they are made* in world-changing technoscientific practices by particular collective actors in particular times and places' (emphasis added). To make things even more precise from her point of view, organisms make themselves and are also made by history. Nature's constructions are affected by history, economics, technology, science and myths of all kinds. The construction of the same biological species as a 'dangerous beast' and the 'endangered' can be better diagnosed from such a perspective. Such perspectives resonate clearly in the work and enterprise of Foucault (1976).

Foucault also makes a case in point by stating in his *Order of Discourse* that 'within its own limits, each discipline recognizes true and false propositions but it pushes back a whole teratology of knowledge beyond its margins'. Even this finds application in our home context, as a wide number of studies are explicitly reconsidering the *locus standi* of a number of scientific 'facts'. For example, Vasant Saberwal (1996) in his article 'Pastoral Politics: Gaddi Grazing, Degradation and Biodiversity Conservation in Himachal Pradesh', brings to light certain key assumptions that underlie conservation focus. It is on the basis of some such assumptions (scientific for most part) that the government has articulated its position as believing that *gaddi* grazing is responsible for the degradation of grazing lands. Saberwal's rigorous method and explorations on the other hand go to prove that, in fact, there is a lack of scientific evidence of this. The claims of the Forest Department are partial, and there has been no attempt to differentiate the erosion caused by natural processes from that resulting from human activities. Saberwal (1996) posits that all human resource use is not incompatible with the conservation of biological diversity, as the sciences are at times eager to contend.

Within the realm of climate change Matt Riddley (2010) in *The Rational Optimist: How Prosperity Evolves*, speaks of how climate change is an unnecessary pessimism of today. In speaking of the anomalies of science, Riddley reminds:

> In the mid 1970s it was briefly fashionable for journalists to write scare stories about the recent cooling of the globe, which was presented as undiluted bad news. Now it is fashionable for them to write scare stories about the recent warming of the globe, which is presented as undiluted bad news (Riddley, 2010: p. 328).

Riddley also questions as to why a host of details are concealed or underplayed as part of the global climate change debate such that: 'the increase in methane has been (erratically) decelerating in the last 20 years, that there were warmer periods in earth's history in medieval times and even 6,000 years ago and yet no accelerations or "tipping points" were reached'. David Demeritt (2001), on his part, in 'The Construction of Global Warming and the Politics of Science', raises a similar concern. Demeritt (2001) does not out rightly dismiss the global warming problem as prematurely as Riddley does, but brings to notice the typically top-down manner in which scientific facts about climate change are being formulated and dispensed. Even if global warming is not completely untrue, its articulation is partial, and the reductionist formulation of the problem, for Demeritt, serves a variety of political purposes. Furthermore, 'instrumental and interest-based critiques of the use of scientific knowledge tend to ignore the ways in which a politics gets built into science'. Not only is there a narrow scientific focus on Green House Gases (GHGs), and the exclusion of social relations producing them and giving them meaning, even the calculations are skewed, in Demeritt's assessment.

It is in the full face of such concerns that it becomes important for green social workers to not simply contend themselves with scientific truth-claims, but realize that a part of their work necessarily demands an engagement with 'knowledge-formations'—for to contemplate knowledge is to contemplate power, a thing we have learnt from Foucault. Post-structural political-ecology as explained by Peet and Watts (1996) is a welcome relief in this sense. As the celebrated authors of *Liberation Ecology*, Peet and Watts are found to be stating that:

> [...] new directions attempt to engage political ecology with certain ideas and concepts derived from post-structuralism and discourse theory. There is in other words an extraordinary vitality within the field, reflecting the engagements within, and between political economy,

> the power-knowledge field and critical approaches to science itself. As a short hand we refer to these confluences and engagements as "liberation ecology". (Peet and Watts, 1996: 16)

Needless to state, Peet and Watts make an attempt to explain how 'discourse' is an area of language use, expressing a particular standpoint and related to a certain set of institutions. Concerned with a limited range of objects, a discourse emphasizes some concepts at the expense of others. The illumination offered by post-structural thinking, in such ways we are told, provides for a broader canvas for the conception of forms of contention (from class struggle to social movements, to everyday resistance) and deeper conception of what is contended (from ownership of productive resources, to control over the human imagination). Peet and Watts eventually suggest, 'that the social imaginaries and discourses which environmental and other social movements contend do not arise on the head of a pin, or a de-natured ivory tower'. Rather, the environment in itself is an active constituent of imagination, and the discourses themselves assume regional forms, which are referred to by Peet and Watts (1996) as 'regional discursive formations'. The area-specific debates of development vs. nature, tiger vs. tribal, dams and displacement—issues in which social workers find themselves embroiled—are awaiting deeper inquiry at the hands of such a perspective, in which the role of science, of discourse, and of power remain to be understood more effectively.

Environment: The Essence of Government

Critical perspectives on the topic of environment, *paryavaran* as it is known, are most prone to a Marxian analysis. Where 'ecology' tends to bend towards scientificisms and 'nature' to spiritualist imaginations as we see in the following section, 'environment' is largely an administrative construct, a thing waiting to be managed. It is perhaps a thematic in which the government deems itself to have the most important role. Perhaps that is why we have repetitive references to the environment, and not ecology or nature, in the title and body of every other act or policy in India. Where the environment is concerned, there are a host of studies that ham-handedly try to fit everything that has happened in India, colonial and post-colonial, into a Marxian frame of analysis. Some of the more pertinent studies look at negotiations and discussions over the environment as a contestation between the developed and underdeveloped countries. The modern environmental discourse in India, according to historians such as Richard Grove (1993, 1996) has its foundations in British colonial India, and stands in contrast to the simultaneous exploitation of our natural resources by the imperial forces, the latter being elaborated by histories such as those provided by Guha (2000). From the point of view of green social work, Alain Lipietz (1995), a French green-economist provides a telling account about how contestations over the global commons (ocean, atmosphere, glaciers, etc.) can be compared with the enclosure movement of the fourteenth and sixteenth centuries. Drawing from a Marxist tradition, Lipietz observes that the global crises would entail some form of 'global enclosure as part of the solution'. This may, however, pave the way for proletarianization of the 'less efficient nations' or the southern countries (very much as Marx had predicted for the workers of the world, mobilised by capital's own forces under factory rooftops). For Lipietz this forms a crucial aspect of the 'North-South aspect of the political economy of global commons'.

In speaking of commons, Andharia and Sengupta (1998) in their 'The Environmental Movement: Global Issues and Indian Reality' provide eight categories of the environmental movement on the basis of issues and examples. These include issues and protests relating to, forest and land, marine resources, industrial pollution, development projects, wildlife parks, tourism, organic farming and related individual campaigns. On the other hand, Agarwal and Narain in their *Green Politics* (1999) discuss at length, the ongoing negotiations over the global environment in a North-South conflictual manner, while affording sufficient attention to the broader thematic of Sustainable Development. Needless to say Sustainable Development criss-crosses with efforts to salvage the environment, deriving much of its impetus and force from that value loaded statement ushered in by the Brundtland report (1984) which allegorically states that: Sustainable Development is 'development that meets the needs of the present generation without compromising the ability of future generations to meet their needs'. Sustainable Development ever since has become one of the most fancied enterprises of NGOs in India, garnering huge amounts of funding, both nationally and inter-nationally. But even where budding social workers remain absorbed in such efforts at the behest of their employer NGOs, the lack of perspective is apparent from the manner in which quite a few studies have tried to ascertain the role that NGOs are in themselves playing. One article titled 'Non-Governmental Organisations in Sustainable Development' (Agrawal, 2008) begins on the premise that NGOs 'are usually a small group of highly motivated, low paid, young persons'! The ambiguity in their operations can be ascertained through Sachs (1999), who pertinently remarks that with Sustainable Development everything goes. In characteristic style he states that, 'since 'development' is conceptually an empty shell which may cover anything from the rate of capital accumulation to the number of latrines, it becomes eternally unclear and contestable just what exactly should be kept sustainable'. Not unlike Sachs, Escobar (1996) treats Sustainable Development like a discourse in which two old enemies—economic growth and the preservation of the environment—are effectively reconciled. With this 'nature is reinvented as environment so that capital, not nature and culture may be sustained' (*Ibid*).[2]

However, we can approach the Foucauldian strands in such thinking in a slightly roundabout way. A Foucauldian perspective broadens our horizons and forces us to consider the work of several other institutions, from scientific laboratories to educational universities, in the shaping of the environmental problematique. The concept of governmentalities, as explained by Foucault (Burcehll, Gordon and Miller, 1991) helps one to examine what we may call in shorthand the "non-governmental versions of the environment", without necessarily thinking that such ideas or thematics are promulgated by what is referred to as NGOs in parlance. In trekking through the dominance of Marxian perspectives where research on the environment is concerned, one need not negate the significance of the same. Likewise, without purporting that the terrain between Marx and Foucault is contiguous in any which way, we find that scholars such as Escobar (1996) have made use of ideas across the board. For instance, the Marxist theory of crisis is based upon the contradiction between capitalist productive forces and production relations, but for Arturo Escobar there is a 'second contradiction of capitalism' that has become pressing with the aggravation of the ecological crisis and the social forms of protest this crisis generates. The 'second contradiction of capitalism' finds fuller expression in the work of James O'Connor (1989) with relation to the subject under review.

It is not overstretching the point, as classical Marxists might think, when Escobar (1997) and O'Connor (1989) both allege the role of scientific truth-making, and knowledge systems that work through a co-ordinated series of institutions. According to them labour is not just educated, as part of the reproduction of production conditions, but positively tamed and moulded through 'normalising' discourses. On the other hand, sciences such as urban planning and the environmental sciences accelerate the capitalisation of space. One finds that capitals' threatening of its own conditions of production, particularly nature, elicits manifold and contradictory attempts at restructuring those conditions in order to reduce costs or defend profits (Escobar 1996). This re-structuring is, needless to say, affected through a variety of discourses. Thus, for Escobar:

> The history of capital not only involves exploitation of production condition. It is also the history of the advance of the scientific discourses of modernity in areas such as health, planning families, education, economy and the like through what Habermas (1987) refers to as the colonisation of the lifeworld and Foucault as the advance of biopower. With this observation we wish to emphasise that the modern form of capital is inevitably mediated by the expert discourses of modernity. (Escobar, 1996, p. 47-48)

This verily demands a closer examination of Foucault's concept of bio-politics, within the realm of green social work. The concept finds detailed mention in the first volume of Foucault's *The History of Sexuality*, and then again in the posthumous publication *The Birth of Biopoltics* (2008). At the cost of some oversimplification, but for all purposes of brevity, bio-power is understood as the exercise of power from multiple points in the social fabric. Foucault (1976) had attempted to distinguish bio-power from the power exercised by monarchies, where the latter wielded absolutist force. In India, however, such expressions of monarchical power were complicated by the role of Brahminism. Notwithstanding, Drekmeier (1962) in his Weberian reading of historical events successfully establishes how Kingship in ancient India became increasingly invested in the person of the king in the centuries following the decline of Mauryan rule.[3] Against the backdrop of such conceptions of kingly power in native India, bio-power as explained by Foucault (1976) becomes a form of power that shapes, moulds, and conditions populations in certain prescribed ways, that they may be rendered both politically and economically useful. For Foucault, this is achieved through a disciplining of individual bodies (*anatomo-politics of the human body*) on the one hand, and regulatory controls extended over populations (*bio-politics of the population*) on the other. For social work researchers the question largely remains if the singling and disciplining of tribals by first tagging them as 'poachers', 'deviants', 'criminals', 'offenders' and the like, and the simultaneous aggregation and settlement of such communities at the behest of state-devised programmes such as the Forest Rights Act of 2005, is not a variant of what Foucault has asserted previously at the level of individuals and populations. Though the FRA is bound to being read in emancipationist terms, Foucault (1980) warns that power is not something that always says 'no', it can be positive and encouraging as well.

Foucault demonstrates that such discourses need not have their original point of reference in the state, but in a number of sub-state institutions (Rabinow and Rose, 2003). Discourses need not always have a unilinear trajectory, always being articulated by the bourgeoisie and imposed upon the proletariat in accordance with Marxian suppositions. For our purpose, Andrée (2002) is able to illustrate the relevance of such ideas of power with reference to the environment through his study on Genetically Modified Organisms. He presents the argument that Genetically Modified Organisms (GMOs) include questions that range from 'food and environmental safety, to moral concerns about playing God, to criticisms of the way in which genetic engineering, along with new interpretations of Intellectual Property Law reinforce the trend towards oligopolies in the global seed and agri-chemical industries'. Even where there is pressure from certain sections to opt for a 'labelling policy' so that consumers may be able to exercise their choice, several state governments are of the opinion that 'no scientifically justifiable reason prevails for singling out GMOs from their non-modified counterparts'. This being the case, Andrée (2002) is at odds to explain, that the debate is squarely placed 'between science and politics' and 'questions in the realm of policy are waiting to be settled by the truth'. But the interesting point for Andrée is that science, in the given instance, is not merely looking to attend to the concerns of the public; instead, it is producing a different kind of political struggle—a discursive struggle that fits within what Foucault calls bio-politics. Just as how Foucault (1977) has explained knowledge-power produces 'docile bodies', Andrée establishes how the genetic engineering research community creates 'a docile productive nature, and consumers as condoning subjects of GM food' (Andrée, 2002).

One fears that the discourse of GMOs in India, IPR in relation to local seeds, hybridisation of local cattle and livestock varieties have not alarmed social workers as much as made ready 'condoning subjects' out of them. Along with other discourses such as that of Sustainable Development, we might state at the cost of some repetition, that we could actively be partaking in the adversarial re-invention of nature as environment, 'so that capital not nature and culture may be sustained' (Escobar, 1996). M. O'Connor (1993) goes to the point of stating that the conquest of social life by expert discourses is being taken a step further, right into the 'heart of nature and life'. Social workers thus, among others, take for granted the normalisation already achieved by the modern discourses of science. Such discourses not only move into new territories, they also develop new modes of operation. This even relies on the semiotic conquest of local indigenous knowledge. In this regard M. O'Connor argues that traditional knowledge systems are seen as something existing in the minds of individual persons (such as shamans or elders) about external objects (such plants, trees, herbs), and the medicinal or economic 'utility' of which their bearers are supposed to transmit to the scientist. Local knowledge is seen not as a complex cultural construction but brought into the politics of modern science, which re-codifies them in utilitarian ways (M. O'Connor, 1993; Escobar, 1996). Going by this, the fears of some grass-root activists in India that 'biodiversity registers' are being maintained at the village level, not so much with the intention of conserving biodiversity but usurping local knowledge, ought to be treated seriously.

In recent times Arun Agrawal's (2005) *Environmentality: technologies of government and the making of subjects,* has emerged as one of the more emphatic readings of environmental issues, by using the Foucauldian concept of 'governmentality'. For Foucault, government becomes in the eighteenth century the designation of 'a field of intervention, through a series of complex processes' in which 'government is the right disposition of things' (Burcehll, Gordon and Miller, 1991; Luke, 1995). Governmentalities are thus not reducible to the state, though they may animate it, emerging from different quarters of the social body. One can verily enquire through this if NGOs intervening in the field of environment constitute such governmentalities, or 'environmentalities' as Agrawal would have it. However, it is important to note that

Timothy W. Luke's (1995) work on the concept of environmentalities precedes that of Agrawal's. Luke makes use of Foucauldian tenets such as governmentality and more, to threadbare the environmental problematique in a way that is significantly useful for the discipline of social work. Luke's sarcasm is intent, when he shares that many individuals who are bent on transforming the world into a better place, not unlike social workers, turn to the 'environment' in order to affect their improvements. Nevertheless, their struggles are often hobbled by a fundamental lack of clarity about what 'environment' actually is (leave alone environmental problems).

Despite the absence of clarity, Luke confirms that there is an ever-increasing reference to the term environment since the 1960s, to prove which he uses a list of expert discourses and newspaper indices. In Nebel's (1990) understanding the environment is 'the combination of all things and factors external to the individual or population of organisms in question', and for that matter Barry Commoner (1971) describes the environment as a 'house created on the earth by living things, for living things'. But such definitions are vague for Luke; Luke explains that environments under consideration are not studied directly, but in specificity to the 'objective relations' and effects they register upon the subjects of study they surround. This is partly on account of the fact that the environment is customarily understood as surroundings. These 'objective relations', Luke argues, are looked at and weighed only to the extent that available measurements make it possible (such as temperature levels, gas concentrations, molecular dispersions, resource variations, or growth rates). What can be measured *is* what can be said of the environment. Luke questions 'whether this vision of 'environment' really captures the actual quality or true quantity of all human beings' interrelations with all of the terrains, waters, climates, soils, architectures, technologies, societies, economies, cultures, or states surrounding them?' For instance it is quite possible that wildlife conservators in India set priorities in a highly complex natural environment comprising a zillion variables on the basis of figures of trafficking and poaching, as this can be measured, assessed, presented and circulated with relative ease and confidence. In addition, such figures also serve a disciplinary function in our society, if we closely follow Foucault on the matter.

One's suspicions are not allayed, when Luke attempts to trace the origins of the word 'environment' and shares that it was borrowed by English from Old French, where 'an environment is an action resulting from, or the state of being produced by a verb: to environ'. We are made to learn that 'To environ is to encircle, encompass, envelop, or enclose. It is the physical activity of surrounding, circumscribing, or ringing around something' (Ibid). Some of the uses of the word even suggest 'stationing guards around, thronging with hostile intent, or standing watch over some person or place' (Ibid). To environ a site or a subject is, therefore, to beset, beleaguer, or besiege that place or person. 'Environment', as either the means of such activity or the product of these actions, can now be read in a more suggestive manner: 'It is the encirclement, circumscription, or beleaguerment of places and persons in a strategic disciplinary policing of space' (Ibid). Environmentalities thus can produce spaces and sites of supervision, where environmentalists can be horrifically directed to fulfill the ends of other economic scripts, managerial directives, and administrative writs (Ibid). The manner in which social work/ workers could be cultured in such environmentalities demands attention. This is bound to take our focus right to the 'grass roots' (that much favoured word amongst social workers) with the added potentiality of revealing what Foucault (1977) calls the 'micro-physics' of power[4] alongside the existing Marxian dialogues that provide a meta-narrative. A focus on environmentalities makes a critical revisioning of the state's role possible than simply believing that the government is the custodian of the environment, as often projected in India; and such reasoning being based on the concept of governmentalities, opens the entire arena of negotiations between the government and the non-government for greater scrutiny on the part of green social workers.

Nature: The Essence of the Timeless

The Philosophy of nature unravels as a concept that derives, in part, from (a) the philosophy of physics (where laws of energy and motion are deemed as laws of nature), and more so (b) from the philosophy of biology (wherein the evolution of life from small systems and hierarchical arrangements are deemed descriptive of nature) (Encyclopaedia Britannica, 2007). In his theory of natural selection, Darwin suggested that 'survival of the fittest' was the basis for organic evolution, namely the modification of living things with time. However, in the Indian context the term 'nature' connotes a socio-cultural construct, and at times a preoccupation with the 'original state of things'. An instance of this can be found in the work of O.P. Dwivedi (2000), who manages an eloquent wedding of 'nature' and 'ecology'. He stresses on the possibilities of resolving the ecological crisis, by reverting to the religious scriptures of the Hindus. The immemorial and timeless scriptures, of course, use 'nature' for purposes of signification (and not ecology or environment, a thing we contemplate in ending). Even in the critical perspectives we have canvassed so far in this review on the thematics of 'ecology' and 'environment', we find that scholars refer to the 'nature as an un-manipulated essence, an innocent entity subject to several types of schemings. A similar reference to 'mother nature' remains to be found among the *vana devtas* that Vandana Shiva (1989) talks about in her celebrated work *Staying Alive*. A quote that Vandana Shiva (1989) verdantly invokes, manages to convey the manner in which the concept of 'nature' is bequeathed into our contemporary context:

> O ye gods, I shall support (i.e. nourish) the whole world with life-sustaining vegetables which shall grow out of my body, during a period of heavy rain. I shall gain fame on earth then as *Shaakambhari* (goddess who feeds the herbs), and in that very period, I shall slay the great *asura* named *Durgama* (a personification of drought). (Devimahatmya, 90:43-44)

Such understandings are reasonably structuralist if we look at them closely. In his celebrated work *Structural Anthropology*, Lévi-Strauss (1963) explains that a myth is a part of speech, for it has to be told. 'But in order to preserve its specificity, we are required to show that it is the same thing as language, and also something different from it' (*Ibid*). What makes a myth different from language is that it is held to be timeless.[5] Interestingly, for Lévi-Strauss, the different ways in which language imagines the world has an impact on nature; and with the power of myths it is only expected that it acquires a quintessential timelessness. It is perhaps in this connection that in any study of nature along Straussian lines, the effort is *not* to explain how men think in myths, but how myths operate in the minds of men without them even being aware of them. 'Myths signify the mind, which evolves them by making use of the world of which it itself is a part' (Ibid). There is no 'I think' in this characterization of the human mind where nature and myths are concerned, yet we find that such a release from Cartesian recidivism should not become a matter of comfort or solace for us.

It is on this cautionary note that the expositions of Michel Foucault become important for us. When we think of the activities of budding naturalists in British India—cemented in journals of yesterday such as the *Indian Forester, The Asiatic Society of Bengal* and most importantly the century-old *Journal of the Bombay Natural History Society*—we can be assured that some of our efforts at protecting nature is a colonial legacy that we have inherited. Could ideas of a timeless nature be retrieved from an ancient past, as Shiva and several others aspire to, without it being tarnished by the colonial impasse? Foucault's reading of the evolving discipline of Natural History, albeit Eurocentric, offers rich perspective, for practitioners and green social workers back in India. From him the possibility arises that the timelessness of myths about nature are perhaps a product, an implantation of colonial discourses. Foucault at the very start of his celebrated work *The Order of Things* (1970) mentions the impossibility of reinstating an idea of nature (which the present day global discourse is trying to achieve through a great many ways). Nature for Foucault has been, 'distorted and masqueraded by the use of categories and patterns that are our own' (Foucault, 1970). He dispels the popular impression that Natural History might have emerged as a response to the limitation of Cartesian mechanisms. For Foucault, it was not simply that the 'laws of rectilinear movement' which failed to contain the entire world, and the complexity of the plant and animal kingdom, that Natural History was born. In radical difference to such notions, Foucault states that for Natural History to be born, 'History had to become Natural':

> For Natural History to appear, it was not necessary for nature to become denser or more obscure, to multiply its mechanisms to the point of acquiring the opaque weight of a history that can only be retraced and described, without any possibility of measuring it, calculating it, explaining it; it was necessary – and this is entirely the opposite – for History to become Natural. (Foucault, 1970, p. 128)

It is from such cautionary notes alone that practitioners in the field can apprehend the surreptitious manner in which our own history is possibly being 'greened'. Such strands are apparent in Shiva (1963) as well, whom subaltern historians have accused of being 'ecologically functional' in her romanticized representation of a past (Hardiman, 1994). As another example we also find that the very same Mughal emperors who were once praised by the Governor of Bombay, Mountstuart Elphinstone (1843), for their 'exuberant courage' in hunting wild animals are re-characterized by the late 1920s as 'lovers of nature' by Salim Ali (1927). The myriad possible ways in which select individuals such as Jim Corbett, apart from the sovereign rulers of a past, are typified as equivocal lovers and protectors of nature nowadays, when they were colonial-subjects equally crazed about sport-hunting, makes for another instance. Foucault makes a green social worker's engagement with Nature profoundly Historical in such ways—and should we think that the contemplation of history is necessarily a contemplation on power in following Guy Debord (1967), then this is an eminent way of rendering green social work more politically sound.

Foucault on his part is relentless. He proceeds to elaborate as to how the manner of recording the history of plants in the seventeenth century necessitated looking at a great many details, including its heraldry, legends associated with it, earlier records and versions of travellers. Thus history, in itself, began to acquire a 'natural' character. More interestingly, the naturalizing of history and the consequent emergence of Natural History necessitated a grid of denominations, a strategic use of language, within which observations could be captured. Only in this way could the project of Natural History be taken any further. The effort was to bridge the so far 'silent gap' between things and words. Natural History soon had to 'bring language as close as possible to the observing gaze, and the things observed as close as possible to words' (Foucault, 1970).

In the contemporary environmental discourse, thinkers and theorists in India have tried to submit their own categories, of not so much nature, but the varied efforts underway to protect it. Almost as though at the auspices of Natural History such classifications may have become the very means of perceiving 'nature', without problematizing it. The possible hazards of proceeding in such fashion can be entertained by looking a little more carefully at how Foucault dashes Darwin's thesis. We are given to understand, through Foucault, that individual species were clubbed (characterized) according to certain structures—size, magnitude, shape, etc. But then the fact that structures are liable to change, or have been undergoing changes in the past, brought several naturalists of the seventeenth century to wonder if the fixed ordering of species was relevant in the first place. Foucault refers to this permanent tabulation of species (i.e. taxonomy) as 'fixism'. Foucault explains that it was this very dilemma that forced naturalists, much before Darwin, to insert the concept of 'continuity' into the pre-existing ordering, thus, hinting that nature has had an immemorial history. This insertion of continuity may well have been heralded as the birth of 'evolutionism', but for Foucault it is only superficial, since it is articulated within a taxonomy that was fixed in its inception. Alas, Darwin's thesis on 'evolution' may never be too far from the current day spiritualist imagination of nature as a timeless and unchanging element in India.

Foucault presents the thesis that 'There is not and cannot be an evolutionism or a transformism in classical thought'. The reason being that for evolutionary thought, time played a crucial role. While in the earlier ordering of nature as propounded by early-day naturalists like Linnaeus, time was extrinsic to the essential reality of things, and in the tables they had generated to classify nature. But this is obviously a performationist view (meaning that everything is set in the seed or sperm) that in no way regards species as emerging from one another in time (Gutting, 1989). For Foucault this is not 'evolutionism' that is beginning to overthrow the old dogma of 'fixism', rather it is a pre-existing system that perforce includes time like an appendage. We investigate a little later as to how this timelessness of nature serves the articulation of what Foucault calls knowledge-power in the context of India, but not before examining Foucault's treatment of another seventeenth century naturalist, Maupertuis.

Maupertuis had asserted that there were two aspects of nature: 'activity' and 'memory'. It was Maupertuis' claim that that 'nature's forms' are a result of attraction and chance between particles, and they disappear if they are unable to survive. Those that do remain in existence give rise to new individuals in which the characters of the parent couple are preserved by memory. Thus, the thought that the living beings that are available for our analysis, contain *all* the characters of their past (thanks to the dint of memory) became the cornerstone for natural history. But then the question arises about the beings that did not survive. Foucault says this was the fundamental assumption: 'Nature has a history only so far as it is susceptible of continuity' (p. 154). The chain of succession, from one character to another, is only traceable through living objects that have been recorded (by some fortune). Perhaps, fossils provide clues about that which did not survive; but even a fossil remains to be understood by looking backwards through the available *taxinomia*, which alone may give it its identity through the grids and categories already created. This is not so remote in its implications as the bid to classify varied social movements, which have perhaps begun to conduce ways of imagining what 'nature' might once have been. For instance Rangarajan (2003) provides three classifications, 'constructive work', 'urban intelligentsia' and 'rural activists', on the basis of which he arguably retrieves select incidents from the past to reconstruct an idea of nature. To paraphrase Foucault (2003) such a Nature has a history that is susceptible to the continuity of social movements into the present.

One may justifiably ask as to how such concerns could be of any relevance to social workers. In India, social workers are often a vexed lot, accused of upholding that stereotype of the tribal as an 'unchanging nature's man'—a thing that has merited criticism at the hands of scholars across the board. But the full face of a paradox, and the resultant vexation, is only revealed when we recognize that a vast segment of social workers are also engaged in rehabilitating and relocating tribes from forested areas on the presumption that this would help return things to their 'original' state, their primordial 'natural-ness' as it was before the arrival of the primitive man. Both competing ideas are negotiated by an idea of nature as being timeless. And it can be justifiably asked if the categorizing undertaken by Indian environmental thinkers, of the varied bids to protect nature do not harbor in themselves an idea of nature that is unchanging and timeless. Referring to Keulartz (1999) at this stage may entail a premature leap from the classical era Foucault is dissecting to a more contemporary day and age. But this does not necessarily entail a loss of relevance to the developments in our home context.

Keulartz (1999), not unaware of Foucauldian ideas, speaks of a project of 'Nature Development' being furthered in the Netherlands. The project embodies most of the dilemmas discussed in so far. Keulartz elaborates as to how the Dutch government is busy with developing nature, more specifically taking nature back to its 'original state', as far back as the 'interglacial period, because from a climatological point of view this era is closest to our own times'. Reconstruction of this 'primeval' nature relies on geological, physical–geographical, and biological-archaeological research, and the emerging plans, Keulartz shares have gone to the extent of deploying bulldozers to make twists and bends in streams and rivers that were once canalized. Very clearly, for Keulartz, the 'nature developers' exclude other interested parties from nature policy-making, owing to which some stakeholders are left to fear that all such plans would cause the old polders to flood, and spell doom for the river landscape as a cultural historical monument. This 'technical reproducibility' of 'new nature', seems as ironic as the anomalies of Natural History laid bare by Foucault, and does not take account of the fact that nature changes. 'Naturalness' is a constant process of transformation rather than control and stability (Keulratz, 1999). Keulartz summarises this in a way that enjoins popular notions of nature in India on the one hand, and the possibilities that Foucault presents in understanding the politics of nature for social workers on the other:

> On the one hand, the phrase (nature development) can refer both to a supreme, quasi-sacred subject—primeval nature—and to a profoundly manipulable object. On the other, it is precisely this ambivalence that gives nature development its strength and has allowed it to become the *cause célèbre* of a wide variety of social groups with diverging and often conflicting interests. (Keulartz, 1999: 84)

In the light of Keulartz's finding, one is forced to reconsider Foucault's earlier thesis. Nature may have occupied a central place in the ongoing global discourse, everyone wants to be on its side; but nature is limited to seeing only that which can be said within a grid of denominations, and even today it is vulnerable before the scientific or theoretical discourse that interprets it. This dependence of the 'original' nature on the discourse that 'successfully' interprets it, as Foucault has elaborated, is what renders it a 'manipulable object' just as Keulartz (1999) establishes in his 'Politics of Nature Development'. Innovative ways of dealing with such issues could emerge by apprehending the discourses of nature, the manner in which they construct ideas of nature, and enlist agencies and organizations across the board in its service. A more nuanced manner of categorizing efforts at protecting nature might emerge out of such an understanding, than what is available to us. The availability of the timelessness of nature as a specific tactic of power and knowledge, the imagination of a pristine nature in time so passed through present politics, and the surreptitious greening of history—all three aspects that we have raised with reference to examples in India—emerge as three concerns for any valid and informed practice of green social work. In the mean time, in India the project of creating national parks as wilderness spaces, cleansed of any living human presence (except perhaps that of the tourist!) continues unabated. The possibility that this has acquired discursive proportions is captured in the proclamation of some authorities on the subject that 'conservation *without* parks is unthinkable' (Shahabuddin and Rangarajan, 2007). Once again there is no 'I think' in such a characterization of the human mind, but as opposed marking a release from Cartesian recidivism as the structuralists might have wished to celebrate, this implies a more severe ensnarement of the human condition.

Conclusion: Nature, Environment and Ecology Reconsidered

In following Foucault we find that the social body opens up as a regime of tactics, technologies of knowledge and power, infinitesimal ways of brining individuals and populations under surveillance, and subjecting human and non-human bodies to disciplining power. To perceive or admit, even if a little presumptuously, that NGOs, green social workers, and several other social-actors function in such an atmosphere, opens up the possibility of engaging, analyzing, interpreting and synthesising their objectives, efforts and achievements along post-structural lines. If 'nature', 'environment' and 'ecology', be treated as tactics of knowledge and power, then green social work in India would stand better deciphered in light of what Foucault has described to be a discourse: 'Indeed it is in discourse that power and knowledge are joined together. And for this very reason we must conceive discourse as a series of discontinuous segments whose tactical function is neither uniform or stable' (Foucault, 1976). In the light of which, it serves to re-present some of the core concerns or emerging issues of this paper.

An early discussion on the thematic of 'ecology' reveals that there was an initial and desperate bid in the West to distinguish ecology from the environment. Within such sites of discussion the environment is described in adverse terms, while ecologism was presented as the true ideological position. Ever since the terrain between environment and ecology as core concepts has been a troubled and contested one, while thinkers and scholars from our home context have turned a blind eye to it in employing such terms in describing events in India. While the social sciences have their own role to play in the murky relations between 'environment' and 'ecology', Foucault helps us to steer away from the theoretical contestations/collaborations, and apprehend the project of ecologists by directly questioning the manner in which ecology as a 'science' submits its 'truths'. Green social work in India has in so far treated 'scientific output' as an objective truth, an indisputable fact, or a given. Events and literature captured in this review shows this is not always true, and any green ideological position as adopted by social work is going to be partial if it is not alert and aware to the processes by which truth is produced.[6]

Likewise, a discussion on the thematic of the 'environment' reveals a preponderance of Marxian perspectives. And even though a number of scholars in India are circumspect in treating Marx and Foucault at par, scholars in the West are not averse to drawing ideas across the board in deepening their understandings. This is not to say that Marx and Foucault make for a contiguous terrain in any which way. However, we get to see that green social work in India can greatly benefit from the expositions of Foucault. A few scholarly works related to the environment, though remote from the field of social work, demonstrate this to be true. A focus on 'environmentalities' makes a critical revisioning of the state's role possible than simply believing that the government is the custodian of the environment, as often projected in India; for such reasoning being based on the Foucauladian concept of governmentalities, stretches open the entire arena of negotiations between the government and the non-government for greater scrutiny on the part of green social workers. Failing which social workers are only bound to become condoning subjects in normalizing discourses that traverse the space between the government, and the non-government. A focus on environmentalities counterbalances some of the meta-narratives written with a Marxian perspective by bringing the 'micro-physics' of power to the fore (Foucault, 1977)

And lastly, with 'nature' we find in reference to the earlier two sections on the environment and ecology, that it thrives as an idea of timeless purity. A critique of the environment as a concept, or even ecology for that matter, becomes possible only by treating 'nature' as a timeless essence, an uncorrupted a-priori. In India prevailing understandings are reasonably Straussian, we find. The present review of literature reveals as to how the concept of a timeless and pure 'nature' can become available for the projects of power. It is equally apparent that in India the timelessness of nature (which assumes the form of a radical critique of evolutionism in Foucault (1970)) is at the root of a number of debates. For instance the depiction and refutation of the tribal as a true and 'unchanging nature's man'; or on the other hand the equally popular bid to remove indigenous populations from select spaces, with the hope that this would return things to their 'original' or natural state, a state of things before the changes began. Both competing ideas, we have argued, are negotiated by an idea of nature as being approached as timeless and "out there". And it can be justifiably asked if the categorizing undertaken by Indian environmental thinkers of the varied bids to protect nature do not harbour in themselves an idea of nature that is unchanging and timeless (and thus the seed of varied debates). This perhaps goes to point to the insufficiency of the existing level of theorizing. It is hoped that such concerns, critical perspectives on the foundational terms of 'nature', 'environment' and 'ecology', will perhaps better inform and direct green social work in India.

Notes

1. Though Bookchin (1996) provides a viewpoint of ecology that invokes popular concepts such as the 'balance of nature', Sachs (1992) provides an interesting contra point in the *Development Reader*. Sachs (1992) claims that a part of the ambivalence surrounding ecology rests on the fact that activists have, rather ironically, adopted theorems like 'the balance of nature' at a moment when they have already been abandoned by the discipline (p. 41).
2. It seems almost inescapable that in critically analyzing the concept of environment, theorists must also reinvent nature as something that is original and innocent. We analyze such aspects and more in the following section.
3. Drekmeier (1962) in his *Kingship and Community in Early India*, establishes that in 'the time of barbarian encounter and religious competition that followed Mauryan rule, the institution of kingship was strengthened. If the invaders were to be repulsed, the king must have full responsibility and the state must be organized to take maximum advantage of its resources'. Drekmeier adds that 'In the acute religious conflict that followed the break-up of the Ashokan empire, the states usually took a strong partisan position (most of them disposed to renascent Brahminism) and the king was rewarded

with a sanctification that had never been equalled earlier in Indian history' (pp. 180-1).

4. Micro-physics of power in this context can be understood as the operation of a power that is strategic, tactical, and heterogeneous and dispersed in select geographies.
5. Levi-Strauss provides an example here of the French revolution. When referred to as an element of the past, by a historian, it does not constitute a myth. But when a politician refers to it as an aspect of the past, as much as an event that has consequences for the future, at once historical and a-historical the revolution acquires the proportions of a myth. Another distinguishing feature of myths is that unlike poetry it can survive even the worst translations without losing much of its intended meaning. (Levi-Strauss, 1963, pp. 205-206).
6. This is not without considering how Foucault (1980) would himself state that ideology itself 'is a notion that cannot be used without circumspection'.

References

Agarwal, A., Narain, S., and Sharma, A. (eds.) (1999). *Green Politics*. New Delhi: Centre for Science and Environment.

Agrawal, S. (2008). Non-Governmental Organisations in Sustainable Development: Theory and Practice, In Bava, N. (eds.) *Non-Governmental Organisations in Development*. Kanishka: Delhi

Andrée, P. (2002). The bio-politics of genetically modified organisms in Cananda. *Journal of Canadian Studies*. Vol. 37, No. 3.

Andharia, J. and Sengupta, C. (1998). The Environmental Movement: Global Issues and the Indian Reality, *Indian Journal of Social Work*, Vol. 59, 422-49.

Barry, J. (1999). *Rethinking Green Politics: Nature, Virtue and Progress*. New Delhi: Sage

Bauer, J. (2011). Review of Arun Agrawal's, Environmentality: Technologis of government and the making of subjects (2005). *Carnegie Council, Voice for ethics in international affairs*. Retrieved on 6 March, 2011, from, http://www.carnegiecouncil.org/resources/journal/19_3/book_reviews/5272.html/:pf_printable

Bookchin, M. (1996). The concept of social ecology. In Merchant, C. (ed.), *Ecology: Key concepts in critical thought*. New Delhi: Rawat Publications.

Burchell, G., Gordon, C. and Miller, P. (eds.) (1991). *The Foucault Effect: Studies in Governmentality*, Hemel Hempstead: Harvester Wheatsheaf.

Commoner, B. (1971). *The Closing Circle: Nature, Man and Technology*. New York: Knopf.

Darrier, E. (ed.). (1999). *Discourses of the Environment*. London: Blackwell.

Debord, G. (1994). *The Society of the Spectacle*. New York: Zone Books.

Drekmeier, C. (1962). *Kingship and Community in Early India*. Stanford University Press.

Demeritt, D. (2001). The construction of global warming and the politics of science. *Annals of the Association of American Geographers*, Vol. 91, No. 2, p. 307-337. Taylor and Francis.

Dobson, A. (1990). *Green Political Thought*. London and New York: Routledge

Dominelli, L. (2012). *Green Social Work: From Environmental Crisis to Environmental Justice*. Polity Press.

Dwivedi, O.P. (2000). Dharmic ecology. In Chapple and Tucker (eds.), *Hinduism and ecology: The intersection of earth, sky and water*. Harvard, Mass: Harvard University Press

Escobar, A. (1996). Constructing nature: Elements for post-structural political ecology. In Peet, R., and Watts, M. (eds.), *Liberation ecologies: Environment, development and social movements*. Routledge: New York.

Foucault, M. (1970). *The order of things: Archaeology of the human sciences*. New York: Vintage Books.

_______, (1976). *The history of sexuality I*. Australia: Penguin.

_______, (1977). *Discpline and Punish*. Harmondsworth: Penguin.

Gadgil, M. and Guha, R. (1998). Towards a Perspective on Environmental Movements in India. *Indian Journal of Social Work*, Vol. 59, p. 450-472.

Giddens, A. (1987). Structuralism, post-structuralism and the production of culture. In A. Giddens, and J. Turner (eds.), *Social Theory Today*, pp. 195-223. California: Stanford University Press.

Grove, R. (1993). Conserving Eden: The (European) East India Companies and Their Environmental Policies on St. Helena, Mauritius and in Western India, 1660 to 1854. *Comparative Studies in Society and History, 35*(2), pp. 318-351

Grove, R. (1996). Indigenous Knowledge and the Significance of South-West India for Portuguese and Dutch Constructions of Tropical Nature. *Modern Asian Studies, 30*(1), pp. 121-143.

Guha, R. (2000): *The Unquiet Wood: Ecological Change and Peasant Resistance in the Himalaya*. Berkeley: University of California Press.

Haraway, D. (1989). *Primate visions*. New York: Routledge.

_______, (1992). The Promises of Monsters: A Regenerative Politics for Inappropriated Others. In Grossberg, L., Nelson, C., and Treichler, P.A. (eds.), *Cultural Studies*, pp. 295-337. New York: Routledge.

Haila, Y. (1999). The north as/and the other: Ecology, domination, solidarity. In Fischer, F., and Hajer, M. (eds.), *Living with Nature. Environmental Politics as Cultural Discourse*. Oxford: Oxford University Press.

Keulartz, J. (1999). Engineering the environment: The politics of nature development. In Fischer, F., and Hajer, M. (eds.), *Living with Nature.*

Environmental Politics as Cultural Discourse. Oxford: Oxford University Press.

Lipietz, A. (1995). Enclosing the global commons: Global environmental negotiations in a north-south conflictual approach. In Bhaskar and Glynn (eds.), *The north, the south and the environment*. London: Earthscan.

Luke, T.W. (1999). Eco-managerialism: Environmental studies as a power/knowledge formation. In Fischer, F., and Hajer, M. (eds.), *Living with Nature. Environmental Politics as Cultural Discourse*. Oxford: Oxford University Press.

Levi-Struss, Claude. (1963). *Strucutral anthropology*. USA: Basic Books.

Lévi-Strauss, C. (1978). Structuralism and ecology. *Graduate Faculty Philosophy Journal*, 7 (2), pp. 153-178.

Luke, T.W. (1995). On environmentality: Geo-power and eco-knowledge in the discourses of contemporary environmentalism. *Cultural Critique*, No. 31, The Politics of Systems and Environments, Part II (Autumn, 1995), pp. 57-81. University of Minnesota Press.

Merchant, C. (1996). Editors Introduction. In Merchant, C. (ed.), *Ecology: Key concepts in critical thought*. New Delhi: Rawat Publications.

Nature, Philosophy of. (2011). Encyclopædia Britannica. *Encyclopaedia Britannica 2007 Ultimate Reference Suite*. Chicago: Encyclopaedia Britannica.

Nebel, B.J. (1990). *Environmental Science: The Way the World Works*. Englewood Cliffs: New Jersey.

O'Connor, M. (ed.). (1993). *Is capitalism sustainable*. Guilford Press: New York.

O'Connor, J. (1989). Political economy of ecology of socialism and capitalism. *Capitalism Nature Socialism* 1, 1, pp. 11-38.

Peet, R., and Watts, M. (1996). Editor's introduction: Liberation ecology: Development, sustainability and environment in an age of market triumphalism. In Peet, R., and Watts, M. (eds.), *Liberation ecologies: Environment, development and social movements*. Routledge: New York.

Rabinow, N., and Rose, P. (2003). *Thoughts on the concept of biopower today*. Publisher unavailable.

Rangarajan, M. (1996). *Fencing the Forest: Conservation and Ecological Change in India's Central Provinces 1860-1914*. New Delhi: OUP.

_______, (1996). The Politics of Ecology: The Debate on Wildlife and People in India, 1970-95. *Economic and Political Weekly*, Vol. 31, pp. 2391-409.

Riddley, M. (2010). *Rational optimist: How prosperity evolves*. London: Fourth Estate.

Saberwal, V. (1996). Pastoral politics: Gaddi grazing, degradation, and biodiversity conservation in Himachal Pradesh. *Conservation Biology*, Vol. 10, No. 3, pp. 741-749.

Sachs, W. (1992). Environment. In Sachs, W. (ed.), *Development Reader: A Guide to knowledge as Power*. London: Zed Books.

Sachs, W. (1999). Sustainable development and the crisis of nature: On the political anatomy of an oxymoron. In Fischer, F., and Hajer, M.

(eds.), *Living with Nature. Environmental Politics as Cultural Discourse*. Oxford: Oxford University Press.

Shahabuddin. G., and Rangarajan, M. (2007). *Making Conservation Work*. Ranikhet: Permanent Black.

Shiva, V. (1989). *Staying Alive: Women, Ecology, and Development*. USA: Zed Books.

Smart, B. (1985). Michel Foucault. In Hamilton, P. (Series Ed.) *Key Sociologists*. London and New York: Routledge.

Sterling, S. (1991). Towards an Ecological Worldview, Sterling (1991). In Engel, J.R., and Engel, J.B. (eds.), *Ethics of environment and development*. USA: University of Arizona Press.

7

Community as the Key for Disaster Recovery

A Case of Long Term Intervention in Kanyakumari District

Subhasis Bhadra

Social work as a profession has made considerable contributions in the field of disaster management and also contributed to a large extent in developing the models of disaster interventions through different phases of disasters by using the basic methods of social work practice. All the three primary methods of social work i.e. case work, group work and community organisation are used simultaneously in various interventions in disaster. Psychological First Aid (PFA) and single session therapy in emergency have been routed through case work theories, while group and community organisation are most common to facilitate recovery as well as to build preparedness among community people. Disaster management is understood through the cycle of disaster, that segregates and conceptualises different phases with the required response strategies of different stakeholders in this process. The stakeholders are multiple, as per the situation, complexity, cause and nature of disasters. For social work practice, disaster is understood by its diversity, intensity, and complexity of impact on the human beings immediately after the event and in the long-term. Disaster can be broadly divided into natural disasters that are due to natural forces and human made disasters that are due to human elements. Though, it is theoretically established that there is no disaster without human hands (Steinberg, 2000) still, disasters are broadly divided as natural and human made disasters. The impact on human beings, living creatures, and environment are the focus of disaster management (GOI-UNDP,

2012). In the phases of disaster intervention, i.e. rescue, relief, rehabilitation and long term recovery, the survivor community becomes the largest stakeholders in the process with other agencies, institutions and government located at different levels. It is the community which has the key role to play in the disaster response programme through the participatory model of disaster management (Bhadra, 2013).

Considering the sociological and anthropological definitions, community is understood as a most close, cohesive unit of human beings with 'we' feelings, close systems and integrated culture (Gisbert, 2006, pp. 38-39). Though the features of community vary and differ, the community becomes the primary strength of living and survival after any disaster. Therefore, for disaster intervention workers or social workers, analysing the features of community based on its history, cultural traits, strength, weakness, vulnerabilities, location, gender role, legal, social, economic, health, institutional, and organisational structure become crucial for intervention and ensuring benefits. When a disaster or emergency strikes the community, it faces multiple impacts and the changes persist for a long time. Every change that takes place in the community is part of a continuum that influences the life of the individuals, family and groups. The changes may be positive or negative in the long term, as it is often debated in academic literature that disasters brings development. However, the caution is that the well planned, participatory disaster intervention and management are the crucial linkage.

The present article is based on a long-term intervention project in the post-Tsunami period with the survivors of the coastal villages for community recovery (IFRC, 2009; IFRC, 2008). The author was involved in the entire duration of the project. He was also involved with the target communities from the time of Tsunami, while working with the CARE India project for Tsunami recovery (Sekar, Biswas, Bhadra, Jayakumar, and Kumar, 2005). In the projects, the role of the author was to design, implement, monitor and document the psycho-social support programme for the survivors of Tsunami. The chapter makes an effort to understand the community in a perspective that can be used by the social workers for post disaster interventions, as well as for encouraging disaster preparedness. It also analyses the community organisation principles and process, the basic method of social work as the key theoretical structure for disaster intervention with the survivors in the community. An exploration is done on the existing national and international policy guidelines on psycho-social support that are heavily drawn on community engagement practices and have close links with social work skills. It is the community which is the key stakeholder in disaster management (IASC, 2007) and intervention process. Cohesiveness, community culture, social capital, socio-political and economic structures are all essential dimensions for social work practice in disaster intervention programmes. These are the key characteristics of the community that the disaster management workers need to understand and analyse.

Cohesiveness of the community is a factor that facilitates the disaster recovery process. Disaster and its aftermath usually lead to a bonding among the people belonging to a specific caste, religion or sect. Rather than being united as one, even though they have stayed in the same village in close proximity with interdependence, people belonging to a specific geographical area usually get divided into various interest based communities in the eventuality of a disaster. This can be religion, caste, occupational group or any other pattern of identity that emerged or prevailed even much before the disaster stuck the community (Bhadra, 2010).

*Traditional knowledge about disaster always helps to deal with disaster situati*ons. The areas affected repeatedly by disaster have certain traditional mechanisms and knowledge to deal with disasters of low or medium intensity. This is seen in various flood prone zones, where the community people have their own traditional methods to cope with the disaster and its aftermath. But if the disaster strikes the community with a higher severity, though it may not be in position to deal with it, but the traditional knowledge becomes a key strength in the phase of recovery. The communities with previous experiences of disaster usually develop some resilience to deal with future uncertainties.

Resilience among the community facilitates recovery at a faster rate. After any disaster, as the survivors start picking up the threads of life to meet the basic survival needs, the common feature that gets reported in media and among the disaster management professionals is about the resilience among the community. A resilient community in disaster is an ideal state of affairs, as it refurbishes the self-initiative among the community to get back to normalcy. A resilient community strives to achieve normalcy by initiatives within, and by developing a better coordination mechanism to navigate help from the external agencies.

Cultural sensitivity is an important consideration for the disaster intervention worker. Communities identify themselves by their unique culture which is part of their living and is shared among the community members. The culture of a community which has evolved over generations may not be similar in case of urban slums, migratory or resettled communities where people start living due to various occupational and personal requirements. However, developing a sense of community always helps in extending and seeking mutual support among the survivor groups.

Political and economic structure of the community influences the outcome of the disaster recovery interventions. A community with strong political influence gets the attention of the government and mobilises funds more easily than a community which has no specific influential political leader or identity. Economic resources may be within the community or beyond the community, but the resources that can be quickly mobilized for the community help in quick recovery. These resources could be the financial or material resources that are crucial for reconstruction and for building new initiatives in a disaster affected community.

Social structure of the community denotes the various organisational and institutional patterns of a community to manage its affairs at large. Every community has a formal or informal structure that facilitates recovery. The existence of support groups, occupational groups, women or youth groups can mobilise support and facilitate change at a faster rate. Similarly, there may be potential threats within the community that may be due to existing community issues and unresolved conflicts. While understanding the structure, the potential hindrances in the development and recovery effort should also be identified.

Social Capital of a community is about the strong networks that the community possesses and uses for the development of the community. Bourdieu (1986) defined social capital as 'the aggregate of the actual or potential resources which are linked to the possession of a durable network of more or less institutionalized relationships of mutual acquaintance or recognition'. Every community usually has social capital, and it is in a position to mobilise more resources for its recovery. The human capital accounts for the specific knowledge, skills and capacity of the local community people, which contributes towards building social capital and establishing networks both within the community and outside, to mobilize support. A community with higher social capital has better chance of faster recovery. Social capital can be created and nurtured through practice to strengthen the community effort towards recovery.

Community for Project Intervention

It is imperative that the project community be placed as the key stakeholder in the recovery process in the aftermath of a disaster. While the community is at the receiver's end, the survivors usually become passive recipients and fail to recognise their own capacity. Social work practice recognizes the importance of community participatory methods and the importance of engaging the community through community organisation practices, but lack of trained social workers in the field of disaster intervention at the community level sometimes causes a higher dependency of the survivors on external agents for their recovery. The presence and support of the external agency is crucial for disaster recovery, but how the support is utilized and maintained for strengthening the community capacity has to be firmly established. The WHO (1991) definition of 'disaster' highlighted that the community affected by disaster needs external help to recover, as the impact of the disaster exceeds the coping capacity of the community. Considering the community as an essential stakeholder means that there is a greater responsibility of the external supporting agencies and professionals to engage the survivors meaningfully in the recovery process, by building their capacity, recognizing their efficiency and identifying the cultural strength of the community. The community as a stakeholder is a continuum of engagement that starts with a higher level of engagement of the external agencies at the initial stage with a gradual decline in engagement towards the end of intervention with the gradual increase of community engagements with higher degree towards the end of the intervention to support autonomous and sustained recovery. In this whole process, the manner in which the community would engage itself depends on the efforts taken by the professionals from external agencies and the techniques used for the same.

Disaster recovery is not just a natural process, rather it needs to be designed, directed and organised in a fashion that can strengthen the community's capacity for dealing with future uncertainty. An approach of empowerment is most crucial for disaster recovery as only that can help the community to gather confidence and cohesion. The vulnerability of a community for disaster is multi-dimensional and includes, geographical location, settlement pattern, use of modern technology, traditional skills to deal with disaster, and ultimately human potential to deal with vulnerabilities. Therefore, in the post disaster recovery phase, designing interventions to reduce the vulnerability by adopting strategies that strengthen the community's capacity and human potential are vital. The rehabilitation in disaster situation can be designed through the community organisation practice models and capability approach (Sen, 1997; Nussbaum, 2011) to empower and include all the survivors through holistic recovery. The capability approach measures the development of the society as a function of the level of well-being or standard of living of individuals within that society. 'Functioning' is what a person actually does and experiences and it may vary from the elementary, such as being adequately nourished and being free from avoidable disease, to complex activities or personal states, such as taking part in the life of the community and having self-respect. 'Capability' refers to the feasible alternative combinations of this functioning. The best possible combinations of functioning help to achieve optimal capability and enhance well-being. Nussbaum (2011) outlined the capabilities classified by types of activities that people are enabled to do in a given situation. Her list included ten distinctive aspects of activities. Some of the important aspects are: living a normal span of life; being able to have good health (bodily health); being able to use the senses; being able to imagine, to think, and to reason (sense, imagination, thought), being able to plan one's own life (practical reason); and control over one's environment. The disaster survivors need to be supported in restoring their capabilities for resuming normalcy for only their own engagement can usher in recovery.

Case Study as a Method

This section describes the community empowerment process in the post-disaster intervention programme in the communities of Kanyakumari district following the devastating Indian Ocean Tsunami in 2004, through the case study method. Case studies are particularly good for providing "holistic and context sensitive" analyses (Patton, 2002, p. 447). The construction of a case study generally involves three steps: (i) The collection of case data; (ii) the organisation of the data into a case record; and (iii) the development of the case record into a narrative (Patton, 2002). Data was collected from sources including publicly available reports and documents, presentation materials, and the experiences, observations and reflections of the author, by virtue of his working closely with the community as a psycho-social expert from the time of onset of the disaster to a subsequent period of five years. The author being a trained social worker worked with social work skills and methodologies as his basic strength. The case data has been organized and presented to explain how the community was empowered to move towards recovery.

Community Engagement Programme

The huge death, destruction and loss of the communities in the coastal villages of Kanyakumari district that bore the worst brunt of the Tsunami, became an immediate attention seeker for humanitarian workers and organisations. The premier mental health institute of India in Bangalore, NIMHANS, where the author was working, became one of the first responders to the disaster. With other team members and professional guidance, the initial strategy of working with the survivors was to train a large number of community volunteers/ community workers in government and non-government sectors for providing emotional or psychological first aid (NIMHANS and WHO, 2006). This is also termed as psycho-social care that includes seven basic principles (ventilation; active listening; empathy; social support; externalisation of interest; relaxation and recreation; spirituality) of providing care to reduce stress reaction due to traumatic experiences and enhance wellbeing. In this phase, a large number of community members who were working with the health, education, children and family welfare departments were trained. The different NGO/CBO workers who were present in the community like teachers, child care personnel, health workers, community leaders, representatives of local self-government, student volunteers, volunteers from different forums, self-help group members, members of religious institutions were also included. The initiative draw a huge response and immediate mobilization which showed the community's inherent capacity to determine its own future. The training was based on sharing of experiences and participatory methodology that helped the participants to relate with their own situation and in building their confidence to deal with the problems emanating out of the tragedy.

At the initial phase of relief, the community engagement that was seen could be identified with few distinctive characteristics.

The spirit of voluntarism was higher among the people in the community as the impact of the Tsunami was overwhelming and people got together to help each other. This feature can be referred to as the 'honeymoon phase' after a disaster (Weaver, 1995). This is what a community experiences roughly from two weeks to two months after the disaster. The crucial aspect within this phase was to sustain the energy of the community and to make it an active partner of the recovery process. Similarly, transforming the skills of training into application largely depends on the use of the same in the actual situation. The trained community level workers (e.g. the teachers, health workers, child care personnel, the SHG members, volunteers) were provided with ongoing handholding support that included structured follow-up, monitoring, refresher course, regular sharing at different levels supervised by the TOTs (trainer of the trainees) and trained mental health social workers. Eventually, different levels of training were designed and implemented that ensured continuous engagement of the survivors at the individual, family or group levels. At this juncture, community organisation principles become most crucial to ensure an integrated, inclusive approach to deal with issues of marginalization of the weaker sections among the survivors. Establishing community control over the resources, both external and internal, depends on how the community as a whole is being empowered to work as a unit. As the community became aware and able to deal with the traumatic experience, it gradually learnt important lessons in joining together to build a better rehabilitation process.

In the government sector, through Education, Women and Child Development, and Health Departments, the programme was able to reach the survivors to a great extent, and through the NGOs, specific integrated development projects were designed. Various training programmes for the restoration of livelihood, microfinance and vocational skills were designed along with other soft skill based projects. The soft skill based projects were largely on water – sanitation, community based first aid, disaster preparedness through community engagement and participation.

The integrated community recovery project was designed for long-term implementation with an aim to enhance the capacity of the tsunami survivors to recover through community and school based interventions. The outcome was envisioned as developing safe, healthy, and competent individuals, families and communities through community engagement processes;

strengthening internal resources of the community; and developing functional community organisations and institutions like, schools, community training centres, and other community based institutions. The objectives were designed to empower the tsunami affected communities and schools and strengthen local resources and support systems (IFRC, 2008).

The programme was taken forward through the interventions that started with the capacity building of the project staff who had to take the main responsibility of implementing the project in the communities. The project staff comprised of social workers, health educators, and community health nurses who could work with the communities and schools in the affected areas. Further, this training was designed to be a TOT (Training of the Trainers) as the main task was of mobilising community level workers from the affected communities and training them for the purpose of rehabilitation. The cascading effect of the training (Sekar, Bhadra & Dyer, 2007; Becker, 2009) is one of the proven modes of transferring the required knowledge and skills to engage the entire community in the long term.

The community volunteers were not paid by the organisation as that could have led to a financial dependency, and may also be derogatory to their status as volunteers in the community. Through regular sessions with the volunteers and the programme staff, the specific factors of joining as volunteers were identified. A large number of volunteers joined and many other regularly participated in different community based programmes, where they joined and contributed for their own development. Voluntarism as a pro-social behaviour in the post disaster situation becomes an important determinant of community participation and needs to be optionally mobilized. Though, the selection and participation of the volunteers is a gradual process, yet the community members, students, women, men and youth of the community were able to engage the community people in various community recovery components like community meetings, awareness rallies, community health fair, community 'sense of place' projects, health and hygiene activities, disaster preparedness activities etc.

The community recovery project was designed in the form of action that addressed both the psychological and social needs of individuals, families and communities. The project targeted at all the three levels to build resiliency and well-being of the Tsunami survivors. Following the mobilization of the community volunteers and their training, the work in health and psycho-social areas started with the analysis of the community situation from the perspective of the survivors in the community. Through the trained staff, participatory research 'community mapping', and making of the seasonal calendar was initiated. These maps were effectively used for programme planning in the communities. Subsequently, a representative group in each of the targeted community was developed and named as Community Committee (CC). The committee comprised of a group of community volunteers, village leaders, and local mass leaders of the community. The CC was involved in various stages of the recovery programme like planning, implementing and monitoring, and to ensure the sustainability of the project activities. The committee met regularly to discuss and design the interventions within the community and also contribute (financially and volunteer time) as per requirement and decisions. The process was maintained in such a manner that the community representatives could take control over the recovery process gradually and the intended programme could be facilitated. Further, various community mobilisation activities were aimed to ensure that the community members join and develop capacities to work together. Engagement of the whole community through an active participation of the community volunteers facilitated the process and the community gradually gained ownership of the programme (Bhadra & Pratheepa, 2009). Simultaneously, there were other health activities to deal with issues regarding water and sanitation, cleanliness, hygiene, prevention of communicable diseases, prevention of malaria and mosquito born diseases in the coastal areas. CBHFA (Community Based Health and First Aid) approach was used to improve the health condition of the target communities' recovery project (Singh & Mini, 2009).

There were a number of community mobilization activities to encourage the community members to join together and plan activities on a regular basis. These reduced stress among the survivors and brought a level of normalization. These mobilization activities were culturally and traditionally appropriate such as, sports and competitions, cultural day celebration, celebration of important days (Human Rights Day, Women's Day, World AIDS day, etc.), ecological activities and awareness rallies on various themes. To ensure appropriate sharing of each of the activities and planning at the community level, community wide meetings were regularly organized, where the community people joined in and shared their feelings and ideas. The local CC members, volunteers, local school teachers, women and youth representatives shared their thoughts, achievements, etc. The community volunteers took the lead role to organize the meetings with support of community committee and other local agencies in the community like local youth club and self-help groups. There were health 'melas' in the community to promote health awareness among the survivors. In these events, the survivors were encouraged to own responsibility for their wellbeing and for disseminating messages to other community members on health and psychosocial wellbeing. Audio visual displays, distribution of pamphlets, cultural events, rallies, community kitchen and exhibitions of various IEC (Information, Education and Communication) were conducted. Through a rigorous participatory process and following behaviour change communication principles, the IEC materials were designed and developed. Health stalls were established and messages on disease prevention and health promotion, hygiene, sanitation, nutrition and the issues related to psycho-social wellbeing were provided to the community members. These positive behaviour changes were encouraged through home visits and group meetings with the community members. There were a number of small projects that were conducted to facilitate 'sense of place' to enhance active participation and sense of ownership over the community programme. These projects were identified, planned, initiated and managed by the communities with the help of volunteers, using one third of financial help from the project budget. Rest of the finance was mobilised from the community. These projects fostered group identity, cohesion, partnership and a spirit of working collectively to identify local problems and find appropriate solutions which were culturally and traditionally appropriate. The various 'sense of place' projects entailed themes like: waste management, refurbishment of library, establishing tailoring unit, computer training, children's park, providing play materials to youth clubs, solid waste management, pond cleaning, and canal cleaning. CBHFA (Community Based Health and First Aid) approach was used to improve the health conditions of the target survivors' communities. CBHFA in action brings action and learning together and ensures that the community responds to adverse events immediately. It widens the base of traditional first aid training and uses a community–based approach to include aspects of community health such as disease prevention, health promotion, control of common diseases and infections. Health assessment was conducted by using different tools such as: Free Listing, Focused Group Discussions, Health Mapping, Seasonal Calendar and Home Visits.

A health action plan was prepared based on the prioritised issues which were further addressed through a participatory methodology.

The recovery project was a combination of such various activities that finally helped in implementing the programme with community participation as the key. Looking at the gradual increase in the participation, it can be said that the community was guided to take the recovery effort in their own hands. The recovery project mobilized a large number of community people and engaged the people in some or the other activities to join and become a stakeholder and partner, through the process of community participation and engagement. The implementation was a long drawn continuous process that needs to be strengthened in the community to continue the developmental activities beyond the life-cycle of the project period. Strengthening the communities' strength was an essential expected outcome for sustaining the community interventions. The sustainability of the project could be ensured by following a rigorous participatory process that facilitated the development of community ownership and ultimate control of the project to sustain the impact beyond the life of the project.

The pre and post assessment that was done specifically for the Red Cross intervention in an interval of 30 months showed that the intervention specifically facilitated a subjective wellbeing, a spirit of voluntarism and quality of life. The programme promoted community cohesion and also facilitated community control for sustainability. Through project monitoring and evaluation system, it was seen that that quantitatively speaking, the project activities achieved almost one hundred per cent of the targeted intervention and project activities, but qualitative changes were essential to understand the process through which the community became the key stakeholder. The evaluation showed five important changes that contributed towards social work knowledge building for practice in disaster intervention:

- First, as a basic method of social work practice, community organisation is most crucial in the post-disaster recovery programme. The IASC-MHPSS (2007) guidelines emphasised on community mobilisation that is based on community organisation practice and principles. Community mobilisation, participatory methodologies and community based assessment and programming are essential to facilitate community control and recovery process in a sustainable mode. The transition of a community from 'victim' to 'victor' can happen only with appropriate community oriented practice.

- Second, community organisation and mobilisation of the community people in the recovery programme is the most vital aspect that can work as a platform for all other interventions in the community. For any kind of intervention in the community, like housing, livelihood, water and sanitation, disaster preparedness or health promotion, community engagement is the key for successful intervention. The community is the ultimate stakeholder and thus, it needs to be engaged for it to own the programme designed for its recovery.
- Third, survivors respond to an active interest and concern (Sekar, *et al.*, 2005) even at the time of the most traumatic event. However, the effort should be to facilitate self strength to gain power by overcoming the traumatic experiences through normalization of stress reactions and by creating social support. Essentially, the process of recovery through engagement is an effort of building social capital (developing social support mechanisms and networks) and human capital (skill building). The circle of support should be built by strengthening individual initiatives, family unity and mobilizing community resources. Community becomes the key factor in this process of rebuilding social support system.
- Fourth, community is at the centre of recovery and the ultimate stakeholder in the disaster intervention. Therefore, ensuring participation in recovery means an active engagement of the survivors in a bottom up approach that empowers the community to take charge of its own recovery process. The participation of the community without power transfer is disempowering. The approach of putting external resources for recovery without engaging the local community does not help the community to develop a sustainable pattern of recovery and development.
- Fifth, the immediate situation of a community after a disaster may call for immediate support that usually does not have room for encouraging survivors' active participation. But from the time of relief onwards, the gradual increase of participation of the community members should be

envisioned and implemented by the responding agencies. The gradual involvement of the community members in recovery finally strengthens the community.

To conclude, it is essential to recognize that disaster intervention and rehabilitation model should be designed and implemented in manner that is essentially an approach to encourage the community to become the key stakeholder of the rehabilitation process through participatory approach based on social work principles and practice. The disaster intervention is essentially a capability building approach for the rehabilitation of the survivors.

References

Anand, P., Hunter, G., and Smith, R. (2005). Capabilities and Well-Being: Evidence Based on the Sen-Nussbaum Approach to Welfare. *Social Indicators Research, 74*(1), 9-55.

Becker, S. M. (2009, April). Psychosocial Care for Women Survivors of the Tsunami Disaster in India. *American Journal of Public Health, 99*(4), 654-658.

Bhadra, S. (2010). Social Work and Disaster Interventions. In B. Gunjal, & G. Molankal, *Fields of Social Work Practice*, pp. 355-386. Bengaluru: Baraha Publishing House.

_______, (2013). Community based psycho-social support programme for resiliency building in Tsunami rehabilitation of Kanyakumari District. *Journal of Social Work, Special issue on Building Resilient Communities: Communitarian Social Work, 3*(8), 66-86.

_______, and Pratheepa, C.M. (2009, November 8th and 9th). *Strengthening Communities and Recovery through Psychosocial Support*. Retrieved June 26, 2013, from National Institute of Disaster Managment: 2nd India Disaster Managment Congress: http://nidm.gov.in/ idmc2/ PDF/Presentations/Psycho_Social/Pres3.pdf

Bourdieu, P. (1986). The Forms of Capital. In J. G. Richardson, *Handbook of Theory and Research for the Sociology of Education* (pp. 241-258). New York: Greenwood.

Brieger, W. R. (2006). *Johns Hopkins Bloomberg School of Public Health*. Retrieved January 4, 2014, from jhsph.edu: http://ocw.jhsph.edu/ courses/socialbehavioralfoundations/ PDFs/Lecture15.pdf

Gisbert, P. (2006). *Fundamentals of Sociology* (3rd ed.). Kolkata: Orient Black Swan.

GOI-UNDP. (2012). *Disaster Managment in India.* New Delhi: Ministry of Home Affairs. Retrieved from http://ndmindia.nic.in/UNDP-020811.pdf

IFRC. (2008). *Report-2004-2008, Federation-wide Tsunami Semi-annual Report: India.* New Delhi: International Federation of Red Cross and Red Crescent Societies.

_______, (2009). *Report 2004-2009: Federation-wide Tsunami 5-Year Progress Report.* Geneva: International Federation of Red Cross and Red Crescent Societies. Retrieved June 26, 2013, from http://reliefweb.int/sites/reliefweb.int/files/resources/3DA9790 D55FAE 3364925768C00203B11-Full_Report.pdf

Inter Agency Standing Committee (IASC). (2007). *Guidelines on Mental Health and Psychosocial Support in Emergency Settings (MHPSS).* Geneva: IASC.

NIMHANS and WHO. (2006). Psycho Social Support in Disaster: Proceedings and Recommendations of NIMHANS-WHO India Workshop. *Psycho Social Support in Disaster*, pp. 1-12. Bangalore: NIMHANS and WHO India Country Office.

Nussbaum, M. (2011). *Creating Capabilities: The Human Development Approach.* Cambridge, MA: Harvard University Press.

Patton, M.Q. (2002). *Qualitative Research & Evaluation Methods* (3rd Edition ed.). California: Thousand Oaks, Sage Publications.

Sekar, K., Bhadra, S., and Dyer, A.R. (2007). A Decade of Disasters: Lessons from the Indian Experience. *Southern Medical Journal, 100*(9), 292-231.

_______, Bhadra, S., Jayakumar, C., Aravindraj, E., Henry, G., and Kumar, K.K. (2005). *Facilitation Manual for Trainers of Trainees in Natural Disaster.* Bangalore: NIMHANS and Care India.

_______, Biswas, G., Bhadra, S., Jayakumar, C., and Kumar, K.K. (2005). *Tsunami Disaster: Psychosocial care for children; Information Manual-3.* Bangalore: NIMHANS-CARE-India.

_______, Dave, A.S., Bhadra, S., Rajsekar, G.P., Kumar, K.K., and Murthy, S. (2002). Psychosocial Care by Community Level Helperfor Survivors. *Informational Manual-2.* Bangalore, Karnataka, India: Books for Change.

Sen, A.K. (1997). Distinguished guest lecture: From income inequality to economic inequality. *Southern Economic Journal, 64*(2), 384-402.

_______, (1999). *Development As Freedom.* Oxford: Oxford University Press.

Singh, N., and Mini, J. (2009, November 8th and 9th). *Important of Community Health Assessment Through Community Based Approach in Post Disaster Period.* Retrieved June 26, 2013, from National Institute of Disaster Managment, 2nd India Disaster Management Congress: http://nidm.gov.in/idmc2/PDF/Presentations/PHE/Pres3.pdf

Steinberg, T. (2000). *The Acts of God: The unnatural history of disasters in America.* New York: Oxford University Press.

Weaver, J.D. (1995). *Disaster: Mental Health Interventions.* Florida: Professional Resource Press.

WHO. (1991). *Psychosocial consequences of disasters: Prevention and managment.* Geneva: World Health Organisation.

8

Social Work and Human Animal Conflict

Opportunities for Interdisciplinary Practice

Mayuri Gogoi

Social work as a human service profession has largely operated within the realms of the social environment, paying scant attention to the biophysical environment. The 'person-in-environment' hypothesis introduced in social work in the early 20th century had for decades focussed only on the individual's interaction with the social environment. Lately, however, the growing acknowledgement of the fact that human well-being is intrinsically related to the well-being of the natural environment has inspired many social work academics to advocate for an integration of the physical environment in social work practice (Hoff and McNutt, 1994; Coates, 2003 & 2005; Besthorn, 2008; Coates and Gray, 2012; Dominelli, 2012). The negative impacts of environmental degradation are differentially borne by the humans and the worst affected are the poor and marginalised living on the periphery of development. As a profession based on the values of social justice and empowerment, it is imperative, therefore, that practice is oriented towards addressing environmental concerns.

> 'While environmental concerns and solutions are complex, it is becoming increasingly clear that realities such as climate change, soil erosion, pollution and deforestation are affecting human health and wellbeing and, as the consequences of environmental devastation, social injustices fall disproportionately upon the most disadvantaged. These realities have raised serious challenges for social work' (Gray & Coates, 2012; p. 239).

Environmental problems are often the results of unmindful human activities driven by motives of capitalist gains and greed. Pollution, deforestation, climate change are raising their ugly heads due to unrestrained growth and development and the breakdown of men's inherent relationship with their natural environment. These environmental problems are not only jeopardising the health and well-being of communities but also at the same time creating conditions of war and strife thereby endangering the lives of millions of people (Orr, 2011). Since humans are an integral part of the entire ecosystem their actions have deleterious effect on other living beings as well. In order, therefore, for holistic and responsive practices, which are environmentally sound and socially just, an interdisciplinary approach is a primary precondition. As Coates and Gray (2012) remarks:

> 'We believe that environmental work should be interdisciplinary as it involves an array of knowledge, including the contested science of global warming, scientific studies on the pollution of air, water and soil and their impact on people, habitat destruction and extinctions, agricultural practices and policies, and globalisation and trade policies, to name a few.' (Coates & Gray, 2012; p. 231)

Practitioners who adopt an interdisciplinary perspective are better equipped at problem solving as they have a "broader range of resources for response" (Schmitz, Stinson & James, 2011, p. 87). Social workers in their varied roles as community workers, change agents, activists and clinical and therapeutic practitioners can be important linkages in bridging the gap between environmental sustainability and promoting social justice and equity. The complexity of problems arising out of a degraded environment calls for interventions which are informed by various disciplines. As Coates and Gray (2012) states that the challenge facing social work, and for that matter other professions as well, is to break free from the confines of their own academic discipline and embrace learnings from other disciplines and work cooperatively to address the varied dimensions of environmental problems. Schmitz, *et al.* (2012) believe that for social work to establish itself as a leader in developing an integrated environmental practice requires going beyond humanistic focus and encompass the ecological environment.

It is in the light of the above developments in social work practice that intervention in Human Animal Conflict (HAC) needs to be undertaken with an interdisciplinary focus. HAC which till recently had been addressed primarily from a biophysical perspective had failed to include the socio-cultural perspective inherent in the problem. Solutions to HAC are therefore ecocentric, biased and, based on expert notions rather than on indigenous wisdom. The addressal of HAC within social work enables practitioners to assess the conditions of hierarchy, domination, poverty, gender, racism and marginalisation that exacerbate conflict. Working on HAC in social work is also imperative to understand how conflict affects the social, emotional and psychological well-being of people, how communities respond to conflict, what role does culture play in defining, coping and mitigating conflict, etc. and thereby design and undertake informed interventions for empowerment and development of HAC affected communities along with conservation of animals.

Human Animal Conflict – Causes and Concerns

As residents of the same planet, human and animals have always coexisted. While some people like to romanticise about the harmonious and peaceful coexistence between humans and animals in early history, but in reality, conflict between the two had been omnipresent. Humans hunted animals for food and at times had themselves fallen prey to animals. In the early agricultural history of mankind, instances of crop depredation and livestock predation by wild animals were also recorded. The question, thus, arises is, why human animal conflict has become a cause of concern today? The answer lies in the changing demographic conditions, changing landscapes and also changing perception of people towards wildlife and damages caused by them. Increased human population combined with rapid urbanisation and industrialisation has been exerting considerable pressures on the natural habitat. Habitat destruction has gone to an extent now where both man and animals are increasingly competing for limited space and resources. This competition for common resources has pitched humans and wildlife as adversaries in a conflict for survival. The World Conservation Union (2004) defines Human Animal Conflict as occurring, *"...when the needs and behaviour of wildlife impact negatively on the goals of humans or when the goals of humans negatively impact the needs of wildlife. These conflicts may result when wildlife damage crops, injure or kill domestic animals or kill people."*

Human Animal Conflict (HAC) or Human Wildlife Conflict (HWC), includes both *competition* and *predation* and take many forms like crop-raiding, livestock predation, human injury or death, competition for wild forage between humans and wild animals or between livestock and wild animals, building infestations, zoonoses, traffic accidents, etc. (Knight, 2000). HAC adversely impacts human welfare, health and safety and is ridden with huge economic and social costs. It also negatively impacts ecosystem equilibrium and biodiversity conservation.

HWC is a universal phenomenon and occurs everywhere but the incidence of conflict tends to be higher in the borderlands of protected areas or forest-edge regions (Hill, 1998; Knight, 2000; Nyhus, Tilson, & Sumianto, 2000). The protected areas around the world have been converted to 'isolated islands of natural habitat in a sea of humanity' (Sitati *et al.*, 2005) where animals are seeking refuge. Consequently, animals inhabiting these spaces come into greater contact and conflict with humans in their efforts to fulfil nutritional, ecological and behavioural needs (Sukumar 1989; Naughton-Treves, 1998).

Studies on human-animal conflict basically regard increased human population and associated habitat changes as being at the root of the problem (Nyhus, Tilson, & Sumianto, 2000; Treves & Karanth, 2003). Growing human population results in extension of anthropogenic activities to erstwhile wild areas leading to complete loss, degradation and/or fragmentation of these areas. In Africa, for instance, the population has almost tripled in the last five decades and agriculture has spread to wildlife habitats leading to an inevitable increase in conflicts between humans and animals (Naughton *et al.*, 1998).

As population increases, the need for conversion of natural habitat to agriculture is uppermost. Agriculture, both subsistence and commercial, has expanded to forested areas in order to meet growing consumption demands. The massive transformation of forests and wild habitat has had a dramatic impact on HWC with more and more people and animals being affected. Apart from agriculture, activities such as collection of wild fruit and berries, fuel wood, fishing, grazing, etc., also expose humans to harmful encounters with wildlife (Rajpurohit & Krausman, 2000; Ogra, 2008). Aside land, water is another resource for which both humans and animals compete for. In rural Africa, people still rely on water bodies such as lakes, rivers, etc. for water. These water bodies are also prime crocodile habitat and as the demand for water is increasing with the rise in population, incidents of human-crocodile conflict are also on a high (Fergusson, 2002). Studies also hint that human-carnivore conflict is on the rise in many parts of the world because of the reduction in the natural prey-base due to hunting, fishing and/or poaching (FAO, 2005).

In addition to agriculture and allied activities, commercial activities such as mining, logging and oil extraction have also destroyed prime animal habitat and given access to remote and inaccessible areas, usually resulting in negative consequences for animals like hunting, poaching etc. (Walsh *et al.*, 2000). Development projects like construction of roads, dams, railways, etc. also destroy wildlife habitat, cause pollution and disturb the natural distribution of species. Construction of development projects on traditional migratory routes of animals also results in disruption of their mobility and often leads to unusually aggressive behaviour among them thus intensifying conflict (Kangwana, 1995).

The problem of HAC has an overtly ecological character to it and both habitat ecology and biological characteristics of animals contribute towards occurrence of conflict. However, a close re-examination of the facts shows that behind these implicit ecological factors lies an array of social conditions which lays the ground for conflict. While habitat loss can be categorised as an ecological phenomenon but the forces inducing such loss are profoundly social and political in nature.

Human Animal Conflict – Exploring the Social Perspective

HAC is one phenomenon where humans and animals are both the perpetrators of harm as well as the victims of it. Irrespective of what causes HAC, the adverse impacts of conflict are borne both by man and animals. The consequences of HAC ranges from crop loss, property damage, loss of livestock and injury and death for humans and is a serious conservation concern for the animals involved. On account of the huge economic costs incurred in HAC, it has become an integral part of development discourse world-wide. The economic costs involved in HAC are the most apparent and 'direct' consequences of conflict and have received the most attention in studies of HWC. Humans have to bear high economic costs resulting from destruction and damage to property and infrastructure (e.g. fencing, pipes, etc.) and livestock depredation.

The fact that most of the wildlife conservation areas are located in nations battling rural poverty and growing population makes it doubly important to focus on the economic costs involved in HAC. In addition, HAC poses significant risks to the well-being and safety of individuals by exposing them to large predator attacks resulting in death or grievous injuries.

Crop damage by wild animals is probably the most widespread, persistent and serious form of human-wildlife conflict. Such damage adversely impacts availability of staple food grains (rice, wheat, maize, sorghum, millet); non-grain food crops (potatoes, peanuts, vegetables, sugarcane, bananas, cassava, coconuts, cacao), and commercial crops (rubber, tea, coffee, spices). Damage results not only from the animals feeding on crops, but also from trampling, uprooting, and other forms of wastage (Madhusudan & Karanth, 2002). Crop damage results in the loss of staple food for the poorest class of rural people by compromising food security and thus exacerbates existing poverty (Ogra & Badola, 2008; Hill & Wallace, 2012). Additionally, destruction of commercial crops may lead to wastage of years of labour and capital investment and may take several years to re-establish (Madhusudan & Karanth, 2002). Because agriculture usually employs a significant proportion of rural workers, such crop losses lead to indirect loss of livelihood opportunities on a wider scale (*ibid*).

Killing of domesticated stock by carnivores is another serious aspect of HAC. Livestock predation by carnivores can negatively affect cattle farming and agricultural production thereby impacting farming livelihood (Treves & Karanth, 2003). A study conducted by Woodroffe *et al.* (2005) estimated that Kenyan farmers lose nearly 22 per cent of average per capita annual income in livestock losses killed by wild dogs.

Apart from livestock losses, HAC also results in loss or damage to infrastructure such as houses, water tanks, fences and property items like household goods etc. (Sukumar, 1994). For instance, baboons in South Africa have been reported for breaking and entering private residences or hi-jacking picnics in tourist resorts (Svotwa *et al.*, 2007). A study by Kumar *et al.* (2004) recorded 117 incidents of elephants damaging school kitchens, ration shops and houses, office equipment and automobiles. The transmission of diseases from wildlife to domestic animals and even humans is also regarded as both a cause and impact of HAC. Zoonotic diseases have had an impact on humans throughout history and have emerged as a major public health problem across continents. For example, bubonic plague, transmitted through rats and fleas has caused illness and death around the world since ancient times (Wheelis, 2002).

Human-wildlife conflict attains its most serious form when people are injured or killed by wild animals. Although big cats, bears, and wolves in Southern Asia are readily recognized and targeted for such manslaughter, wild elephants probably kill more people than large carnivores in this region (Madhusudan, & Karanth, 2002). World Wide Fund for Nature (WWF) estimates that in India, over 100 people are killed by elephants each year, and over 200 people have been killed in Kenya over the last seven years (www.wwf.org). Rajpurohit and Krausman's (2000) study on HWC in Bihar showed that from 1989 to 1995, 242 individuals had been killed by elephants, 50 by sloth bear and, 92 people were killed by wolves. Various studies have reported man-slaughter and attacks by carnivores on humans in several parts of the world such as, lions in Gir, India (Saberwal *et al.*, 1994) and Africa (Treves & Naughton-Treves, 1999); tigers in the Sunderbans (Hendrichs, 1975); brown bears in North America (Herrero & Higgins, 1999); and, wolves in Alaska and Canada (McNay, 2002).

Apart from these 'direct' costs, HAC also involves what Ogra (2008) calls 'hidden' costs. She defines 'hidden' costs as those characterized by one or more of the following traits: (a) uncompensated, (b) temporally delayed, or (c) psychological or social in nature (p.1409). Hoare (1999) also made a reference to such 'hidden' costs when he wrote, "*economic assessments exclude many of the social 'opportunity costs' associated with living with elephants*" such as loss of sleep and disrupted school attendance (p.700). Catherine Hill (2004) has elaborated on the understanding that economic causes do not sufficiently cover the entire range of costs incurred by farmers in HAC. She writes that crop losses to animals are not just economically draining for the household experiencing conflict but such losses can also generate other costs to household members, including: (i) an increased need to guard fields, which creates labour bottlenecks in certain seasons, (ii) disruption of schooling because children are needed to help guard family fields, (iii) increased risk of injury from wildlife, and (iv) increased risk of contracting diseases (e.g., malaria) if people are required to guard their fields at night (p. 280). Due to the undeniable social costs involved in HAC, the 2003 World Parks Congress recommended that conflict mitigation approaches must address the "social" issues associated with HWC in addition to economic and ecological ones (IUCN, 2004).

Social Work with HAC Affected Communities

Lessons in Interdisciplinary Practice

Communities affected by HAC have to battle an array of negative consequences in living their everyday lives. For communities living in the periphery of Protected Areas (PAs), impacts of HAC are exacerbated by the stringent laws which disallow the continuation of their traditional resource use within the PAs in the name of conservation. The wildlife legislations in many countries prescribe strict norms for the maintenance of certain areas as wilderness areas that are bereft of human presence. In their bid to conserve wildlife and forests, the forest bureaucracy also prohibits indigenous communities from using PA resources which were being traditionally used by them. Under such circumstances, when protected wildlife engages in crop or property depredation the safety net provided by PA resources are also not available to people. Households whose primary occupation is subsistence agriculture faces economic hardships when they have to buy food grains to sustain themselves till the next harvest. In the absence of any supplementary means of income and non-availability of liquid cash, people often have to borrow money from others or sell household goods to obtain money and buy food grains.

It is not only the government agencies that are alienating the local population but most non-governmental wildlife conservation organisations have also been criticised by forest fringe villagers for initiating programmes which further accentuates the policy of exclusionary conservation and disregards the welfare of the people. It has been observed that most of the non-governmental organisations engaged in wildlife conservation in the HAC affected areas have minimal association with the communities and thus have come to be regarded as agents of government. The role of the wildlife organisations is again driven by the ideological influences of the philanthropic business elites funding their programmes. The neoliberal conservationist agenda followed by these business elites through non-governmental organisations appears, "to facilitate the combination of fierce capitalism with overwhelming philanthropic generosity" (Spierenburg & Wels, 2010).

Social workers working with HAC affected communities can advocate for participatory conservation involving local communities. They can work closely with the government in developing community based mitigation measures and encourage greater participation of community members in these schemes. Social workers can be effective agents in brokering relations of trust and dependence among the local communities, government authorities and wildlife conservation organisations and thereby put into motion a system of mitigation which is effective and where the responsibility is shared equally by all. Making people equal partners in the mitigation and conservation processes will reduce the feelings of animosity among stakeholders and pave way for better implementation of forest policies.

HAC also has damaging consequences on the physical and mental health of communities particularly women, children and elderly. Death in animal attacks generates immense trauma and shock among family members because it is sudden and violent. For women whose husbands are killed in this manner, the initial trauma is very often compounded by drudgery, economic hardships and emotional stress. Researches have shown that widowhood is among one of the most stressful events in the life of a woman (Holmes & Rahe, 1967) and can cause severe psychological problems owing to a sense of loneliness and loss of emotional support. It also remains an important risk factor for transition into poverty and women in households that are least prepared financially for widowhood are at greatest risk (Sevak *et al.*, 2003-2004).

Death of an individual in conflict with animals can also have far-reaching negative consequences on the lives of her/his surviving children. In instances where the child was a witness to the violent death of a parent, or saw an injured or dead parent could cause distress, fear and disorganisation in the child (Pynoos, 1994). Elaborating on the impact of parental death on young children, Lieberman *et al.* (2003) writes,

> 'Children in the first five years of life need to trust that the parent will be reliably available and protective in order to develop a sense of physical and emotional integrity. When an attachment figure dies, the child loses intimate patterns of interaction that organise key developmental

domains and constitute the building blocks for the child's sense of self. The loss produces intense and long-lasting grief, and represents a risk factor for healthy development unless the child is supported in the protracted process of mourning' (p. 6).

Similarly, HAC also heightens the vulnerability of elderly by exposing them to physical danger of animal attacks. Apart from the immediate physical threat to their own safety, death or injury of a family member, or loss of crops and property in animal attacks can be emotionally devastating for the elderly or even push them back to a state where they are required to do additional labour to make up for the loss. For elderly people living alone and/or without any family support system in HEC affected areas, conflict severely compromises their well-being and coping becomes arduous.

Death of an individual by wild animals not only traumatises the victim's family but also creates fear and uncertainty in the minds of fellow community members. While fear is a natural emotion induced in both humans and animals when a threat is perceived, it becomes unnatural when the emotion takes the form of phobia that can severely disrupt routine life.

Social workers, thus, have a significant role to play in alleviating the adverse effects of HAC on different socio-demographic groups. Prevailing symptoms of mental and psychiatric illness among affected community members call for specialised therapeutic interventions in areas experiencing conflict. Social workers can also include a gendered perspective in HAC mitigation by addressing concerns pertaining to women who are burdened by conflict either by virtue of the gendered dimensions of their work (e.g. collecting firewood from forests) or by the absence of social security due to death of the male member(s) of the household in conflict or both. On the same note, social workers also have a responsibility towards children living in conflict-ridden areas. The care and protection of children from physical harm, which is considered as an important right of children, is being violated in societies experiencing conflict with animals, particularly large-bodied animals. Social workers can contribute immensely towards restitution of this basic right along with improving the mental and psychological well-being of children traumatised in conflict. Planning school based interventions, establishing therapeutic play groups, providing accessible mental health and counselling services at the grassroots are few options which social workers practising in HAC affected areas can explore for working with children.

The scope of geriatric social work which is basically inclined towards institutional settings needs to extend Community and family-based interventions to strengthen the coping and functioning of these support systems are some of the ways in which social workers can help the elderly caught in the vicious cycle of conflict, poverty and suffering. Social workers can be instrumental in planning and implementing integrated efforts at rehabilitation of HAC affected elderly, ensuring provision of regular and adequate pension, providing accessible medical care etc.

Apart from these specialised interventions, social workers role is inevitable in creating social policies which take into consideration the needs and concerns of communities living in conflict with animals. Social workers informed about ecological causes of conflict and social impacts of conflict can help bring a multidimensional focus to policies which promote both social and environmental justice. Advocacy for human rights, endorsing animal rights, capacity building of communities, organising communities to mitigate conflict, creating social networks and support systems and generating awareness about the issues through research and documentation are other opportunities for engagement for social workers in HAC.

It can be said in conclusion that HAC has multiple traits and thus can be the subject matter in various disciplines, be it anthropology, geography, conservation biology, ecology or social work. Irrespective of the differences in perspective of different disciplines, what is required is a convergence of ideas and understandings which can be applied to practice solutions that are balanced and not prejudiced either towards animals or towards humans.

References

Besthorn, F.H. (2008). Environment and social work practice. In *Encyclopedia of Social Work*, pp. 132–136, 20th ed., Vol. 2. New York: Oxford University Press.

Coates, J. (2003). *Ecology and social work: Toward a new paradigm*. Halifax: Fernwood.

_______, (2005). The environmental crisis: Implications for social work. *Journal of Progressive Human Services*, 16(1), 25–49.

_______, and Gray, M. (2012). The environment and social work: An overview and introduction. *International Journal of Social Welfare*, 21, 230-238.

Dominelli, L. (2012). *Green Social Work: From Environmental Crisis to Environmental Justice.* Cambridge: Polity Press.

FAO. (2005). *Strategies to mitigate human-wildlife conflict in Mozambique*, by J. Anderson & F. Pariela. Report for the National Directorate of Forests and Wildlife, Mozambique.

Fergusson, R.A. (2002). *Living with a wild predator: Managing human/ crocodile conflict in Africa.* A proposal for an IUCN/SSC Crocodile Specialist Group initiative to provide technical support for the investigation and alleviation of human/crocodile conflict in several African countries. *Crocodile Specialist Group Newsletter*, 21: 4.

Gray, M. and Coates, J. (2012). Environmental ethics for social work: Social work's responsibility to the non-human world. *International Journal of Social Welfare*, 21, 239–247.

Hendrichs, H. (1975). The status of the tiger Panthera tigris (Linn 6, 1758) in the Sundarbans mangrove forest (Bay of Bengal). *Saugetierikd. Mitt.*, 23: 161-99.

Herrero, S. & Higgins, A. (1999). Human injuries inflicted by bears in British Columbia: 1960–97. *Ursus*, 11: 209–218.

Hill, C.M. (1998). Conflicting attitude towards elephants around the Budongo forest reserve, Uganda. *Environmental Conservation*, 25(3): 244-250.

_______, (2004). Farmers' perspectives of conflict at the wildlife–agriculture boundary: Some lessons learned from African subsistence farmers. *Human Dimensions of Wildlife*, 9: 279–286.

_______, and Wallace, G.E. (2012). Crop protection and conflict mitigation: reducing the costs of living alongside non-human primates. *Biodiversity and Conservation*, 21(10): 2569-2587.

Hoare, R. (1999). Determinants of human-elephant conflict in a land-use mosaic. *Journal of Applied Ecology*, 36: 689-700.

Hoff, M.D. and McNutt, J.G. (eds.). (1994). *The Global Environmental Crisis: Implications for social welfare and social work.* Aldershot: Ashgate Publishers.

Holmes, J.H., & Rahe, R.H. (1967). The social readjustment scale. *Journal of Psychosomatic Research*, 11: 213-228.

IUCN. (2004). Preventing and Mitigating Human-Wildlife Conflicts: World Parks Congress Recommendation. *Human Dimensions of Wildlife*, 9(4): 259–260.

Kangwana, K. (1995). Human-elephant conflict: The challenge ahead. *Pachyderm*, 19: 11-14.

Knight, J. (2000). Introduction. In J. Knight (Ed.), *Natural enemies: People–wildlife conflicts in anthropological perspective*, pp. 1-35. London: Routledge.

Kumar, M.A., Mudappa, D., Raman, T.R.S. and Madhusudan, M.D. (2004). *The elephant hills: Conservation of wild Asian elephants in a landscape of fragmented rainforests and plantations in the Anamalais, India.* CERC Technical Report No. 10, Nature Conservation Foundation, Mysore, India.

Liebermen, A.F. Compton, N.C. Van Horn, P. and Ippen, C.G. (2003). *Guidelines for the Treatment of Traumatic Bereavement in Infancy and Early Childhood.* Child Trauma Research Project, University of California San Francisco.

Madhusudan, M.D. and Karanth, K.U. (2002). Local hunting and the conservation of large mammals in India. *Ambio,* 31: 49-54.

McNay, M.E. (2002). Wolf-human interactions in Alaska and Canada: review of the case history. *Wildlife Society Bulletin,* 30(3): 831-843.

Naughton-Treves, L. (1998). Predicting patterns of crop damage by wildlife around Kibale National Park, Uganda. *Conservation Biology,* 12(1): 156-168.

_______, Treves, A. Chapman, C. and Wrangham, R. (1998). temporal patterns of crop-raiding by primates: linking food availability in croplands and adjacent forests. *Journal of Applied Ecology,* 35, 596-606.

Nyhus, P.J. Tilson, R. and Sumianto. (2000). Crop-raiding elephants and conservation implications at Way Kambas National Park, Sumatra, Indonesia. *Oryx,* 34 (4): 262-274.

Ogra, M.V. (2008). Human–wildlife conflict and gender in protected area borderlands: A case study of costs, perceptions, and vulnerabilities from Uttarakhand (Uttaranchal), India. *Geoforum,* 39(3): 1408-1422.

_______, and Badola, R. (2008). Compensating Human-wildlife conflict in Protected Area Communities: Ground Level Perspectives from Uttarakhand, India. *Human Ecology,* 36: 717-729.

Orr, D. W. (2011). *Down to the wire: Confronting climate collapse.* Washington, DC, Island Press.

Pynoos, R.S. (1994). Traumatic Stress and Developmental Psychopathology in Children and Adolescents. In R.S. Pynoos (Ed.), *Posttraumatic Stress Disorder: A Clinical Review* (pp. 65-98). Lutherville, Madison: The Sidran Press.

Rajpurohit, K.S. and Krausman, P.R. (2000). Human – sloth-bear conflicts in Madhya Pradesh, India. *Wildlife Society Bulletin, 28 (2)*: 393-399.

Saberwal, V.K., Gibbs, J.P., Chellam, R., and Johnsingh, A.J.T. (1994). Lion-human conflict in the Gir Forest, India. *Conservation Biology,* 8(2): 501-507.

Schmitz, C.L., Stinson, C.H. and James, C.D. (2011). Reclaiming community: Multidisciplinary approaches to environmental sustainability. *Critical Social Work* 11(3): 83–95. Retrieved from http://www.uwindsor.ca/criticalsocialwork/community-and-environmental-sustainability-collaborationand-interdisciplinary-education.

Schmitz, C.L., Matyók, T., Sloan, L.M. and James, C. (2012). The relationship between social work and environmental sustainability: Implications for interdisciplinary practice. *International Journal of Social Welfare,* 21, 278-286.

Sevak, P. Weir, D.R. and Willis, R.J. (2003-2004). The economic consequences of a husband's death: Evidence from the HRS and AHEAD. *Social Security Bulletin*, 65(3): 31-44.

Sitati, N.W. Walpole, M.J. and Leader-Williams, N. (2005). Factors affecting susceptibility of farms to crop raiding by African elephants: using a predictive model to mitigate conflict. *Journal of Applied Ecology*, 42: 1175-1182.

Spierenburg, M. and Wels, H. (2010). Conservative Philanthropists, Royalty and Business Elites in Nature Conservation in Southern Africa. *Antipode*, 42(3): 647-670.

Sukumar, R. (1989). *The Asian Elephant: Ecology and Management*. Cambridge, UK: Cambridge University Press.

Sukumar, R. (1994). Wildlife-human conflict in India: an ecological and social perspective. In R. Guha (ed.), *Social Ecology* (pp. 303-317), New Delhi: Oxford University Press.

Svotwa, E. Ngwenya, J. Manyanhaire, O.T. and Jiyane, J. (2007). Residents perception of the human/wildlife conflict in Kariba urban. *Journal of Sustainable Development in Africa, 9 (2):* 178-191.

Treves, A. and Naughton-Treves, L. (1999). Risk and opportunity for humans coexisting with large carnivores. *Journal of Human Evolution*, 36(3): 275-282.

Treves, A. and Karanth, K.U. (2003). Human–carnivore conflict and perspectives on carnivore management worldwide. *Conservation Biology*, 17: 1491-1499.

Walsh, P.D. Thibault, M. Mihindou, Y. Idiata, D. Mbina, C. and White, L.J.T. (2000). A statistical framework for monitoring forest elephants. *Natural Resource Modelling*, 13, 89-134.

Wheelis, M. (2002) Biological warfare at the 1346 Siege of Caffa. *Emerging Infectious Disease*, 8: 971–975.

Woodroffe, R., Thirgood, S. and Rabinowitz, A. (2005). The Impact of Human Wildlife conflict and natural systems. In R., Woodroffe, S. Thirgood, and A. Rabinowitz (Eds.), *People and wildlife: Conflict or coexistence?* (pp. 1-12) New York: Cambridge University Press.

World Conservation Union-IUCN. (2004). The Durban Action Plan. Proceedings of the fifth World Park Congress. World Conservation Union, Cambridge, UK. Retrieved from http://cmsdata.iucn.org/downloads/durbanactionen.pdf

9

Disaster Management

An Emerging Field in Social Work Education

Aruna Gajbhiye and *Ravindra Gajbhiye*

Communities in India continue to be plagued by disasters such as droughts, windstorms, heavy rains, floods, and many other types of disaster. During the last few years, India has witnessed serious effects of disasters which are unpredictable in nature. There has been an increase in the incidence of natural disasters worldwide with increasing loss of life and damage to property. The risk of disasters can also be expected to rise in the future, particularly for developing countries' populations. There are two reasons for this trend: (i) An increase in extreme natural events, primarily due to climatic change, and (ii) Increased vulnerability of populations to disasters.

India is one of the most disaster prone countries, due to its unique geographical location and cultural diversity. The country has witnessed many calamitous disasters, which required the immediate attention of the national and international institutions. Table 1 reflects India's vulnerability to disasters and highlights the necessity of disaster prevention, mitigation and management practices to build resilience and minimize the losses stemming from disasters. The Government of India initiated efforts through the enactment of the Disaster Management Act, 2005. The tenth and eleventh Five Year Plans gave emphasis on disaster management and made mandatory provisions for it. With the ushering in of the National Disaster Management Act, institutes like the National Disaster Management Authority and the National Institute of Disaster Management came into force. The Ministry of Home affairs issued, guidelines for school safety after the fire tragedy in Kubhkonam and the Ministry of Human Resource

Development initiated efforts to implement the subject of disaster management as a frontline curriculum through the CBSE. It also forwarded suggestions to the institutes of higher learning to include disaster management within their main curriculum. All these efforts aimed to inculcate a culture of safety, as also to increase the overall disaster resilience of the country. Being resilient to disasters is the basic premise for the minimization of the devastating impacts of disasters.

Table 9.1: Disasters and India

	Total Number of People Reported Killed (1992-2001)	*Total Number of People Reported Affected (1992-2001)*	*Total Number of People Reported Killed (2002-2011)*	*Total Number of People Reported Affected (2002-2011)*	*Total Number of People Reported Killed (2011)*	*Total Number of People Reported Affected (2011)*
India	76876479	479611794	43530	499366763	1304	12829814
Asia	73357	1965633824	786159	2294859811	28751	176453329
Japan	6476	1803262	21414	1452867	19975	392615

Impact of Disasters on Individuals and Communities

After every disaster, natural or man-made, the communities adjacent to the disaster site suffer the greatest loss. Loss of life, livelihood, employment opportunities, economic resources, property, agricultural land, educational loss and several other losses have to be borne by the communities. The effects of disasters are not limited to individuals and communities. These are also extended to the economy, society and polity of the country. Survivors of disasters are traumatised by impending threats, losses, injuries from incidents and experience different psychological crises. Siginificant crisis arises from the loss of property, fear of further harm, subsequent life threatening incidents, and continued threat from impending disasters. It has been established by psychologists that the combination of stress factors predisposes a person to a major life crisis (Morris, 1990). This can be compounded by the prior disaster events suffered by individuals, groups, and communities. As such, the disaster responders primarily provide food and other items to the survivors, but do not address the psychological needs of the affected. Desjarlais (1995) argues that roughly 36 per cent of people affected by disasters suffer from some form of mental distress. The Indian approach to deal with the disasters has been subject to change, and now there is a mainstreaming of prevention, preparedness and quick and effective response in the disaster management cycle. Presently, increasing disaster resilience is on the agenda of every nation and rightly so. In India the NDMA ensures the mainstreaming of disaster risk reduction in the developmental agenda of all existing and new developmental programmes and projects which are expected to incorporate disaster resilient specifications in design and construction along with planning.

Need of Disaster Management Education and Social Work Profession

To implement, inculcate and induce a culture of prevention, education is the best option. The countries of Japan, Indonesia, Canada, Germany, New Zealand, Netherlands, Somalia, Russia, US, and the UK have included disaster management education and training right from the primary level of education. India has also attempted this, but only up to the secondary level. However, it is imperative that we reexamine the way in which we impart this education. Recently the author conducted a study regarding the impact of disaster management education on students and school and found that due to the low weightage of marks, the schools ignore the objective of this curriculum and limit this course to a scrap book activity or project work only. Mock drills are also not conducted by most schools due to ignorance regarding hazards and risks. In higher education, very few disciplines of studies have included disaster management in their course curriculum. Engineering, Medicine, Law, Social Work, Architecture, Nursing, Management, Anthropology and all Science and Humanities courses need to integrate disaster management with their specialized focus and subject oriented approaches. In all these disciplines, the component of disaster management should be mandatory.

The social work profession has for long been involved with disaster relief, both through the profession's roots in wartime relief, and its concern with the physical, social and psychological environment of individuals, groups, communities and populations. Social work as a profession is committed to providing relief and support to vulnerable populations within many contexts.

Within the disaster arena, social workers can assume multiple roles through which they might offer multi-level interventions to address the unmet needs of such groups. Increased access to disaster services can be facilitated through a number of approaches. For example, in order to increase the capacity to provide effective disaster services, social workers can offer culturally relevant training of volunteers (Zakour & Harrell, 2003). Increasingly, social workers are getting involved in international relief services through organisations such as the Red Cross, Oxfam India, SEEDS, UNICEF and UNDP. All the above mentioned organisations have initiated school disaster management programmes through their team of experts and social workers are beginning to play an important role in this team.

Disaster management has evolved as a multidimensional and interdisciplinary science that includes the fields of public health administration, geography, engineering, computer science, psychology and social work. Effective disaster management includes – hazard identification, vulnerability assessment, risk analysis, response plan, training, rescue, relief and rehabilitation. The focus of social work in disaster management is also at all the levels of intervention, that is, individual, family, community and society. The responsibility of disaster management lies both with the government and civil society and social workers are engaged in both these arenas.

They are involved in providing social services and cooperate with the government to help the victims of disasters. They can have their own specific roles in each stage of the disaster management cycle. From preparedness plans to recovery plans, social workers can take active part in helping the diverse stakeholders to shoulder their responsibilities in all stages, from preparedness to rehabilitation.

The study conducted by Wenger (1978) found that social workers have significant roles and functions in both rescue and recovery stages, especially in linking the victims' needs and resources. Social workers also have unique disaster mandates to support vulnerable groups such as people with disabilities, poor, women, children and the elderly. They can assist the agencies and organisations to organise effective relief and response interventions; provide therapeutic support to survivors, and help organise need based recovery programmes for the community. Social workers can also contribute by evolving context specific approaches by working with the many professionals and organisations that are active in disaster management services. The coordination and case management skills of social work can be suitably applied to disaster aid procedures.

Shahar (1993) stated that the theories and practices that social workers apply in disaster situations, such as crisis theory, needs assessment, resources mobilisation, networking trauma counselling and others are exactly those that they apply during their work in the other fields of their employment. Moreover, social workers, by virtue of their training have the ability to work under critical conditions during emergencies. They possess the ability for creative thinking, innovative work, and productive self investment. They are also equipped to address and intervene in the social and psychological issues that can block the individual's normal functioning. Social work offers a set of approaches, methods, tools, techniques, skills and strategies to deal with crisis and emergency situations. Social work intervention emphasizes the active, purposeful and planned participation of both the client and social worker in all the stages of crises intervention. Social worker can also play a very significant role as a liason between authorities, communities, and government and non-government organisations and local communities.

Disaster Management in Social Work Education

UGC curriculum development report suggested including disaster management in social work. Tata Institute of Social Sciences initiated and started two years postgraduate programme in Disaster Management, Devi Ahilya Vishvavidyalaya, Indore is offering an MBA in Disaster Management. Many Social Work Colleges and Departments in the various universities have included disaster management in their graduate and postgraduate curricula.

Disaster Management education requires some specific skills based inputs which are not visible in these courses. If social workers feel that they must be identified as specialized professionals in this area, it is highly required that we revise our curriculum through learning exercises and past experiences of our involvement in the disaster management field. Skill based training is required to be inculcated through Skill Laboratories, Rural Camps, Social Work Practicum, Exposure Visits with theoretical inputs in class room lectures. Disaster Management education can bridge the gap in terms of qualified manpower that can mobilize vulnerable group and communities for disaster preparedness, mitigation and management. Working for disaster prevention, risk reduction as also recovery and rehabilitation work in the post disaster context are indeed upcoming areas of engagement for social work professionals.

References

Banerjee, M., and Gillespie, D.F. (1994). Linking Disaster Preparedness and Organisational Response Effectiveness. *Journal of Community Practice, 1*(3), 129-142.

Barton, H.A. (1969). *Communities in Disaster: A Sociological Analysis of Collective Stress Situations.* Garden City, NY: Doubleday.

Bell, L. (1995). Traumatic Event Debriefing: Service Delivery Designs and the Role of Social Work. *Social Work, 40*(1), 36-43.

Bell, L., Sang, Y., Park, J., and Shin, G. (2000). The Second Injury/Social Wound: The Villagers' Experience of the Crash of South Korea's Asiana Flight 733. *Tulane Studies in Social Welfare, 21/22,* 311-321.

Benight, C.C. (2004). Collective efficacy following a series of natural disasters. *Anxiety, Stress, and Coping,* 17(4), 401-420.

Chen, A., Airriess, C., Li, W., and Leong, K.J. (2007). Economic vulnerability, discrimination, and Hurricane Katrina: Health among black Katrina survivors in Eastern New Orleans. *Journal of the American Psychiatric Nurses Association, 13*(5), 257-266.

Cherry, L., and Mary E.C. (1996). Research as Social Action in the Aftermath of Hurricane Andrew. *Journal of Social Service Research,* 22(1/2), 71-87.

Cosgrove, J.G. (2000). Social Workers in Disaster Mental Health Services: The American Red Cross. *Tulane Studies in Social Welfare, 21/22,* 117-128.

Davidson, J.R.T. (2006). After the tsunami: Mental health challenges to the community for today and tomorrow. *Journal of Clinical Psychiatry, 67*(Suppl. 2), 3-8.

Dodds, S., and Nuehring, E. (1996). A Primer for Social Work Research on Disaster. *Journal of Social Service Research, 22,* 27-56.

Drabek, E., and McEntire, D. (2002). Emergent Phenomena and Multiorganisational Coordination in Disasters: Lessons from the Research Literature. *International Journal of Mass Emergencies and Disasters, 20*(2), 197-224.

Drabek, E. (1970). Methodology of Studying Disaster. *American Behavioral Scientist, 13*(3), 331-343.

Drumm, D., Sharon, W., and Shelly, P. (2003). *Social Work Interventions in Refugee Camps: An Ecosystems Approach. Journal of Social Service Research, 30*(2), 67-92.

Fairbank, J.A., Friedman, M.J., Green, B.L., and Solomon, S.D. (2003).

Intervention options for societies, communities, families, and individuals. In B.L. Green, M.J. Friedman, J. de Jong, S, Solomon, T. Keane and J.A. Fairbank *et al.* (Eds.), *Trauma Interventions in War and Peace* (57-72), New York: Kluwer Academic/Plenum Publishers.

Gillespie, F. (1991). Coordinating Community Resources. In T.E. Drabek and G.J. Hoetmer (eds.), *Emergency Management: Principles and Practice for Local Government* (55-78). Washington, DC: International City Management Association.

Gillespie, F., Richard, A., Colignon, Banerjee., Susan, A., and Rogge, M. (1993). *Partnerships for Community Preparedness*. Boulder, CO: University of Colorado, Institute of Behavioral Science.

Gilligan, C., Spencer, R., Weinberg, M.K., and Bertsch, T., (2003). On the listening guide: A voice-centered relational method. In M. Paul, J.E. Rhodes, and L. Yardley (Eds.), *Qualitative research in psychology: Expanding perspectives in methodology and design* (pp. 157-172). Washington, DC: American Psychological Association.

Johnson, K.W., Susan, A., and David, C. (2002). An Evaluation Strategy for Improving Disaster Victim Services: Blueprint for Change. *International Journal of Mass Emergencies and Disasters, 20*(1), 69-100.

Kreuger, L., and John Stretch. (2003). *Identifying and Helping Long Term Child and Adolescent Disaster Victims: Model and Method."* Retrieved from: Journal of Social Service Research *30*(2): 93-108.

Liu, Li-Wen., Gillespie, D.F., and Murty, S.A. (2000). Service Coordination as Intergovernmental Strategies in Service Delivery. *Tulane Studies in Social Welfare, 21/22*, 85-103.

Miller, J. (2003). Critical Incident Debriefing and Social Work: Expanding the Frame. *Journal of Social Service Research, 30*(2), 7-25.

Minahan, A., and Pincus, A. (1977). Conceptual Framework for Social Work Practice. *Social Work, 22*(5), 347-352.

Mitchell, J.T. (1983). When Disaster Strikes: The Critical Incident Stress Debriefing Process. *Journal of Emergency Medical Services, 8*(1), 36-39.

Padgett, K., (2002). *"Social Work Research on Disasters in the Aftermath of the September 11 Tragedy: Reflections from New York City."* Retrieved from: Social Work Research 26(3): 185-192.

Quarantelli, E.L. (1998). *What is a Disaster? Perspectives on the Question*. New York: Routledge.

Rogge, M.E. (2003). The Future is Now: Social Work, Disaster Management, and Traumatic Stress in the 21st Century. *Journal of Social Service Research, 30*(2), 1-6.

Soliman, H.H., and Mary E.R. (2002). Ethical Considerations in Disaster Services: A Social Work Perspective. *Electronic Journal of Social Work, 1*(1), 1-23.

Soliman, H., and Paula T. (2003). Preface. *Journal of Social Service Research,* 30(2), xiii-xv.

Streeter, L. (1991). Disasters and Development: Disaster Preparedness and Mitigation as an Essential Component of Development Planning. *Social Development Issues. 13*(3), 100-110.

Streeter, L. (1992). Redundancy in Organizational Systems. *Social Service Review, 66*(1), 97-111.

Zakour, M.J. (1996). Disaster research in social work. *Journal of Social Service Research. 22*(1/2), 7-25.

_______, and Harrell, E.B. (2003). Access to disaster services: Social work interventions for vulnerable populations. *Journal of Social Service Research, 30*(2), 27-54.

_______, (1994). Measuring Career-Development Volunteerism: Guttman Scale Analysis Using Red Cross Volunteers. *Journal of Social Service Research, 19*(3/4), 103-120.

_______, (1996). Disaster Research in Social Work. *Journal of Social Service Research 22*(1/2): 7-25.

_______, and Evelyn, B.H. (2003). Access to Disaster Services: Social Work Interventions for Vulnerable Populations. *Journal of Social Service Research. 30*(2), 27-54.

_______, David, F., Michael, W., and Calvin, L. (1991). Volunteer Organizations in Disasters. *The Journal of Volunteer Administration. 9*(2), 18-28.

10

Exploring the Climate Change Discourse in India through the Lens of Social Work Practice

Vinay Kumar and *Digvijoy Phukan*

Change is the rule of nature, every species of flora and fauna on the earth follows this thumb rule at its own pace, but we humans have lost the harmony with nature in our quest of self-gratification and changing lifestyle patterns through exploiting the nature as per our convenience at a exponentially rapid pace. Earth, the only planet existing in our known part of universe, to sustain life is unable to balance with these rapid changes today and the repercussions of these are reflected in various forms of frequent disasters like earthquakes, floods, cyclones, heat storms, droughts etc., with significant loss of lives and property all over the planet. Several breed of flora and fauna have become extinct and lot many are on the verge of extinction. One such visible event due to human activities which has the ability of upsetting natural cycles and popping up frequently in global discourse is climate change. This has gained popularity due to its harsh consequences for the present and the future generations to come.

Climate Change has become a universal reality and will have a long term effect on the human civilization. It has already started showing its impact on land, rivers, oceans and people across cultures and national boundaries. Climate is basically the average weather for a particular region with time period taken over 30 years or more, while weather denotes the familiar happenings of atmosphere (rain, winds, humidity, snow, etc.) at a place over a short time period. The difference between weather and climate is a measure of time (Shepherd, Shindell, and O'Carroll, 2005). Earth's climate is changing contrary to its natural climatic cycle in ways that are affecting our weather, oceans, snow, ice, ecosystems, and society. Environmental causes alone cannot explain all of these changes. Man made actions are contributing to climate change, mainly by discharging billions of tons of carbon dioxide (CO_2) and other heat-absorbing gases, which are greenhouse gases (GHGs), into the atmosphere every year (NRC, 2010). More and more frequent extreme weather events, record of increasing annual global average temperatures, and unruly recurrent changes all provide substantial growing proof of human induced climate change. What is notable is the fact that since the commencement of the industrial age, while global average surface temperature has fluctuated over the initial 100 years or so, the last five or six decades have clearly been marked by a clear trend of rising temperatures. This is evidently the result of human actions and is based on highly reliable models that are being used currently to stimulate past actions with the inclusion of both natural as well as anthropogenic forcings (IPCC, 2007).

Globally, the most accepted definition of Climate Change is of the United Nations Framework Convention on Climate Change (UNFCCC, 1992) which defines *Climate Change* as a change of climate which is attributed directly or indirectly to human activity that alters the composition of the global atmosphere and which is in addition to the natural climate variability observed over comparable time periods. *Climate Change* within the Intergovernmental Panel on Climate Change (IPCC)[1] usage refers to a change in the state of the climate that can be identified (e.g. using statistical tests) by changes in the mean and/or the variability of its properties, and that persists for an extended period, typically decades or longer. It refers to any change in climate over time, whether due to natural variability or as a result of human activity.

In the twenty first century, Climate Change has emerged at the helm of global affairs of the human world and poses a complex developmental challenge. Even, scientific evidence has established that the rapid warming has been the product of rampant exploitation of nature through human activities in the past five decades (IPCC, 2001). The world metrological department (WMO, 2013) in its report declared the decade (2001-2010) as "a decade of climate extremes", being the warmest decade for both land and ocean temperatures. It reported a loss of Artic sea ice, and a decline in the Greenland and Antarctic ice sheets. The global average sea level over the decade was 20 cm higher than that in 1880. Floods were the most frequent climate extreme with big floods in eastern Europe, India, Africa, Asia and Australia creating huge loss of life and economy. At the same time, many countries in East Africa and the Amazon basin, and Australia were visited by severe droughts. The decade recorded an astounding increase in deaths from the heat waves from less than 6000 in 1991-2000 to 136000 in 2001-2010. In India, most recently in the year 2013, the state of Uttarakhand witnessed exceptional damage and destruction of life and property, where by flashfloods and landslides killed more than 5000 people and several persons were reported missing. The just released summary report for policy makers (IPCC, 2013) emphasises that "warming of climate is irrevocable". It confirms that both ocean and land temperatures have witnessed rise and that the anthropogenic contribution is also irrevocable. It demands intensive action without a day of delay from nations across the world.

Historical Milestones on Issue of Climate Change

The contemporary civilization officially woke up to the challenge of Climate Change as an issue of concern when in 1972 the UN Conference on Environment was held in Stockholm. Today, Climate Change has become a dominant subject of international discourse; the deliberations of the international community have been marked by political deadlocks, scientific uncertainties, lack of trust, inadequate leadership, political regrouping, influence of business lobbies and geo political considerations. Though, Stockholm Conference, 1972, is considered to be the first international endeavor on environment, which politically awakened the world towards preservation and enhancement of the Human Environment, but, if we track history, the first major conference which came up in context to climate change was the World Climate Conference (WCC) of 1979, held in Geneva. The time line below, detailing the international response to climate change provides a contextual entry point to the essential background on climate change (UNFCCC, 2013).

1988: On the recommendation of World Climate Conference, the Intergovernmental Panel on Climate Change is set up.

1990: IPCC's first assessment report released. IPCC and second World Climate Conference calls for a global treaty on Climate Change. United Nations General Assembly negotiations on a framework convention begin.

1991: First meeting of the Intergovernmental Negotiating Committee (INC) takes place.

1992: The INC adopts United Nations Framework Convention on Climate Change (UNFCCC), text. At the Earth Summit in Rio, the UNFCCC is opened for signature.

1994: UNFCCC enters into force.

1995: The first Conference of the Parties (COP1) takes place in Berlin, Germany

1996: The UNFCCC Secretariat is set up to support action under the Convention.

1997: Kyoto Protocol is formally adopted in December at COP3, Kyoto, Japan.

2001: Release of IPCC's Third Assessment Report. Bonn Agreements adopted, based on the Buenos Aires Plan of Action of 1998. Marrakesh Accords adopted at COP7, detailing rules for implementation of Kyoto Protocol, setting up new funding and planning instruments for adaptation, and establishing a technology transfer framework.

2005: The Kyoto Protocol enters into force. The first Meeting of the Parties to the Kyoto Protocol (MOP 1) takes place in Montreal. In accordance with Kyoto Protocol requirements, parties launched negotiations on the next phase of the KP under the Ad-Hoc Working Group on Further Commitments for Annex I Parties under the Kyoto Protocol (AWG-KP). Later in 2006, was named the Nairobi Work Programme on Adaptation.

2007: IPCC's Fourth Assessment Report (AR4) released. Climate science entered into popular consciousness. At COP13, parties agreed on the Bali Road Map, which charted the way towards a post-2012 outcome in two work streams: the AWG-KP, and another under the Convention, known as the Ad-Hoc Working Group on Long-Term Cooperative Action under the Convention.

2009: Copenhagen Accord drafted at COP15 in Copenhagen. Countries later submitted emissions reduction pledges or mitigation action pledges, all non-binding.

2010: Cancun Agreement drafted and largely accepted by the COP, at COP16.

2011: The Durban Platform for Enhanced Action drafted and accepted by the COP, at COP17.

2012: The Doha Amendment to the Kyoto Protocol is adopted by the CMP at CMP8.

2013: Key decisions adopted at COP19/CMP9 include decisions on further advancing the Durban Platform, the Green Climate Fund and Long-Term Finance, the Warsaw Framework for REDD Plus and the Warsaw International Mechanism for Loss and Damage.

Today, the three key problems of sustainable development are water; climate change and energy; and trade for sustainable development. All these need to be kept on priority while undertaking any discourse on the subject. Even the UNFCCC and Kyoto Protocol explicitly advocate integrating sustainable development and Climate Change goals.

Climate Change and India

India's journey on the path of sustainable development and within it, the country's concern for environment has so far been marked, both by reasons for celebration and introspection. The Indian Constitution provided for special provisions by the 42nd Constitutional Amendment Act of 1976, ***Article 48A***[2] under the Directive Principles of State Policy (DPSP) to highlight the duty of the Governments, both at Central and State level, and ***Article 51A(g)***[3] under the Fundamental Duties for every citizen of India, an obligation for the protection of the environment. The Green Revolution and White Revolution of the 1970's paved the way towards food sustainability. The 1980's and early 1990's marked the beginning of economic reforms which acted as a catalyst for India's faster growth rates and coincidentally, at the same time, the world started talking about Climate Change on a serious note.

The State of the Environment Report (MoEF, 2009), identified five key challenges faced by India. These were: climate change, food security, water security, energy security, and rapid urbanization. Climate Change is impacting the natural ecosystems and is expected to have substantial adverse effects in India, mainly on agriculture (on which around 58 per cent of the population directly depends for livelihood) water storage in the Himalayan glaciers (which are the source of major perennial rivers), ground water recharge, sea level rise, and threats to the long coastline and habitations.

Precisely at a time when India is confronted with development imperatives[4], it is severely impacted by Climate Change. Like other developing countries, several sections of the Indian populace will not be able to buffer themselves from impacts of global warming. With its economy dependent on natural resources and climate-sensitive sectors such as agriculture, water and forestry, India may face a major threat and require serious adaptive capacity to combat Climate Change. As a developing country, India can little afford the risks and economic backlashes that industrialized nations can. With 27.5 per cent of the population still below the poverty line, reducing vulnerability to the impacts of Climate Change is essential. In this regard, the India's Initial National Communications (NATCOM)[5] very well articulated its approach to Climate Change stating that, 'since the goals of sustainable development are favourable to the issue of Climate Change, the achievement of these goals would accrue a double dividend in terms of added Climate Change benefits. The cascading effects of sustainable development would reduce emissions and moderate the adverse impacts of Climate Change, and thereby alleviate the resulting loss in welfare.'

Potential Impacts of Climate Change in India

The Intergovernmental Panel on Climate Change (IPCC) in its 4th assessment report projects that the global mean temperature may increase between 1.4 and 5.8 degree Celsius by 2100. This unprecedented increase is expected to have severe impacts on the global hydrological system, ecosystems, sea level, crop production and related processes. The impact would be particularly severe in the tropical areas, which mainly consists of developing countries, including India (Sathaye, Shukla, and Ravindrnath, 2006). Considerable researches have been undertaken in India on climate change related impact assessment and indicate the vulnerability of Indian populations to climate change. Most recently in the Second National Communications (NATCOM) submitted by India to the UNFCCC, it is projected that the annual mean surface air temperature rise, by the end of the century ranges from 3.5 degree Celsius to 4.3 degree Celsius whereas the sea level along the Indian coast has been rising at the rate of about 1.3 mm/year on an average (MoEF, 2012).

With changes in key climate variables, namely temperature, precipitation and humidity, crucial sectors like agriculture and rural development are likely to be affected in a major way. Impacts are already being seen in the unprecedented heat waves, cyclones, floods, salinisation of the coastline and effects on agriculture, fisheries and health[6] which further may lead to a major threat of food insecurity. India is home to a third of the world's poor, and

Climate Change will hit this section of society the hardest. Set to be the most populous nation in the world by 2045, the economic, social and ecological price of Climate Change will be massive.

The future impacts of Climate Change, identified by the Government of India's National Communications (NATCOM) include decreased snow cover, affecting snow-fed and glacial systems such as the Ganges and Brahmaputra. Seventy per cent of the summer flow of the Ganges comes from melt water. An erratic monsoon with serious effects on rain-fed agriculture, peninsular rivers, water and power supply, drop in wheat production by 4-5 million tones, with even a 1°C rise in temperature, rising sea levels causing displacement along one of the most densely populated coastlines in the world, threatened freshwater sources and mangrove ecosystems, increased frequency and intensity of floods, increased vulnerability of people in coastal, arid and semi-arid zones of the country are the looming threats staring India in the face. Studies indicate that over 50 per cent of India's forests are likely to experience shift in forest types, adversely impacting associated biodiversity, regional climate dynamics as well as livelihoods based on forest products.

India currently has one of the fastest growing economies in the world. With a government target of 8 per cent GDP to achieve developmental priorities[7], a share of one sixth of the global population, and changing consumption patterns, India's emissions are set to increase dramatically. Growing at an almost breakneck pace, and guzzling coal, gas and oil in large quantities[8] , India today is the third largest emitter of greenhouse gases worldwide making five per cent of the total global emission. Although our per-capita emissions are among the lowest in the world, India's growth rates imply that the past is no predictor of the future. The most recent IPCC report suggests that India will experience the greatest increase in energy and greenhouse gas emissions in the world if it sustains a high annual economic growth rate (IPCC, 2007).

The government recognises that 'global warming will affect India seriously' but maintains that the 'most important adaptation measure to Climate Change is development itself'. This has ensured that India's position at the UNFCC has remained 'common but differentiated responsibility'. Under the UNFCCC agreement, India has not taken any binding emission reduction targets. In spite of this guarded stand, India has 'declared' that even as it pursues its social and development objectives, it will not allow its per capita emissions to exceed those of developed countries. The government of India needs to capitalize on India's position as a developing giant, and take the lead and engage with governments of the world and the private sector for a low-carbon future. India requires strong policy initiatives by government on the issue of Climate change at international, regional as well as national levels on the issues of Green House Gases (GHGs) Emissions, Energy, Clean Development Mechanisms, Climate Change Mitigation and Adaptation Strategies and Climate Finance (Sathaye, Shukla, and Ravindrnath, 2006).

Convergence of Perceptions of Law Makers and People

Based on a review of two studies (Kumar, 2012) and (Yale Project on Climate Change Communication, 2012) on perceptions of lawmakers and Indian people, the general picture which emerged is mentioned below:

- More than 50 per cent lawmakers are aware about Climate Change while less than 25 per cent people are aware of it. Thus, there is a strong need to make people aware about the issue of climate change.
- There is a high level of dissatisfaction in both the lawmakers and people regarding the government's role at the national level. In fact the lawmakers want a separate ministry to manage climate change.
- There is a strong need to have climate change laws, stringent policies and NAPCC implementation.
- In general, there was a level of satisfaction on India's stand at International platforms like UNFCCC.
- Both expressed that the government is not spending much on climate change mitigation and adaptation, which will affect the future generations.
- There is a strong need to generate momentum in public perceptions and priorities on the various aspects of climate change as they confront the state.

In democratic societies, policy changes can only come about if the public desires them. Governments sit up and take notice of what the public demands only when such a manifestation is widespread and strong (Pachauri in Yale Project on Climate Change Communication, 2012).

Adaptation to Climate Change

Vulnerability to climate change is generally understood to be a function of a range of biophysical and socio economic factors. The most recent report of the Intergovernmental Panel on Climate Change (IPCC, 2007) provides a useful typology suggesting that vulnerability may be characterized as a function of three components: adaptive capacity, sensitivity, and exposure. Adaptive capacity describes the ability of a system to adjust to actual or expected climate stresses, or to cope with the consequences. It is considered "a function of wealth, technology, education, information, skills, infrastructure, access to resources, and stability and management capabilities" (McCarthy, J., Canziani, O.S., Leary, N., Dokken, D., and White, K.L., 2001). Sensitivity refers to the degree to which a system will respond to a change in climate, either positively or negatively. Exposure relates to the degree of climate stress upon a particular unit of analysis; it may be represented as either long-term change in climate conditions, or by changes in climate variability, including the magnitude and frequency of extreme events.

Adger (2003) is of the view that adaptation processes that are built from the bottom up and are based on social capital can alter the perceptions of climate change from a global to a local problem. When actors perceive adaptation to and the risk of climate change as being within their powers to alter, they will be more likely to make the connection to the causes of climate change, thereby enhancing their mitigative, as well as adaptive capacity. Special emphasis is needed to develop social capital at individual or group level as a tool for a better adaptation to climate change. Rural India has strong social capital and it can be channelized towards better utilization of resources and evolving people centric policy for adaptation to climate change in various situations and based on regional demand.

Adaptation decisions are also shaped by the policy environment in which decision-makers operate, i.e. social safety nets, trade policies, market price support and stockholding, land tenure and water rights, and the ability of stakeholders to participate in political processes (Adger, 2010). Societies can respond to climate change both by reducing the rate and magnitude of change by reducing GHG emissions (mitigation), and by adapting to its impacts.

Many impacts can be avoided, reduced or delayed by mitigation, but adaptation will be necessary to address impacts resulting from the warming which is already unavoidable due to past emissions. Some of the national policies and institutions set up to combat climate impacts are mentioned in the following section.

National Policies and Institutions

The planning process, while targeting an accelerated economic growth, needs to be guided by the principle of sustainable development with a commitment to a cleaner and greener environment. The past few years have witnessed the introduction of landmark environmental measures in India that have targeted conservation of rivers, improvement of urban air, improved forestation and a major increase in the installed capacity of renewable energy technologies. These and similar measures, affirmed by democratic and legislative processes, have been implemented by committing additional resources, as well as by realigning new investments. Few important policies and institutions are mentioned here,

The National Forest Policy, 1988, envisages active measures for expanding carbon sinks through increase in forest and tree cover to 25 per cent by 2007 and 33 per cent by 2012.

The National Environment policy of 2006 provides for several measures and policy initiatives to create awareness about Climate Change and help capacity building for taking adaptation measures. Several major programmes addressing climate variability concern have been undertaken. These include cyclone warning and protection, costal protection, floods and drought control and relief, major and minor irrigation projects, control of malaria, food security measures, research on drought resistant crops and several others. Several other climate friendly measures that have a direct bearing on mitigation of climate change have been taken. Some such measures are those aimed at improving energy efficiency and conservation measures (including setting up of Bureau of Energy Efficiency), power sector reforms, promoting hydro and renewable energy, reduction of gas flaring, and environmental quality management.

National Action Plan on Climate Change (NAPCC)

In 2008, the Prime Minister unveiled a policy document on climate change: *"The National Action Plan on Climate Change"* (NAPCC), which encompasses a range of measures through its eight missions, they have been specifically outlined to simultaneously advance

India's development and climate change related objectives of adaptation and GHG mitigation.

National Solar Mission: The NAPCC aims to promote the development and use of solar energy for power generation and other uses, with the ultimate objective of making solar energy competitive with fossil-based energy options. It also includes the establishment of a solar research centre, increased international collaboration on technology development, strengthening of domestic manufacturing capacity, and increased government funding and international support.

National Mission for Enhanced Energy Efficiency: The NAPCC recommends mandating specific energy consumption decreases in large energy-consuming industries, with a system for companies to trade energy-saving certificates, financing for public-private partnerships to reduce energy consumption through demand side management programmes in the municipal, buildings, and agricultural sectors, and energy incentives, including reduced taxes on energy-efficient appliances.

National Mission on Sustainable Habitat: The NAPCC also aims at promoting energy efficiency as a core component of urban planning by extending the existing Energy Conservation Building Code, strengthening the enforcement of automotive fuel economy standards, and using pricing measures to encourage the purchase of efficient vehicles and incentives for the use of public transportation. The NAPCC also emphasizes on waste management and recycling.

National Mission on Strategic Knowledge for Climate Change: To gain a better understanding of climate science, impacts, and challenges, the plan envisions a new Climate Science Research Fund, improved climate modeling, and increased international collaboration. It also encourages private sector initiatives to develop adaptation and mitigation technologies through venture capital funds.

Green India Mission: The NAPCC also aims at afforestation of 6 million hectares of degraded forest lands and expanding forest cover from 23 to 33 per cent of India's territory.

National Water Mission: The NAPCC sets a goal of a 20 per cent improvement in water use efficiency through pricing and other measures to deal with water scarcity as a result of climate change.

National Mission for Sustaining the Himalayan Ecosystem: This particular mission sets the goal to prevent melting of the

Himalayan glaciers and to protect biodiversity in the Himalayan region.

National Mission for Sustainable Agriculture: The NAPCC aims to support climate adaptation in agriculture through the development of climate-resilient crops, expansion of weather insurance mechanisms, and agricultural practices.

India's Five Year Plans

India has announced that it will endeavour to reduce emission intensity of its GDP by 20 to 25 per cent by 2020 in comparison to the 2005 level without reckoning emission from the agriculture sector. This will be achieved through actions in specific sector with necessary provision of financial and technological resources including the domestic and international support. India has a large segment of poor population that is vulnerable to climate change. Ensuring the sustainability of their livelihoods and protecting them for additional burden of climate change is of primary concern to India. India spends almost 2 per cent of its GDP on measures that facilitate adaptation to climate change. In fact, the Planning Commission of India understands climate change as a major area of environmental intervention and had approved a new umbrella scheme *"Climate Change Action Programme"* for inclusion in the 12th Five Year Plan, launched from the year 2012-13.[9]

Prime Minister's Council

It was set up in 2007 and consists of representatives from the government, industry, civil society, NGOs, media and eminent persons under the chairmanship of the Prime Minister to evolve a coordinated response to issue relating to climate change at the national level and provide oversight for formulation of action plans in the area of assessment.

Recently in January 2013, the Government has also constituted an Executive Committee on Climate Change, under the chairmanship of Principal Secretary to Prime Minister to assist the Prime Minister's Council on Climate Change in evolving a coordinated response to issues relating to climate change at the national level, and to monitor the implementation of the eight National Missions and other initiatives under the NAPCC.

National Clean Development Mechanism Authority

This was setup in the year 2003 for the purpose of protecting and improving the strategy of environment. The Authority registers projects for assessment and evaluation as per the guidelines of the UNFCCC. India has the highest number of projects registered for any country. If all projects of India are registered, this will offset almost 10 per cent of India's total emissions per year by 2012.

Expert Group on Low Carbon Strategy for Inclusive Growth

This has been setup with representation from industries, leading think tanks, research institutions, civil society and government. The group has been given the mandate to develop a road map for India for low carbon development. The group's recommendation will become a central part of India's plans.

National Mission for Enhanced Energy Efficiency

This includes several new initiatives — the most important being the Perform, Achieves and Trade (PAT) mechanism, which will cover facilities that account for more than 50 per cent of the fossil fuel used in India, and help reduce CO_2 emission by 25 million tonnes per year by 2014-15. About 700 of the most energy intensive industrial units and power stations in India would be mandated to reduce their energy consumption by a specified percentage. Energy Efficiency rating has been mandatory for four key appliances — refrigerators, air conditioners, tube lights and transformers from 7 January 2010.

Jawaharlal Nehru National Solar Mission

The Mission was launched recently as an ambitious mission to make India a global leader in solar energy. The national solar mission aims to generate 20,000 MW of solar power by 2022. The mission also has other targets: 2000 MW of off-grid solar plants, and 20 million sq. metres of solar collector to be installed. In addition, 20 million solar lighting systems will be created and distributed in rural areas, saving about one billion litres of kerosene every year.

Green India Mission

This has been launched with an overreaching target to double the area to be taken up for aforestation/eco-restoration in India in next 10 years, taking the total area to be afforested or eco-restored to 20 million ha.

India Network for Climate Change Assessment (INCCA)

The Network has been established to undertake a major "4 × 4" assessment of the impact of climate change on four sectors: water resources, agriculture, forest and human health – in four critical regions of India—the Himalayan region, North East, Western Ghats and the Coastal India.

National Clean Energy Fund

A fund with potential of generating about Rs. 3,000 crores of revenue annually has been setup with effect from July 2010 with levy of a cess of Rs. 50 per tonne on production of domestic and imported coal. The fund will be used for supporting initiatives for clean energy and environmental management.

National Green Tribunal

National Green Tribunal Act was passed in the Parliament in 2010. The Tribunal shall not be bound by the procedure laid down under the Code of Civil Procedure, 1908, but shall be guided by principles of natural justice. New Delhi is the Principal Place of sitting of the Tribunal and Bhopal, Pune, Kolkata and Chennai shall be the other four places of sitting of the Tribunal. After India's move with Carbon credits, such tribunal will play a vital role in ensuring the control of emissions and maintaining the desired levels. This is the first body of its kind that is required by its parent statute to apply the "polluter pays" principle and the principle of sustainable development.

Avenues for Social Work Profession

Every event brings along with it opportunities and threats, and this has also been the case with climate change. It is imperative that the opportunities be harnessed and the country prepares itself for resilience. The social work profession can play significant role in bridging the existing gaps and building bridges towards a climate resilient India.

Some major themes and areas of focus and engagement with regard to climate change include: Climate Financing and Budgeting, Advocacy, Policy Planning and Implementation, Disaster Mitigation and Management, Sustainable Livelihoods, Natural Resource Management and Community Development. All of the above figure in the realm of work of social work professionals. The profession, with its special mandate on social justice and human rights needs to be drawn in meaningful interventions to counter climate change and its impact on people, especially those who belong to the vulnerable and marginalized constituencies, for it is them who are potentially the most threatened.

The most prominent areas of intervention for professional social workers are highlighted in the following section.

Awareness Generation

- Information Education and Communication through various media;
- Climate Change Education in schools, colleges, and other educational institutions.

Advocacy

- Lobbying among civil society organisations, and policy makers;
- Linking people with the policy makers through consultations; and
- Climate Justice and Human rights.

Research and Documentation

- Policy research and policy planning;
- Preparing knowledge/study modules for knowledge dissemination;
- Develop and document traditional adaptation methodologies among communities; and
- Linking scientific models with the human systems in order to provide better understanding of cause-effect-cause patterns.

Monitoring and Evaluation

- Impact and Risk Assessment;
- Vulnerability mapping of communities; and
- Social Cost Benefit Evaluation of mitigation options in context to sustainable development.

Training and Capacity Building

- Linking people with policy benefits (Insurance schemes, micro finance, etc.);
- Promoting adoption of climate friendly technologies among people;
- Alternative livelihood development support to communities;
- Efficient utilization of available knowledge towards resilient practices; and
- Develop social capital at local and national levels.

Conclusion

Climate change possesses great developmental challenges to humanity and especially to developing and island countries which are most vulnerable to it. Certainly, larger changes in global climate have taken place in the past, but these have occurred over much longer time periods. The danger facing the global society today is that anthropogenic global warming, which is happening very fast is preventing humans, and other species, to adapt to its damaging impacts. If climate model projections prove to be even moderately accurate, global temperatures by the end of the next century will be higher than at any time during the last 120,000 years. With such unprecedented climate change, impacts to all parts of the world are likely to be extensive, and these will have critical implications on food production, water supply, biodiversity and livelihoods. Failure to accept some strong legally binding agreements on global greenhouse gas emission reduction strategy by the international political community will merely extend the time frame of anthropogenic global warming and climate change that the future generations will have to bear and witness.

Finally, we need to acknowledge that climate change is a global phenomenon that we all have to address in a spirit of cooperation and taking into account the historical responsibilities and capabilities of countries. Only this will to the future generations the same nurturing earth that we bequeath received from our forefathers.

Notes

1. The role of IPCC (established in 1988) is to assess the scientific, technical and socio-economic information relevant for the understanding of the risk of human-induced Climate Change. The IPCC's first assessment report (1990) played an important role in establishing the UNFCCC. The Fourth Assessment Report (AR4) was published in 2007.
2. "The state shall endeavor to protect and improve the environment and to safeguard the forests and wild life of the country."
3. "To protect and improve the natural environment including forests, lakes, rivers and wild life, and to have compassion for living creatures".
4. Climate Change and India: Impacts, Policy Responses and a Framework for EU-India Cooperation. 2008. Policy Department Economic and Scientific Policy, European Parliament.
5. India's initial National communications to the UNFCCC, MoEF, New Delhi, 2004.
6. Malini Mehra, India Starts to take on Climate Change.
7. Sharma S., Bhattacharya S. and A. Garg. Greenhouse gas emissions from India: A perspective. *Current Science*, Vol. 90, No. 3, pp. 326-333.
8. Imagining India: Nandan Nilekani.
9. MoEF, Govt. of India, Annual Report 2011-12, Chapter: Sustainable Development and Climate Change, p. 288.

References

Adger W.N. (2003). *Social Capital, Collective Action, and Adaptation to Climate Change.* Economic Geography, Vol. 79, No. 4, pp. 387-404

______, (2010). "*Climate Change, Human Well-Being and Insecurity.*" *New Political Economy* 15 (2): 2-16.

IPCC (2001). *Climate Change: Synthesis Report*, Geneva, Switzerland: IPCC.

______, *Climate Change*, Geneva, Switzerland: IPCC.

______, (2013). *Climate Change 2013: Summary for Policymakers*, Switzerland: IPCC.

Kumar, V. (2012). *Parliaments and Climate Change: Towards Greener Policies.* New Delhi: Lok Sabha Publication.

McCarthy, J., Canziani, O.S., Leary, N., Dokken, D., and White, K. (2001). *Climate Change 2001: Impacts, Adaptation, and Vulnerability.* Cambridge: Cambridge University Press.

MoLJ. (2008). *Constitution of India.* New Delhi: Ministry of Law and Justice, Government of India.

MoEF. (2009). *State of Environment Report*. New Delhi: MoEF, Govt. of India.

______, (2012). National Communications to UNFCCC. New Delhi: Ministry of Environment and Forests, Government of India.

NRC. (2010). *Advancing the Science of Climate Change*. National Research Council. The National Academies Press, Washington, DC, USA.

Sathaye, J., Shukla, P., and Ravindrnath, N. (2006). Climate change, sustainable development and India: Global and national concerns. *Current Science*, pp. 314-325.

Shepherd, D.J., Shindell, D., & O'Carroll, C.M. (eds.). (2005, January 2). *Climate and Global Change*. Retrieved 2013, from www.nasa.gov: http://www.nasa.gov/mission_pages/noaa-n/climate/climate_weather.html

UNFCCC. (1992). *United National Framework Convention on Climate Change*. New York: United Nations.

______, (2013). *Essential Background*. Retrieved 2013, from www.unfccc.int: http://unfccc.int/essential_background/items/6031.php

WMO. (2013). *The Global Climate (2001-2010) — A Decade of Climate Extremes*. Geneva, Switzerland: World Metrological Organisation.

Yale Project on Climate Change Communication. (2012). *Climate Change in Indian Mind*. http://pmindia.gov.in/Climate_change_english.pdf, [Retrieved on 20 January 2013]

11

Social Work Education and Practice in Climate Change Adaptation

Realities and Gaps

Nivedita Mishra Thapliyal

The consequences of climate change may be comprehended by many but not seriously, including the planning and policies of sustainable development (Aggarwal, 2003). The concept is always linked with the meteorological part and envisages the role of scientists to interpret the temperature and rainfall data. The concept is understood without knowing the best adaptability mode and people are forgetting that it is not just a subject of scientific origin for dealing only with temperature and rainfall, but it figures in the conception of sustainable development, which is the critical link between development and environment. Many of the policy makers and scientists are involved in the work for analyzing and fine tuning the existing policies for better implementation and adaptation of climate change strategies. Climate Change (CC) is recognized as the greatest challenge for societies in the coming years and also for the future generations for survival. Although in recent years, important advances have been made for future projection in terms of rainfall, temperature, crop productivity, however, there are still many aspects to be looked after. The implementation of the concept of mitigation and adaptation and raising the economic standard of the communities is vital for addressing the climate change issue and the responsibilities lies with all sections of society.

Various assessments carried out by the Intergovernmental Panel on Climate Change (IPCC) over the years reiterate the fact that the adverse change in global climate system is contributed by unscrupulous and unsustainable consumption pattern of natural resources, the implications of which are now being felt as dramatic transformations of the biophysical environment that are affecting ecosystem services, water resources, food production and lives and livelihood security of millions of people. It is also obvious that these negative impacts will be skewed towards the poor and the deprived through a vicious cycle that illustrates the connectivity dimension of climate change. Connectivity dimension is increasingly linked across time and space as the outcome of the activity of one group or community in terms of development at one region is increasingly being felt as a threat at another region over time. Less developed countries are likely to suffer more as they are financially and technically constrained for better adaptation options. According to Parikh and Parikh (2002), climate change is one of the many manifestations of a larger malady of economic development and cannot be "fixed" by technological solutions alone. In this context, sustainable management of ecosystems becomes all the more pertinent.

A particular climate hazard, such as a drought, does not affect all people within a community – or even the same household – equally because some people have greater capacity than others to manage the crisis (Aggarwal *et al.*, 1994). The inequitable distribution of rights, resources and power, as well as repressive cultural rules and norms, constrain many people's ability to take action on climate change. This is especially true for women, and therefore, gender is a critical factor in understanding the vulnerability to climate change. There is a reason to believe that climate change will hit women disproportionately hard. Lack of political power, small economic resources, gender-bound patterns in the division of labour and entrenched cultural patterns contribute to making women and girls particularly vulnerable to extreme weather and other climate-related events. Gender needs to be mainstreamed throughout the adaptation decision-making process, from the stage where climate threats and vulnerabilities are mapped and adaptation options identified, to the stage where options are assessed, implemented and evaluated.

The United Nations and many other gender responsive institutions are formally committed to gender mainstreaming within all policies and programmes on climate change. As predicted by the Intergovernmental Panel on Climate Change (IPCC), "climate change impacts will be differently distributed among different regions, generations, age classes, income groups, occupations and gender" (IPCC, 2001). The IPCC also notes that the impacts of climate change will hamper development and harm human living conditions and lifestyles. The effects will fall disproportionately upon developing countries and the poor within all countries, and thereby exacerbate inequities in health status and access to adequate food, clean water, and other resources (FSI Report, 2009).

Today, women represent about 70 per cent of the poor throughout the world. Most of the key areas of the negative consequences of climate change are strongly connected to gender equality issues (Singh *et al.*, 2010). Women in developing and developed countries are generally considered part of the vulnerable groups. High dependence from agriculture, forest resources, fisheries and bio-fuels can increase the vulnerability and the risk of environmental depletion (NAIP 2011). Moreover, the problems relating to the management of the environmental common assets can become worse under the pressure of global warming (Singh *et al.*, 2002). These problems include food security, freshwater supply, rural and urban settlements and their infrastructures. In terms of the role that they have to perform women are highly dependent on the environment and are therefore likely to be impacted the most. The impact on women's lives varies between regions and cultures, thus planning for adaptation to climate change need to take a close look at each individual and concrete situation (Thornthwaite, 1994).

Social work education helps the social specialist to link with the people for bringing change and avenues for development. The current changes from welfare to development in the planning period have forced the policy makers to look on the sustainability side of the development, which shall last longer and leave benefits for the future generation. The social workers will need to keep this perspective centre stage and work towards establishing a balance between the environment and community needs.

The Conference of the Parties (COP15) meeting in Copenhagen in 2009 also outlined the role of social work, though not much discussion was made in this regard. The social work profession no doubt has an important role to play in helping people understand the issues of climate change; promoting sustainable energy production and consumption; mobilizing people to protect their futures through community social work; and proposing solutions to greenhouse gas emissions.

The most significant role of the social worker in the context of climate change is as under:

- The problems like global warming will mean much more severe weather events like extended periods of drought leading to recurrent famines, unprecedented rainfall and consequent flooding; increased sea temperatures causing severity of storms, and this will have adverse affect on farmers (Suresh, 2010). The social worker can help develop different innovative sustainable agriculture practices like the land shaping practices of agriculture in coastal regions, mulching practices, system root intensification techniques as also different watershed approaches like bunding, check dams and trenches. They can propagate mixed cropping, organic farming, integrated farm development model, etc. Different awareness programmes on climate change as well as development of outreach materials in local languages can be undertaken.
- Different projects and research are appreciated in REDD+ on reducing effect related to deforestation and degradation which again encourage sustainable management of land (Aishwath, 2010). In this area, the social work practitioner can develop projects under the REDD+ and work on the relevant issues.
- Poverty is another key factor which shall worsen due to the impact of climate changes (Michlik, *et al.*, 2008). The most socially and economically disadvantaged people are more likely to live in areas liable to flood; have increased risk from heat waves due to poorer health and housing; have limited access to information about the environment and less access to transport to escape the effects of severe weather events. Achieving social justice through the reduction of poverty and inequality are therefore a key part of reducing the risks from climate change, and these fall in the work realm of social workers.

  The contribution of social workers is also in the mitigation processes level such as involvement in the wider environmental social movements against climate change and in the effective implementation of the State as well as National action plans on climate change. The involvement of the local bodies can be enhanced and they can be made aware and trained for their participation in action plans on climate change.
- Social work has a long tradition of not only looking on the needs but also on the right based approach of the

development. Today climate change is perhaps the biggest challenge that humanity faces. Lord Stern suggested in his Review of the Economics of Climate Change, that hundreds of millions of people could suffer hunger, water shortages and coastal flooding as the world warms. The change in role to address development from social justice and ecological justice requires training and understanding of these perspective. Moreover, all the universities and colleges must encourage students to take up research and study in the field of climate change adaptation and mitigation.

The Cancun Forestry decisions on REDD+ agreed on conservation of forest carbon stocks, sustainable management of forest and enhancement of forest carbon stocks along with the decision for reducing emissions from deforestation and reducing emissions from forest degradation. These decision is to be implemented under three phases: (i) Development of national strategies or action plans, policies and measures, capacity-building; (ii) Implementation of national strategies and action plans through results-based demonstration activities; (iii) Evolving into results-based actions that should be fully measured, reported and verified (MRVable) along with Safeguards (Burton *et al*, 2005). The safeguards consist of 'environmental' and 'social', which focus on the protection and conservation of natural forests and their ecosystem services, as well as respect for the knowledge and rights of indigenous people and members of local communities (ILCs) and full and effective participation of all relevant stakeholders, through Free Prior Informed Consent (FPIC). Emphasis is also to provide information on how safeguards for REDD+ activities are addressed and respected so that stakeholders are informed and there is enhancement in confidence building among stakeholders as also the creation of a learning platform for continuous improvement for governance. Social workers can play an important role in REDD+ by involving the community in the decision-making for improved benefit sharing and protection and conservation of traditional knowledge which otherwise is declining, thus minimizing the livelihood opportunities for the communities who are dependant on traditional avenues of environment based livelihoods. Social workers can help develop a road map for implementation of REDD+ projects like development of strategy and action plan; identification of partners for collaboration; mainstreaming REDD+ in Forest Management;

defining the enabling situations, establishing or carrying out baseline study; capacity building in MRV, SIS, Benefit Sharing; identifying the drivers of deforestation and degradation; and ways to address them.

The challenges faced by social workers in climate change are challenging, yet are urgently called for. The social work professionals are not only required to facilitate grassroots development, but also reexamine the current perspectives of development. Research and development based on climate change needs to be encouraged at the university level as well as field level action, so that the role of the social worker is understood not only in community mobilization but also pro active negotiation for addressing climate change.

References

Aggarwal, K.K., Upadhyay, S.D., and Upadhyay, A.P. (2008). Impact of Climate Change on Agro-ecosystem over Madhya Pradesh. In G.S.L.H.V. Prasada Rao, G.G.S.N. Rao, V.U.M. Rao, Y.S. Ramakrishna (eds.), *Climate Change and Agriculture over India* (pp. 176-190). New Delhi: PHI Learning Private Limited.

Aggarwal, P.K., and Sinha, S.K. (1994). Effect of probable increase in carbon dioxide and temperature on wheat yields in India. *Journal of Agriculture Meteorology, 48*(5), 811-814.

______, (2003). Impact of climate change on Indian agriculture. *Journal of Plant Biology, 30*, 189-198.

Aishwath, O.P., Meena, S.S., Kant, K., and Anwer, M.M. (2010). Climate change and seed species In: *Challenges of climate change: India Horticulture*. Eds. H.P. Singh, J.P. Singh, S.S. Lal. New Delhi. Westville Publishing House, pp. 85-90.

Burton, I., Malone, E., and Huq, S. (2005). *Adaptation Policy Frameworks for Climate Change: Developing Strategies, Policies and Measures.* Washington: UNDP-GEF.

IPCC. (2007). *Third Assessment Report: Synthesis Report.* Geneva: WMO-UNEP.

Michlik, A., Liu, C., and Kelkar, U. (2008). *Global Warming and Climate Change: Ten years after Kyoto and Still Counting,* In Velma I Grover (ed.). US: Science Publishers.

NAIP. (2011). *Annual Report.* New Delhi: ICAR Publication.

Parikh, J., Parikh, K., 2002, Climate change: India's perceptions, positions, policies and possibilities, Paper commissioned by OECD. Mumbai, Indira Gandhi Institute of Development Research.

Singh, J.P., Lal, S.S., Govindakrishnan, P.M., Dua, V.K. and Pandey, S.K. (2010). *Impact of Climate Change on Potato in India.* In: *Challenges of*

Climate Change: India Horticulture. Eds. H.P. Singh, J.P. Singh, S.S. Lal. New Delhi: Westville Publishing House, pp. 90-99.

Singh, N., and Sontakke, N.A. (2002). Climatic Fluctuations and Environmental Changes of the Indo-Gangetic Plains, India. *Climatic Change, 52*(3), 287-313.

Sinha, S.K., and Swaminathan, M.S. (1991). Deforestation, Climate Change and Sustainable Nutrition Security: A Case Study of India. *Climate Change, 19* (1-2), 201-209.

Sukumar, R., Suresh, H.S., and Ramesh, R. (1995). Climate change and its impact on tropical mountain ecosystems in southern India. *Journal of Biogeography, 22,* 533-536.

Suresh, K., and Babu Kochu, M. (2010). *Impact of Climate Change on Oil palm in India.* In: *Challenges of climate change: India Horticulture.* Eds. H.P. Singh, J.P. Singh, S.S. Lal. New Delhi: Westville Publishing House, pp. 36-41

Government of India. (2009). *State of Forest Report.* New Delhi: Ministry of Environment and Forests.

Thornthwaite, C.W., and Mather, J.R. (1955). *The Water Balance.* New Jersey: Drexel Institute of Technology.

12

UDAI: A Social Work Response to Managing the Aftermath of a Disaster

Sanjai Bhatt

At 8.46 a.m. (IST) on 26 January 2001, when India was celebrating its Republic Day, a disastrous earthquake of 6.9 magnitude on the Richter scale, shook the Kutchh region of Gujarat. The earthquake affected a large area of the state, damaging buildings and other manmade structures in many big towns and cities. It left behind a trail of destruction with several thousands of human casualties apart from economic losses worth billions in Indian currency in the form of damaged buildings and other structures. The Indian economy suffered a severe jolt as the industrial structure at many places gave way to the fury of the earthquake in a state which was at the forefront of industrial activity in the country.

Genesis of the Project

The community of University of Delhi shared a sense of deep concern with the fate of the people in various parts of Gujarat. The then Vice Chancellor, Prof. Deepak Nayar held discussions with a group of select members which was later formed into a Core Committee. Meetings were also held with the office-bearers of various bodies representing the university community, Delhi University Students' Union (DUSU), Delhi University Researchers' Association (DURA), Delhi University Karmchari Union (DUCKU), Delhi University Teachers' Association (DUTA) and DUPA as well as Deans, Heads and Principals of different Faculties, Departments and Colleges respectively. It was decided that the Core Committee would formulate, plan, develop and execute a short and long-term intervention in Gujarat. It was also decided to create a Vice-Chancellor's Relief Fund, visualized to be a durable one, that could be used for the relief and rehabilitation of the affected victims. In addition, the University also proposed to generate, collate and disseminate a corpus of knowledge. The Vice Chancellor, Prof. Deepak Nayar urged the university community to recognize its social obligation as an instrument of higher learning. Prof. Nayar underscored the need to respond beyond individualism in a culture of materialism and an era of marketisation. As a result of this consultative process, it was decided to conduct a need assessment in the affected area. Subsequently, the project was launched on 15 May 2001.

The project was named UDAI, *University for Development and Integrated Learning*, in keeping with the idea with which it was conceived, which was essentially an intervention for rehabilitation by bringing experiential learning back to the university system through the integration of the youth in disaster management and prevention. With this line of action, a multi-disciplinary team was constituted, consisting of the following members: Prof. Anil Sadgopal (Central Institute of Education), Prof. Ved Kumari (Faculty of Law), Dr. Ashok Nagpal (Department of Psychology), Dr. Azra Razzack (Central Institute of Education), Dr. Alok Verma (Delhi College of Engineering), Ms. Honey Oberoi (Department of Psychology), Mr. Nilanjan Das, Mr. Manish Jha and Dr. Sanjai Bhatt (Delhi School of Social Work). Prof. Sanjai Bhatt was given the responsibility of coordinating the visit. The team was given the following terms of reference:

(a) To identify a particular locality which would be the main area of operation based on the extent of devastation, services rendered by different agencies and presence of suitable agencies with which the university could coordinate
(b) To conduct a needs-assessment of the area
(c) To prepare a plan of action based on the needs-assessment
(d) To identify local governmental and voluntary organizations for the purpose of partnering for long term intervention during the process of relief and rehabilitation

The team broadly identified six different areas of Gujarat for selecting the proposed area of operation. These areas were: Nilpar in Rapar Taluka (sub-division), Kanthkot and Motichirai in Bhachau Taluka, Radhanpur in Patan Taluka, Megllpar in Maliya Miana Taluka and Dhrangadhrain Surendranagar Taluka. These sites were visited to enable a broad assessment of the extent of damage and the quantum of relief disbursed among the village population. The place and the partner agency for the rehabilitation work were decided by employing SWOT (Strength, Weakness, Opportunity and Threat) analysis. The main criteria considered for analysis were: (i) the extent of devastation in the area; (ii) relief and rehabilitation undertaken; (iii) presence of a support organisation in the area; and (iv) the presence of infrastructural facilities. Five organizations were scrutinized, based on these criteria and among them finally, Gram Swaraj Sangh (GSS) of Nilpar was selected as the partner agency for the proposed rehabilitation project.

Gram Swaraj Sangh as Partner Agency

Gram Swaraj Sangh (GSS), a not-for-profit, non-political organisation established in the year 1978, was a part of the *Kutchh Navnirman Abhiyan* meaning 'Kutchh Reconstruction Initiative'. Firmly believing in the Gandhian philosophy of self help, GSS, since its inception has been working for the overall development of the Kutchh region of the Gujarat state and has become the focal point for relief and rehabilitation activities in the Rapar Taluka and Bhachau Taluka. The activities and interventions of GSS are based on a fundamental belief in self-help leading to community capacity building with the overall objective of enabling the villagers to assess, plan, organise and implement their own development process. The organisation believes in providing facilitation with an overall aim of making people autonomous and self reliant. Activities related to rural development, with emphasis on watershed development, rural housing, employment generation, education, agriculture and animal husbandry, as also disaster mitigation work, especially to deal with the menace of earthquakes, cyclones and drought, were being undertaken by Gram Swaraj Sangh. The Kutchh area in Gujarat is home to drought, cyclones and earthquakes and it falls in seismic zone V, which is the most seismically vulnerable area.

The main cognizable needs of the disaster victims identified by the University team after the initial need assessment exercise were: support for earthquake resistant housing, employment, trauma counseling and support and education for children. The rehabilitation programme undertaken by the University consisted of activities aimed at fulfilling these needs. Although at the level of the University, the initiative was intended to restrict itself up to public education, however in view of the felt needs of the impacted community, the focus incorporated the aforementioned needs. These activities tried to enable the local population to derive requisite knowledge, skills and competencies for recovery and rehabilitation. Preliminary estimates suggested a damage to the extent of Rs. 20,875 Crores (US$ 4.5 Billion) to private and public properties of the State. The nature, extent and magnitude of the damages accruing from the Bhuj earthquake are shown in various tables (Table 12.1-12.3).

Table 12.1: Quake affected Villages Zone-wise

Zones	*Number of Villages*
Zone-V	881 Villages of Kutchh District
Zone-IV	1062 Villages of 6 Districts
Zone-III	5690 Villages of other Districts
Total in 21 Districts	7633 Villages affected by Earthquake

Table 12.2: Details of Affected Districts (as on 12-03-2001)

District	*Affected Talukas*	*Affected Village*	*Total Population*	*Affected Population*	*Human Deaths*	*No. of Injured*	*Cattle Death*
Kutchh	10	949	1262507	1262507	18414	136048	19470
Ahmedabad	11	392	4687491	3894000	751	4040	20
Rajkot	14	686	2514122	1594000	433	11951	171
Jamnagar	11	685	1563558	1563000	119	4930	549
Surat	8	94	3397900	397989	46	190	1
Surendranagar	10	661	1208872	1154000	113	2909	121
Banaskantha	8	452	2013519	719000	32	2770	162
Kheda	10	350	1793038	35121	0	28	4
Bharuch	4	248	1148052	460000	9	44	76
Gandhinagar	8	210	1026728	35000	8	241	2
Patan	14	349	935203	664000	38	1695	15
Junagadh	5	554	2018446	597787	8	89	3
Navsari	3	331	1085692	87783	17	52	1
Porbandar	6	157	376113	376113	9	90	8
Vadodara	11	85	3039127	186092	1	270	1
Bhavnagar	8	535	2030615	445226	4	45	4
Anand	9	124	1647759	4687	1	20	6
Mehsana	11	611	1648251	1648251	0	1339	6
Sabarkantha	5	68	1761086	128000	0	56	1
Amreli	4	273	1484300	599000	0	5	2
Valsad	5	108	1087680	5985	0	0	0
Total	182	7904	37759859	15857541	20003	166812	20623

Table 12.3: Summary of Damage caused due to the Earthquake

S.N.	*Details*	*Number*
1.	Affected Talukas	182
2.	Affected Villages	7633
3.	Human Casualties	20003
4.	Injured Persons (in Lakhs)	1.66
5.	Completely Damaged Houses and Huts	367293
6.	Partially Damaged Houses and Huts	885891
7.	Animals Deaths	20623
8.	Affected Population (in Crores)	1.59
9.	Missing Persons in Kutch	247

Nature of the UDAI Project

The data presented in the above tables reveal that the task of relief and long term rehabilitation was gigantic and required assistance and contribution of everyone concerned. This project was conceived within the University with the idea that the expertise available at the different Departments/Faculties could be pooled for the ultimate goals of the project. Accordingly, a Memorandum of Understanding (MoU) was signed with Gram Swaraj Sangh and the stage was set for the formal launch of the proposed rehabilitation project under the name of UDAI, with two main objectives: (i) to be part of the rehabilitation process of the earthquake affected people in few selected villages; and (ii) to bring experiential learning back to the University system. The Gujarat earthquake presented an opportunity, an unfortunate one though, to learn how to understand and manage such a tragic disaster event. This kind of a disaster raises many questions, concerns and such issues that require us to seriously look into established theories and models of work related with disaster management and rehabilitation and compare all possible options. It was with this perspective and after considering the situation analysis, need assessment and the observations of study teams that a plan of action was proposed at two levels — at the level of the field and at the University level. The rehabilitation project was to be a joint venture of the University of Delhi and the Gram Swaraj Sangh. The project intended to make a humble contribution in the field of housing, education, health, psycho-social support, employment generation, environment and legal awareness for the victims of the disaster.

Modus Operandi *of the UDAI Project*

To ensure better implementation and coordination of the project, different project activities were undertaken in the following phases: (i) Preparatory Phase (April 2001), (ii) Action Phase (May 2001 to October 2001), (iii) Consolidation Phase (November 2001 to December 2001), and (iv) Termination or Renewal Phase (January 2002 to March 2002).

In the preparatory phase, the main issues of disaster affected areas and victims were considered. The need assessment and study reports indicated that the distribution of relief materials was not adequate. It was highlighted that the Muslims and Harijans were the worst affected and they were discriminated even in relief. Most of the relief materials was sent to the Kutchh area and the moderately affected areas like Rajkot and Surendranagar were neglected. During this period, the project also received insights about networking with organisations and federations like *Janpath and Kutchh Navnirman Abhiyan.*

The modus operandi of the project was based on volunteerism, learning and integration. The project was executed for the achievement of the aforementioned objectives for about 1250 to 1500 families in the chosen area in collaboration with the partner agency. The project established a *'Village Reconstruction Centre'* (VRC) in each village, covering around 200 to 250 families in the village and its hamlets. Normally, the population of the villages in this area was almost the same and in all, six such VRCs were set up with student volunteers and one village level worker from the partner agency. The *'Village Reconstruction Group'* (VRG) was expected to design, and execute different type of activities like imparting public awareness for different fields of activities, education, planning for damaged houses and creating designs for new houses, among other things. The project intended to ensure total community participation, and to achieve this, the project managers were asked to create a participatory decision-making body called the *'Village Reconstruction Group'* (VRG).

As the heart of the project, the VRG was the main decision-making body to decide the future plan of action in the field on a weekly or monthly basis. Realising the social divisions in the rural society, along caste and religion lines, it was decided to give representation to people from all the sections in the constitution of these groups. Considering one representative from 20 families, the group was constituted by around ten to fifteen members including the project volunteers. It was the view of the planners that a participatory approach and structures that respect the knowledge, wisdom and freedom of the people would be more effective in achieving the aims and objectives of the project. The project activities were planned to be volunteer based. A programme coordinator at the university level was responsible for smooth implementation of the project and the programme organiser at the field level was expected to take care of logistics and liaison with the partner agency.

The project was planned to ensure a continuous presence of volunteers in the field on rotation basis in a batch size of a minimum of 15 volunteers at a time. It was expected to benefit a total of 450 volunteers with the experience of rehabilitation work. Since the task of rehabilitation was monumental and the terrain was quite difficult, it was decided to teach the volunteers to distinguish between disaster tourism and disaster rehabilitation. Prior to sending the batch in the field, they were rigorously trained in different aspect of disasters, relief, life and trauma of the disaster victims, rehabilitation, team management, volunteerism, group living and even local dialect. Each batch stayed at the rehabilitation site for fifteen days, where the volunteers had to spend two days in the beginning and at the end of their stay with the outgoing and the incoming batch, especially for stocktaking and experiential sharing. The UDAI project benefitted 256 student volunteers and 60 teachers who worked in 26 batches. Each batch worked for 13 to 15 days with an overlapping period where the outgoing and incoming batches worked together to facilitate an adequate handover of the responsibilities. The first batch oriented the second batch with the ground realities for three days after which they came back to Delhi. The total financial requirement of this project was calculated in consonance with the partner agency. It was estimated to be in the tune of around Rs. 15 lakhs. However, Rs. 9 lakhs were spent on volunteers during the entire project period. The project was quite cost effective and proved to be a learning model for low cost rehabilitation intervention.

Activities at the University Level

In order to disseminate information updates about the intervention within the University, activities were undertaken at regular intervals. At the Department of Social Work, a project office was created. The project office assumed responsibility for coordinating the diverse activities of the project with its partner agency through the volunteer teams participating in the rehabilitation project. A short orientation programme focusing on basic information and skills required for volunteering in the project was organised for each batch of selected volunteers. Necessary inputs were provided within the orientation programme by including new theme based information requisite in different phases of the project. Inputs were fine tuned on the basis of the feedback received from the field.

Over the temporal span of the project, the following measures were undertaken for generating and sustaining interest of the University community:

- Wide publicity to the project through appropriate means in the University departments, colleges, offices and student hostels;
- Small fund raising and volunteer registration drives;
- Mobilising non-teaching staff during the examinations;
- Seeking the services of the faculty members for the project with the facility of duty leave for this purpose;
- Involving National Service Scheme (NSS) volunteers for disaster preparedness by giving first aid kits and emergency response training;
- Rotation of the autumn and winter break in different colleges and departments in consultation with concerned authorities for facilitating the year round participation of teachers and students in the programme.

Activities Undertaken in UDAI

This project was to be implemented in five villages namely, Kalyanpur, Ratneshwar, Selari, Sangramsur, and Sonapur, in Rapar Tehsil and Bhuj districts. The following activities were undertaken in these villages:

1. Construction of temporary shelters for stay of Delhi University volunteers during the tenure of the project;
2. Supervision of ongoing construction work in coordination with workers of Kutch Navnirman Abhiyan;
3. Conducting awareness programmes for villages about the rehabilitation packages announced by the government;
4. Organising villagers to form village councils/associations for redressal of legal issues including claims for compensation and other entitlements;
5. Awareness generation and training in construction of

seismic resistant housing (SRH) structures to villages and masons;

6. Organising recreational and educational activities for children at the village level;
7. Mobilising and organising youth through games and discussion sessions in different villages;
8. Generating awareness regarding balanced and appropriate diet and physiotherapy;
9. Developing an eco-garden by planting and maintaining trees at the VRC.

Volunteerism: The Core of UDAI Project

The project outline of UDAI had envisioned that batches of 25-30 volunteers from teaching, non-teaching and student members of University of Delhi would undertake activities in the field for a period of one year. Each batch was expected to stay in the field for a minimum of fifteen days and the travel and food expenses were to be borne by the project. The schedule of the batches going to the field was prepared in a manner as to ensure continuity and handing over of responsibilities to the next incoming batch. Before leaving for the field, every batch underwent a three-day orientation and training course, conducted at the Department of Social Work, with resource persons from within and outside the Department. Hence, volunteerism was the main essence of the UDAI project, involving the University community in different ways. Volunteers were encouraged:

- To acquire an understanding of disasters and disaster-centric projects, their relevance, aims and objectives;
- To organise a *'Remembering Gujarat Earthquake'* programme on 26th of every month by holding seminars, exhibitions, debates, shows publicising project activities, selling stickers with UDAI related slogans, competitions for slogan writing, project logo, essay writing, etc.;
- To motivate student unions/associations/groups of departments/colleges/hostels of the university in organising innovative programmes for generating support for UDAI project;
- To help in fundraising and volunteer registration drive;
- To conduct research and documentation of the UDAI activities, and to provide constructive suggestions for project activities.

The First Batch of the volunteers started work in the field, covering the following tasks:

- Public Health – Health camps were organised and involvement of medical students was sought to facilitate the work.
- Rural Housing – Sustainable Rural Housing (SRH) measures were suggested as per the socio-economic condition of families, besides generating awareness about the rehabilitation packages announced by the government.
- Water Management – Campaigns were initiated to facilitate the communities to cope with water shortages. Involvement of watershed management personnel was sought for future.
- Employment – To check migration of local youth, vocational training inputs were imparted.
- Education – Adult education was started and a library resource was created.
- Ecology – Plantation activities was undertaken and recycling of garbage was initiated.

The initial batch of volunteers also prepared village profiles of all the three villages through PRA techniques. Surveys and participatory methods mere employed to collect data about geographic location, demographic stratification, caste composition, village infrastructure, economic status, occupational pattern, impacts of earthquake, relief measures, and compensation received. The subsequent batch continued the work that was started by the first batch and also began some new activities like income generation programme, yoga exercises, formation of youth clubs, etc. The subsequent batches continued the work done by the previous batches and also initiated some additional work like arranging trekking tour, athletic meet at schools, cleaning of dwelling units, construction of an eighty meter approach road through *shramdan*. The later batches started a self help group (SHG) and Mahila Mandal in Selari village, imparted vocational training, organised 'Inter-class Cultural Fest' in Selari, imparted training of SRH, generated awareness about the harms of plastic ('say no to plastic' campaign), held the Kisan Vikas Shivir in Selari and conducted a technical survey of the three villages. Problems specific to these three villages were identified and efforts were made to overcome these handicaps with the cooperation of official authorities. Supply of fodder emerged as a major problem and was brought to the notice of the concerned officials.

The students observed and learnt about group dynamics, role and nature of leadership, importance of democratic functioning through real life exposure. They were also involved in the construction of permanent shelters for the volunteers of UDAI project, information collection during visit to villages, need assessment and prioritisation of needs. For the smoother day-to-day functioning, volunteers formed four groups with a convener and co-convener to decentralise their tasks and responsibilities – Food Committee, Living Arrangement Committee, Work Plan Committee, and Discipline Committee. A daily briefing was done in the morning to roll out a daily work plan. A review meeting was held every evening by the convener and the co-convener. All the responsibilities were held in rotation, thereby giving each of them a chance to assume leadership roles.

Some functional problems were also revealed during the course of the project. These included lack of adequate systems of communication, problems of transport and other infrastructural lacunae. In addition, the absence of a lady volunteer led to the disruption of the adult education programme (as most beneficiaries were women). The smaller size of the batches came in the way of expanding the scope of the project activities. Lack of time to facilitate a comprehensive orientation to rural life and gender disparity within batches emerged as the other major hurdles in the implementation of the project.

Tasks Accomplished under the UDAI Project

The complete range of tasks accomplished under the UDAI project are being summarised below:

Education

- Schools were started in the five villages.
- Enrollment drive campaign.
- Recreational activities with children.
- Basic health education.
- Promotion of parent's participation in school.

Rural Housing

- Awareness generation and training in SRH and cyclone-resistant construction and retrofitting to village communities and masons.

- Supervision of ongoing construction work.

Public Health

- Medical camps with follow-up of earthquake affected persons.
- Identification of major health problems and psycho-social support needs.
- Awareness generation about hygiene, sanitation and reproductive health.
- Malaria prevention.
- Networking with public health centres.
- Counseling and psycho-support services.

Income Generation Programmes with Special Focus on Women

- Initiation of self-help groups.
- Exploring market options for traditional embroidery.
- Organising Kisan Vikas Mela (Farmers' camp).

Legal Aid

- Identification of families facing problems in getting compensation.
- Legal awareness and guidance with regard to compensation packages and procedures.

Environmental Conservation

- Plantation drive in monsoon season.
- Environmental awareness generation.

Social Harmony

- Creation of respect for socio-cultural diversity.
- Communal Harmony.

Outcomes of the UDAI Project

The UDAI project has succeeded in attaining the following outcomes:

- Community building and rehabilitation of target groups and villages.
- Community management of services implemented under the project.
- Developing the University as a partner of a caring community.

- Acquisition of expertise in developing an academic/ training course in disaster management.
- Opening new vistas for real life education and learning.

Learning from the Project

The UDAI project provided an array of learning opportunities for the volunteers. It facilitated the acquisition of skills as also experiential learning for the resource persons and group leaders. The University participated in the mobilisation of human and financial resources to initiate and sustain rehabilitation work in Selari with a commitment for a year. The uniqueness of this project draws from its voluntary base. At the end of three months, seventy-six students in six batches volunteered and participated in this project by visiting and working in Gujarat for a period of fifteen days. Likewise, fourteen resource persons (teachers, staff and research scholars) had volunteered. The non-teaching staff of the Department of Social Work contributed their time and energy to ensure the smooth functioning of the project. Resource persons from other universities like Jamia Milia Islamia also shared their experience of the earthquake-affected areas and participated in the Orientation Programme. The major learning outcomes of the project were:

a. Learning of the Volunteers

All the volunteers and batches were encouraged to record their experiences in Gujarat. In addition, there were a number of formal and informal interactions with different batches that were encouraged to undertake a sharing of experiences. An attempt is made to discuss the learning insights of these volunteers in the ensuing section. This is based on their written and verbal reports. The volunteers acquired knowledge in many forms and ways. Each of the six orientation programmes enabled the student volunteers to develop an understanding with regard to the concept and locale of the disaster. The learning specifically was with reference to:

1. *Disaster:* Types of disaster, problems related to disaster, effects of disaster in relation to housing, property, education, family life, environment, livelihood, etc.
2. *Knowledge of life and living condition in Earthquake Affected Areas (EAA):* The volunteers gained an understanding of life and living conditions of the people of Kutch following

the earthquake, and an understanding the coping and resilience parameters.

3. *Knowledge of the role of Government and non-government sector:* The students developed an understanding of the roles played by different agencies in the rehabilitation of the people affected by earthquakes. They developed an appreciation of the problems related to relief and rehabilitation work as also issues related to networking and problems in service delivery.
4. *Learning to understand the need and problems of community:* The exposure of volunteers to the different villages in Kutch helped them to comprehend the rural reality. Immediate and long term needs were expressed by the people of Kalyanpar, Sangramsar and Selari and the volunteers used different methods including Participatory Research Appraisals (PRA) method to arrive at the conceptualisation of needs and problems faced by the people. This significantly helped in developing their abilities to conceptualise plans and prioritise the problems and needs that require attention immediately and develop strategies wherever possible to address these.

b. Acquisition of Skills by Volunteers

Participation in the intervention provided the volunteers a tremendous opportunity to develop and strengthen the following skill sets:

1. *Skills related to living in rural Areas:* This project helped the volunteers build skills to function in an area where basic amenities were not available. The girls of the first few batches were privileged to use the toilets and bathing facilities at the school campus in Selari as the school principal was gracious enough to allow them the use of these. However, the boys in these batches had to use the open fields and bathe in a stagnant tank of water, which they did very unhesitatingly despite the fact that it was neither easy nor hygienic. In addition, due to the sheer physical nature of the work involved, many of the volunteers developed blisters and boils. There were hardly any complaints from these batches regarding the problems they faced although many of them expressed that this was so because they were so cognizant of the realities in Kutchh

and would feel ashamed to complain about minor problems. The skills building also extended to their learning the local language. The Orientation programme of all batches did have at least two sessions of language learning, where they were equipped with basic phrases that they would require in the field. However, the fortnight in the field gave them the opportunity to further enhance these skills.

2. *Skills Related to Group Living:* Almost all batches reported that the most unique learning from this project was with regard to group living. This project was able to provide the volunteers an opportunity to relate to others in the context of a group and learn the importance of group work. The volunteers of batch I and IV were drawn from the same Department, with resource persons also being largely drawn from the same Department. The other batches were mixed batches comprising of students from various Departments and colleges. Skills related to rapport building and rapport maintenance among themselves, sharing resources that are precious, adjustment and learning to handle inter-group conflict, learning to relate to each other were among the lessons learnt by them. In addition to this, batches that had volunteers from more than one Department/college reported that they had learnt to appreciate and accommodate each other's views and develop an inter-disciplinary perspective. The learning of many of these students went beyond the narrow confines of the discipline that they belonged to and the experience of being part of UDAI project had provided to them learning beyond classrooms. Volunteers were encouraged to write down their personal reflections of their experiences. They have written about the satisfaction of being able to work with community members and being able to make a difference.
3. *Skills Related to Working in a Team:* The student volunteers have expressed their gratitude to the University of Delhi for this opportunity as they have learnt to think and function as a team. They were always conscious of their role as representatives of the University of Delhi and their batch as a link with the other batches. Some reported that they have learnt objectivity with regard to work performance, the importance of appreciation and 'giving

a pat on the back' and the importance of cooperative and coordinated work. Working in the team has meant developing the capacity to sacrifice or compromise individual objectives for the sake of the group or collective objectives.

c. Learning for the Resource Persons

Just like the student volunteers, the resource persons also acquired immense learning. As group leaders, the learning has been with regard to group management skills, organisational skills, learning to handle intra-group conflict, learning to boost group morale and keep the team spirit alive when necessary as also to manage individual and group problems. The most important aspect of their learning however has been with regard to handling finance, project planning and implementation.

Benefits/Learning at the Level of the University

The experience of running this project has clearly had several benefits. There emerged a clear appreciation by the University on the nature of role that it can play in response to disasters. Being the first such organised venture, it was not without initial hesitations and doubts. The university was however able to surmount the initial hiccups and demonstrate the manner in which an active role in rehabilitation work could be undertaken. It moved from merely generating financial resources to playing an emphatic and active role in rehabilitation work.

The University was able to motivate volunteers from among the University community to join the UDAI project thereby sensitising large groups to think how they could play a more decisive role with regard to rehabilitation work. The vast academic and field expertise of the university was tapped to plan and implement this project. However, it needs to be emphasized that this and such initiatives should be extended to further motivate the larger University community to get integrated within disaster response and rehabilitation interventions.

The Contributors

The Editors

Sanjai Bhatt is a Professor of Social Work at the Delhi School of Social Work, University of Delhi. He is a highly proactive academician, social work educator, trainer and development consultant. He had earlier taught at the University of Lucknow, MG Kashi Vidyapeeth Varanasi, Kurukshetra University and Chitrakoot Gramodaya Vishwavidyalaya. He has authored/ edited four books and 60 research papers on varied themes. He has also conducted a number of evaluation and impact assessments for national and international organisations. Prof Bhatt is associated with a number of social movements and civil society organisations in various capacities. He has a rich experience of mobilizing the participation of Delhi University students and faculty in multiple disaster responses in different parts of the country. The UDAI-I and UDAI-II initiatives of the Department of Social Work, under the aegis of the University of Delhi were a result of his initiative and innovativeness to create and establish effective practice models and approaches for social work practitioners. Prof Bhatt is President of National Association of Professional Social Workers in India (NAPSWI) and Organizing Secretary of 1st Indian Social Work Congress 2013 held at Delhi.

Neera Agnimitra is an Associate Professor of Social Work at the Delhi School of Social Work, University of Delhi. She has designed the courses on 'Social Work and Disaster Management' and 'Environment and Social Work' taught in the University and has been teaching both the courses since their introduction at the post graduate level. An academic of great repute, her doctoral thesis based on her ethnographic work in the Bhilangana block of Uttarakhand is one of the pioneering works in social work education on human ecology. Through her continuous engagement with women groups in Uttarakhand, her writings and lectures delivered in several international and national conferences, she has contributed immensely to the acceptance of human ecology and disaster management as areas of social work practice. She has also played a pivotal role in the disaster engagements of the University of Delhi and has a rich experience and expertise in this domain. She is a part of many core committees of the National Institute of Disaster Management and National Disaster Management Authority, including the core committee for drafting the National Guidelines on Community Based Disaster Management and Member, Expert Group on Draft Policy Guidelines on Role of NGOs in Community Based Disaster Management (NDMA, Govt. of India). She is also associated with a number of non-governmental organisations working in the disaster impacted areas of Uttarakhand, including Chamoli, Uttarkashi, Rudraprayag and Tehri; Bihar, and Sikkim. She has acted as Joint Organizing Secretary of 1st Indian Social Work Congress, 2013 held at Delhi.

The Contributors

Ajay Kumar Jha, is working as Executive Director, Public Advocacy Initiatives for Rights and Values in India (PAIRVI) which is a known advocacy group, capacity building and support organization working at the intersection of development and rights. He also coordinates a Pan Indian Collective known as *Beyond Copenhagen*, which is an initiative to promote sustainable development, and climate justice and equity. A lawyer by education and development policy analyst by practice, he has engaged extensively with issues of sustainable development; climate change; agriculture and food sovereignty; trade in agriculture; and human rights based approach to development. He has also worked on right to information, Dalit rights and affirmative action, food and nutrition, access to justice and strengthening human rights infrastructure.

Aruna Gajbhiye is an Associate Professor in Social Work at Tirpude College of Social Work, Nagpur. She is also the Head of the Women Development Centre of the college and a member of the advisory committee on Disaster Management Cell of R.T.M. Nagpur University. She has a Master's degree in Social Work and a P.G. Diploma in Disaster Management from IGNOU. She has also submitted her Ph.D. thesis on Disaster Management to R.T.M. Nagpur University. In addition to teaching, she also has a vast experience of working with NGOs in several capacities. She has received recognition at local, state and national levels for her training programmes and preparation of modules for training in various issues related to social development and has presented papers in several national and international conferences.

Digvijoy Phukan is an M.A, Ph.D from University of Delhi. He is faculty member of the Department of Social Work, Central University of Jammu. For his doctoral work, he has explored the issue of livelihood and conservation conflict involving the Agarias of Little Rann of Kachchh, Gujarat. He has also worked as a team member of the several monitoring and evaluation projects and is actively engaged in civil society's initiatives across the country on health related issues.

Mayuri Gogoi is a social work academic, researching and writing on issues of environmental protection and biodiversity conservation within the contours of the profession. She has attained her doctoral degree from University of Delhi. She has recently joined her alma mater as an Assistant Professor after working as Senior Research associate with British Council. In her career spanning nearly a decade, she has worked as a grass root community worker, as a research assistant, as a development professional, teacher and most recently as a monitoring and evaluation researcher.

Nivedita Thapliyal is a trained social worker with ten years of professional experience of direct field implementation in the areas of community development, gender and governance in different parts of country. She has worked extensively in the state of Uttarakhand. She has completed her Bachelor's and Master's degree in Social Work from Visva Bharati, West Bengal and is currently pursuing her Ph.D. from the Department of Social Work, University of Delhi.

Ravindra Gajbhiye is currently working as the Director, Social Awareness and Action for Development, Nagpur. He has completed his Master's degree in Social work and is presently pursuing his Ph.D. in Disaster Management from R.T.M. Nagpur University, India. He has been invited as a trainer for many national level development programmes, mainstreaming workshops and SHG trainings by National Rural Livelihood Mission (NRLM), DAPCU, State Agriculture Department, etc. He has also presented several papers in international, national and state level conferences on Disaster Management and has been involved in disaster response work in and around Nagpur.

Santosh Kumar is a Professor and Director of the SAARC Disaster Management Center. He has a Ph.D. in Economics and a Diploma in Gender and Development, IDS, Sussex, UK. He is trained in disaster management at the Risk Control Institute and Israel Defense Force, Israel. He is an expert in Disaster Risk Reduction, Policy Planning and Capacity Development expert with more than twenty-three years of experience in different positions in the Development Planning and Disaster Risk Reduction Sector. Prof. Kumar has actively worked with the World Bank as a Disaster Management Specialist in its South Asia Energy and Infrastructure Group. He has been in-charge of three major national reconstruction projects – the Gujarat earthquake, the Orissa super cyclone and the Andhra Pradesh Cyclone Emergency Project – Funded by the Word Bank.

Subhasis Bhadra is an Assistant Professor and Head in Department of Social Work in the Gautam Buddha University, Greater NOIDA, Uttar Pradesh, India. He has completed his Masters in Social Work and holds an M.Phil and Ph.D. degree. He began his career working with people affected by the Gujarat earthquake (2001) and subsequently worked in areas affected by riots, Indian Ocean Tsunami (2004), earthquakes (Kashmir, 2005), terrorist attacks (Mumbai serial Train Blast, 2006), Myanmar cyclone (2008) and Japanese Tsunami (2011). He has developed and implemented psycho-social programmes with organisations like Care India, American Red Cross, Oxfam India, Action Aid, International Medical Corps, etc.

Varun Sharma has obtained his education from M.A.(TISS), M.Phil (University of Delhi) and is presently pursuing his research on forest crimes. He worked with Federation of Ecological Security for five years and also has significant work in the domain of dynamics and politics of water management in the drought prone districts of southern India. His interest areas are: post-structural political ecology, the modern history of scientific conservation discourse and the ecological concerns in Social Work.

Vinay Kumar is a Junior Research Fellow (UGC) at the Department of Social Work, University of Delhi. He worked as parliamentary intern at the Parliament of India, where he undertook research on parliaments and climate change. His current areas of interest include environment, climate change discourse, disaster management and society.

Index